İstanbul 1432 / 2011

© Erkam Publications 2011 / 1432 H

Erkam Publications
Ikitelli Organize Sanayi Bölgesi
Turgut Özal Cd. No: 117/4
Başakşehir, Istanbul, Turkey
Tel: (90-212) 671-0700 pbx
Fax: (90-212) 671-0717
E-mail: info@islamicpublishing.net
Web site: http://islamicpublishing.net

ISBN: 978-9944-83-314-1

The author   : Osman Nûri Topbaş
Translator   : Erdinç Atasever
Redactor   : Kely Dale
Copy Editor   : Süleyman Derin
Graphics   : Mustafa Kayan (Worldgraphics)
Printed by   : Erkam Printhouse

CONTEMPLATION IN ISLAM

OSMAN NÛRİ TOPBAŞ

ERKAM PUBLICATIONS

FOREWORD

*"There is no worship
like contemplation."*

(Hadith, Bayhaki, Shuab, IV, 157)

An everlasting praise and thanks to our Lord, the eternally Benevolent and Munificent, who has opened for us a path to know Him, by endowing us with the ability to contemplate and be spiritually sensitive (*tahassus*) of Him.[1]

An everlasting salute to our Beloved Prophet –upon him blessings and peace- as well as his family and Companions, who contemplated the universe, humanity and the Holy Quran in the profoundest, most beautiful and feeling manner and taught his followers to read all of these with the eye of the heart.

Among all creation, only humans and to a certain extent *jinn* have been given the ability by the Almighty to derive their share of wisdom from the

---

1   *Tahassus* is to become delicate and sensitive and for the heart to become receptive.

depths of Quran, the universe and humanity, and acquire from their depths the pearls of truth to shed a guiding light on the path of life. The only means to do so, however, lies in contemplation and spiritual sensing.

Contemplating and spiritual sensing are irrefutable conditions for attaining the truth and raising ones heart to the desired level. At every given opportunity from its first verse to its last, the Holy Quran, the unique road map to guidance and happiness, invites us to contemplate and commands us to reflect on the wisdom underlying the creation of man, the splendid order of the universe, the signs of Allah, glory unto Him; to discern the Divine threads of power, manifestations of Divine Majesty and the absolute sovereignty of the Almighty impressed upon the universe throughout.

At every given opportunity in the Holy Quran, the Almighty sends out a word of warning to the Believers, with expressions such as, "Do you not ever contemplate?", "Do they not ever think?" or "Do they not understand?"[2]

Correlated are the questions:

---

2   See, al-Anam, 50; al-Baqara, 219, 266; Muhammad, 24; an-Nisa, 82; Yâsîn, 68...

"Do they not observe the camel?"[3] where the Almighty draws attention to creation;

"Do they not observe the clouds, the rain, the mountains and how greenery dies away in winter only to be resurrected in spring?"[4] which puts emphasis on ecological phenomena;

"Do they not reflect on the doom of bygone nations?"[5] underlining historical events. The Almighty thereby invites us to contemplate the Divine Laws effective throughout the universe and grasp the *adatullah*, or the norms of Allah, glory unto Him, that are the conditions for the manifesting of these laws.

Again, the Almighty states the need for humanity to observe the universe with a perceptive and prudential gaze, not with a fleeting look that is empty

---

3   *al-Bari* and *al-Musawwir*, two of the attributes of Allah, glory unto Him, express how the Almighty creates all beings in different shapes and forms and endows them with abilities proper to their environments and the duties they are meant to carry out. Perfect examples of this among the entire animal kingdom are camels. Obliged to live in the harsh desert climate, where food and water are scarce, a camel is able to reserve a sizable stock of water in its humps for weeks and being able to feed even on thorns, can keep its food fresh for an extended period of time. It is furthermore resilient against desert storms and the blistering desert heat. Doubtless, this is just one manifestation of Divine Power and Artwork among innumerable others.

4   See, Qaf, 6; Yunus, 101; al-Ghashiyah, 17-20; an-Nur, 43; al-Hajj, 63; ar-Ra'd, 3; al-Anbiyâ, 31; an-Nahl, 65; ar-Rûm, 50...

5   Muhammad, 10...

7

and thoughtless. A mention of the gifts bestowed upon humankind in the Quran is capped off by the Almighty referring to the said people as "possessors of prudence and reflection".[6]

Allah, glory unto Him, persistently urges us to contemplate both ourselves and nature, with a firm command to reflect on the threads of Divine Power and Majesty, there are nearly 150 separate occasions in the Holy Quran, making use of concepts like reasoning (اَلتَّعَقُّل), forethought (اَلتَّدَبُّر), remembrance (اَلتَّذَكُّر) and contemplation (اَلتَّفَكُّر).

The zone in which such concepts reach their peaks in practice so as to become a method in spiritual training is *tasawwuf*. *Tasawwuf* is the name given to the path of maturity and perfection which aims toward guiding one towards reaching the pinnacle of reality, to the degree of one's spiritual aptitude, and in addition, the blessings provided by Allah, glory unto Him. Therefore, wisdom as expressed in the maxim "He who knows himself knows his Lord" constitutes one of the most vital principles adhered to by Sufis en route to spiritual perfection.

For a person blessed with an open heart, there is no particle in the universe that does not provide a glimpse of his Creator and His artistic power. From the smallest

8

part of the universe to the arc of creation, every single thing stands as a witness to Divine Majesty.

Creation possesses a way of expression known as *lisan'ul-hal*, a soundless articulation of their states through the way they are, through which every existent thing is active in revelation. For those who are able to properly comprehend what is revealed, the Almighty becomes the *qibla* of their hearts, just as Kabah is the *qibla* of their bodies.

So is stated in the Holy Quran:

"Those who remember Allah standing and sitting and lying on their sides and reflect on the creation of the heavens and the earth: Our Lord! You have not created this in vain! Glory be to You; save us then from the punishment of the fire." (Al-i Imran, 191)

One who is able to duly contemplate the manifestations of Divine Power and Splendor expressed in the universe will first acknowledge his own utter weakness, and then by completely surrendering and obeying, every breath he takes thereafter will be in the nature of *dhikr*. The heart, thereby, becomes filled with the light of *taqwa*, with which contemplation achieves its most consummate blend.

In Divine Sight, the worth of a person is not through his external appearance or through his financial standing in life but rather through the maturity of his heart, his depth of spirit and his spiritual attributes and capabilities. It is for that reason that the Holy Quran rescues the believers' contemplation from being stuck in the narrow straits of matter and ego, by way of reinforcing it with the feeling of faith, after which it further guides it to the boundless horizons of the spiritual realm. Only then does the contemplation of a believer, who is able to gaze at the Divine displays set up in the universe, gain a spiritual dimension. A deep and comprehensive contemplation of the kind which reaches its pinnacle through the sense of the heart, in turn, is the most beautiful key, faith can provide.

One who on the other hand is unable to perfect his or her spirituality lies trapped amid the lowly appearances of a self-centered life, and squanders the natural ability for contemplation in the whirlpool of fleeting desires. Enslaved by the desires of his ego, a lazy heart of the kind always plunges towards these fleeting displays, instead of turning to the true and the good. Never does he think that the shroud, the final piece of clothing he is bound to wear to the grave, will surely envelope him, and that death will come to stamp its ending seal over all passing desires, allures and glimmers of pleasure and the world's deceit.

While a contemplation reinforced by the depth of spiritual feeling always provides one with peace and harmony, constraining oneself within the dry borders of reason only fuels the flames of greed and selfishness. It weakens the heart, sending it to the pits of ignorance.

Just as fingerprints are forms of identity that discern one person from the other, the quality of a believer's contemplation and spiritual sensing is equivalent to his spiritual identity. A Muslim, who therefore wants to achieve a depth of spirit as befits the honor of humankind and compliant with the reason of existence, is obliged to enter the realm of contemplation as laid down by the Holy Quran. Only through a contemplation of such caliber will he acquire focus in deeds of worship, a refined heart and propriety in social interactions.

Despite the importance Islam places on contemplation and spiritual sensing, owing to the ignorance that comes with prioritizing worldly activities over the things that truly matter, human beings, on the whole, lead a life remote from both. As a consequence, they tend to completely forget death and the fact of that the world is a mere place of testing.

Believers, on the other hand, who lead their lives compliant with the gist of *taqwa* and who are able to engage in contemplating and spiritual sensing –and they are always in the minority– transcend their egos and acquire a maturity in which they are able to acknowledge their human condition and grasp their shortcomings and virtues, in tandem.

In spite of the external life in which they continue to take part, such persons achieve the eternal vivacity of having gained for themselves a profound inner realm. Consequent upon the broadening of their hearts, they reach a sublime form of comprehension that exceeds the horizons of the physical world, well past the threshold that sees them acquire a perfected faith, a Divine Blessing that is only given at the end of this path.

A believer triumphant in attaining this character no longer perceives this fleeting life as a blessing he feels dependent upon. The days of live, in the eyes of such a Muslim, resemble a loose string continuously flying forth from a reel that could come to an end anytime, who knows when.

Having said that, the asset that is life holds an enormous importance, for it is the only means to gain a life of eternity. A believer who truly comprehends just what this means knows that the end will loom as a tragic remorse unless he is, as the Holy Quran states, "upright as has been commanded".[7] To avoid becoming inflicted with such remorse, he is never oblivious to the below words of caution sent out by the Almighty, of which he constantly reminds himself:

"And spend out of what We have given you before death comes to one of you, so that he should say: My Lord! Why did You not respite me to a near term, so that I should have given alms and been of the doers of good deeds? And Allah does not respite a soul when its appointed term has come, and Allah is Aware of what you do." (al-Munafiqun, 10-11)

7   See, Hud, 112.

In short, Allah, glory unto Him, wills for a believer to properly come to terms with Divine Splendor and the mysteries and wisdoms underlying this great order. He wishes for the believer a life of *taqwa*, a safe haven from becoming a victim of arrogance that comes with worldly possessions, and thus become a servant worthy of his place in Paradise.

In this humble work at hand, we will therefore attempt to focus on the importance of contemplating and sensing, a primary legacy of the Blessed Prophet –upon him blessings and peace-, their benefits and their proper way of actualization.

I would like to thank Dr. Murat Kaya and M. Akif Günay for the labor they exerted during the preparation of this book and sincerely wish for their efforts to be regarded as a never-ending charity in the sight of the Almighty.

May our Lord unite all our feelings and thoughts with His Will! May He render all of us triumphant in this passing life by elevating us to the peak of His knowledge and love!

Amin!...

Osman Nûri Topbaş

June 2010

Üsküdar

CONTEMPLATION IN ISLAM

The Limits of Reason

An everlasting salute to our Beloved Prophet –upon him blessings and peace- as well as his family and Companions, who contemplated the universe, humanity and the Holy Quran in the profoundest, most beautiful and feeling manner and taught his followers to read all of these with the eye of the heart.

Islam places great importance on reason; so much so that it regards reason as one of the two prime requisites of being held accountable for actions.[1] At every opportunity, it advises one how to utilize reason in a befitting manner. But it also states that the capability

---

1   One of the prerequisites of being held accountable in the sight of Allah, glory unto Him, is to have reached puberty, while the other is to be sane, that is to have the rational aptitude developed enough to discern right from wrong. In line with this criterion, children and the insane are not considered by Islam to be liable for their actions.

boasted by reason to comprehend is not unlimited, as Allah, glory unto Him, has not endowed any creation with unlimited powers.

Similarly to how vision and hearing are limited in their exercise, so also is the power of rational comprehension. Just as the existence of countless beings is not exhausted by the fact they elude eyesight, and there are a host of sounds that are inaudible simply because they exceed the power of hearing, there is a myriad of truths that, remaining outside the capacity of reason, transcend reason's attempts of comprehension. Reason therefore does not suffice on its own to grasp reality in its totality.

While they have promised happiness, rationally inclined philosophers, who have regarded reason as the font of unlimited powers, have only ended up dragging the people they were able influence into a state of distress.[2]

---

2 An incident reported to have taken place in Ancient Greece is emblematic in displaying the shortcomings of reason. Accordingly, a young man once requested a reputed philosopher to train him in legal matters. As agreed, half the philosopher's wage was to be paid in advance, while the other half after the young man succeeded in his first court case. Triumph in his first court case would supposedly show that he received a perfect legal training, meaning his teacher would rightfully deserve the second installment. At the end of his legal training, however, the young man requested his teacher give up his rights to the second installment, suggesting the payment he had already received in advance was duly sufficient. Because of this dispute, the first court case took place between the

Allah, glory unto Him, who indisputably knows the flaws and shortcomings of His servants infinitely better than the servants can ever hope of knowing in themselves, sent throughout the history of human-kind –according to tradition- over 124,000 prophets, all of whom were subjected to Divine Revelation, and reinforced them with scriptures, books and the most potent of aids to guide humankind to the truth and to help them rectify the flaws they cannot by themselves overcome.

---

young man and his teacher. So the hearing began. The young man, addressing the panel of judges, said:

"Whether I win or lose this case, I should not be paying the second installment regardless."

"Why is that?" asked the high judge, upon which the youth replied:

"If I win, I will not be paying due to your ruling. If I lose, I will not be held liable with the payment according to our prior agreement with the claimant."

In response, his teacher, the philosopher, spoke with a similar tone.

"Whether I win or lose", he said, "I should be taking the second installment of my payment."

"Why?" asked the high judge, once more.

"If I win, I will be receiving the payment due to your ruling. If I lose, I will be receiving it according to our prior agreement with the young man."

Evidently, both cases are sound and logical, which goes to show that reason and logic can, time and again, become imprisoned between walls they themselves erect and become stranded in a dead end road. For reason, which miserably breaks down even when trying to find a solution for many a human predicament, it is impossible to grasp the infinite Divine truths in all their aspects. The deliverance of reason from these dead ends therefore lies in coming under the training of Revelation and recognizing the need to spiritually surrender to truths that surpass its limits of comprehension.

It is therefore imperative for reason to undergo training under *wahy*, Divine revelation. Reason untouched by the guidance of Divine revelation is like a wild, untamed horse that not only does not comply with his rider in his hope of reaching his destination, but flings him over the edge of a cliff to perish. Just as the best way to tame a horse is to bridle it and train it, it is necessary to subject reason to the spiritual training of *wahy* and its clarification, the *Sunnah* of the Blessed Prophet –upon him blessings and peace-, and thereby set reason right. Until this is done, reason is like a weapon; it may strike for the better, but also and detrimentally, for the worse...

The Role of the Heart

In Islam, *iman*, that is faith, takes place through the affirmation of the heart and pronouncement of the tongue. What that means is that the true precinct where faith becomes manifest is not reason, but the heart, the center of spiritual sensing and feeling. This point is very important, for faith is a sublime feeling, whereas reason, in contrast, consists in providing means to overcome certain initial phases of understanding to reach that feeling of faith.

True faith is not accomplished unless the Divine truths accepted by reason receive their affirmation in the heart. A faith not entrenched in the heart does not transform into deeds and provide a direction to ones behavior. A faith as such carries no worth in the sight of the Almighty, who condemned the past scholars of the people of Israel for not practicing what they studied and learned of the Divine truths due to not having digested those truths in their hearts, comparing them with donkeys burdened with volumes of books.[3]

Knowing Divine truths, therefore, does not mean stashing them in the mind. To know is to decipher, through contemplating and sensing, the mystery of the tremendous order in the universe and in life and acting accordingly. And only a heart enlightened with the light of faith can live up to that.

What reason reaps through contemplating man, the universe and the Holy Quran, is comparable to raw minerals acquired from the earth. Processing these minerals into things of value, on the other hand, is part and parcel of the heart.

The heart is the center of spiritual sensing, of feeling. The function of the heart, also indicated by the terms intuition and inspiration, is to unify the proofs presented by reason and thereby enable a perfect comprehension of the truth, a process comparable to bringing the pieces of a broken vase together and revealing its true shape and pattern.

---

3   See, al-Juma, 5.

It is thus clear that the most perfect manner to reach the true and the good requires reason to be trained under revelation and a heart with a maturity of faith to step in and make amends for its inadequacy.

The value of contemplation, too, depends on it being reinforced with spiritual sense. Simply put, it rests upon a harmonious and balanced exertion of both the heart and reason. A balance swinging heavily in the way of reason may make someone a good man of the world, a self-seeking person. But in order to be a refined Muslim, it is imperative for the heart, the center of feeling and sensing, to receive spiritual training and act as a guide to reason; for the heart gives direction to thinking, while thinking provides direction to willpower. This effectively means that deeds of intent have their primary incentive in the heart; in effect, they are nothing but feelings embedded therein. Rectifying the heart in accordance with Divine commands is therefore of greater importance than setting other parts of the body in proper balance.

A kind of pseudo contemplation, based on desires egotistic in nature, vulnerable to spiritual diseases like pride and conceit and devoid of the guidance of the heart, digresses from its natural course, misleading man to devilish transgressions and depravity.

Mawlana Rumi says:

"Had Lucifer's love been as immense as his reason, he would not have been the Satan he is today."

It is therefore clear that reason alone holds no value. To take the helms of reason and give it an unswerving direction, it is vital to spiritually refine the feelings embedded in the heart.

To be concise, true contemplation begins at the point where a revelation inspired reason meets with a spiritually matured heart. Our use of the concept 'contemplation' throughout this book should therefore strictly be taken in its most perfected form: contemplation trained under Divine truths and reinforced with the sense of the heart.

Contemplation (اَلتَّفَكُّر) means to derive a lesson from any given thing or experience and focus on it, so as to gain a depth of understanding.

Deliberation (اَلتَّأَمُّل) means to stop and think and to further the investigation by virtue of persisting in contemplation. It denotes a process of delicate thought conducted on the universe and surrounding events, with the aim of deriving a lesson and thereby reaching the core of the given matter.

Forethought (اَلتَّدَبُّر) is to reflect on the pending consequences of a given event.

21

The Importance of Contemplation

Both the Book of Allah, glory unto Him, and the sayings of the Blessed Prophet –upon him blessings and peace- emphatically command and encourage investigating, contemplating and deriving lessons from one's surroundings. In just two verses from among hundreds of others mentioned in the Holy Quran in this regard, the Almighty states:

"Do they not reflect within themselves: Allah did not create the heavens and the earth and what is between them two but with truth, and (for) an appointed term? And most surely most of the people are deniers of the meeting of their Lord." (ar-Rum, 8)

"Say: I exhort you only to one thing, that rise up for Allah's sake in twos and singly, then ponder: there is no madness in your companion; he is only a warner to you before a severe chastisement." (as-Saba', 46)

In the above, humans are enjoined to serve the Almighty, both individually and communally, and contemplate and focus on reality.[4] Those who do this are promised salvation even if this be the only command they adhere to.

---

4 Opinions held by society or the majority can tend to exert their influence on personal opinion, Relief from this influence and finding a pathway to the truth lies in requesting the guidance of the experts of that path and spending time alone with the heart so as to enter the domain of contemplation. Each person must therefore voice his own opinion and critically assess the accuracy of general opinion.

The Prophet of Allah was in a Constant State of Contemplation

The Blessed Prophet –upon him blessings and peace- loved silence and contemplation. In the times just prior to his prophethood, he had grown even a more intense desire to retreat. He would remain for days on end in the Cave of Hira, approximately around 5 kilometers away from Mecca. His worship in these times of retreat was comprised of contemplation, gazing at the Kabah and reflecting on the treasures of the heavens and earth in the footsteps of his great ancestor Ibrahim –upon him peace-.[5] Through this manner, the Almighty was preparing him for his sacred mission.

The contemplation of the universe, its Creator and creation in which the Prophet –upon him blessings and peace- immersed himself during those days, did not cease for the remainder of his life.

Hind ibn Abi Hala –Allah be well-pleased with him- explains:

"The Messenger of Allah was in a continuous state of sorrow and thought. Comfort for him was irrelevant. He never spoke in vain. His silence was longer than his speech. He would always begin and

---

end his talk by mentioning the name of Allah…" (Ibn Sa'd, I, 422-423)

To encourage Muslims to embark upon contemplation, The Prophet of Allah –upon him blessings and peace- has said:

"*My Lord has commanded my silence to be of contemplation.*" (İbrahim Canan, *Hadis Ansiklopedisi*, XVI, 252/5838)

"*There is no worship like contemplation.*" (Bayhakî, *Shuab*, IV, 157; Ali al-Muttaqî, XVI, 121)

"*Be like wayfarers on this earth! Adopt mosques as homes! Accustom your hearts to sensitivity! Contemplate and cry in lots! Let not your desires of the ego change you!*" (Ebû Nuaym, *Hilye,* I, 358)

The Blessed Prophet –upon him blessings and peace- again narrates from the ten leaves of Revelation given to Ibrahim –upon him peace-:

"*An intelligent man ought to have certain hours: A portion of those hours ought to be spared for praying to and seeking from the Lord, another portion for contemplating the sublime art and power of the Almighty, another portion to reflect on what has been committed in the past and planning what to do in the future and another for earning a living in a manner permissible.*"

(Ebû Nuaym, *Hilye*, I, 167; İbn-i Esîr, *el-Kâmil*, I, 124)

Luqman –upon him peace- used to love sitting by himself in a secluded place to contemplate, something he frequently did. Upon being asked, "You keep to your self most of the time. Would not it be better if you mixed in with people and spoke with them?" Luqman –upon him peace- gave the following response:

"Remaining alone for long period of time is more suitable for contemplation. And remaining in contemplation for a long period of time is a guide that leads one to Paradise."[6]

Abu'd-Darda –Allah be well-pleased with him- used to say:

"An hour of contemplation is superior to forty nights of supererogatory worship." (Deylemî, II, 70-71, no: 2397, 2400)

Said ibn Musayyab, a prominent scholar of the Tabiun generation, was once asked which deed of worship held greater virtue.

"Contemplating the creation of Allah", he replied, "and growing insightful into His religion." (Bursevî, Rûhu'l-Bayân, [an-Nûr, 44])

---

6   Imam Ghazzali, Ihya-u Ulumi'd-Din, Beirut1990, Daru'l-Khayr, VI, 45. The place inside a historical mosque in Tarsus where Luqman –upon him peace- retreated to itiqaf to contemplate is still visited today.

Bishr ibn Khafiy used to emphasize the significance of contemplation in the following words:

"Had human beings properly contemplated the majesty of Allah, they would not have been able to rebel against him and commit sins." (Ibn Kathir, I, 448, [Âl-i İmrân, 190])

As explained earlier, contemplation that leads one to an understanding of the majesty of Allah, glory unto Him, is an activity of reason. But it is the heart that culminates this activity in a perfect result. Since the heart is the noblest part of the body, it is only natural for its deeds to stand in greater worth than those carried out by other parts. The heart, after all, is the precinct of Divine Sight.

It remains an incontestable fact that a contemplation exerted by a reason trained under revelation is the first glimmer of the rays that enlighten the heart. It is the first and only means on the path that leads one to prudence and wisdom. Again, a contemplation of such caliber is a means to purge the heart from everything except for the Almighty (*masiwallah*) and thereby attain Divine Love.

The most beneficial of all contemplation is to reflect on Divine Majesty, Splendor and Sovereignty, by which one begins to think of ways of setting his or her life right and leaving all things detrimental to her or his eternal happiness.

Contemplating the blessings, commands, prohibitions, names and attributes of Allah, glory unto Him, flourishes love and wisdom in the heart and begins to elevate one spiritually. The thought of the Hereafter, its honor and eternality compared to the stage of test that is the life of the world increases desire for the life after and enables one to value the world only as much as is merited. One then realizes that the life of the world is but a sprint race from the mother's womb to the grave. Grasping the fact that life is a precious asset for earning the bliss of eternity, allows the person to increase his solemnity and effort to render life more meaningful. He treats the time he has in his hands like treasure, making sure to make the most of it through good and beneficial deeds.

Abu'l-Hasan Harakani says it beautifully:

"At any given time, it is necessary for at least one limb of a Believer to be preoccupied with the remembrance of the Almighty. A Muslim ought to remember Allah either with the heart or the tongue, or see something the Almighty would like him to see, or do deeds of generosity with the hand, or visit people with his feet, or put his mind to service of fellow Muslims, or offer a prayer with an unwavering faith, or contemplate so as to attain wisdom, or do a sincere deed, or warn people of the adversities of Judgment Day.

27

Such a person will surely enter Paradise the moment he raises his head from the grave, dragging his shroud from behind him; of that I am his guarantor!"[7]

7   Abu'l-Hasan Harakânî, *Seyr ü Sülûk Risâlesi*, prepared by Sadık Yalsızuçanlar, p. 107, Sufi Kitap, Istanbul, 2006.

CONTEMPLATION IN THE UNIVERSE

How amazing it is that man becomes infatuated upon seeing an ostentatious, embellished palace. The sight never leaves his mind, as he keeps on spreading the news of its beauty to others for the rest of his life. Yet, in spite of constantly seeing the grand Divine masterpiece of art that is the universe, he shrinks back from thoroughly reflecting on it and shies away from making an adequate mention of it. He takes no notice of it and carries on, as if it is an ordinary thing. Little is he aware that the palace he admires so much is but a tiny particle of Earth, which in turn is one of the smallest specks of the grand universe…

CONTEMPLATION IN THE UNIVERSE

From the smallest particle to the grandest planet, everything in the universe is a Divine masterpiece of art. With countless manifestations of wisdom presented to the appreciation of the human mind, the universe is an exhibition of Divine Majesty.

For the thinking mind, the universe provides an evocative display of creative order and harmony. Countless verses in the Holy Quran give expression to this. To mention only a couple:

"Do they not then look up to heaven above them how We have made it and adorned it and it has no gaps? And the earth, We have made it plain and cast in it mountains and We have made to grow therein of all beautiful kinds. To give sight and as a reminder to every servant who turns frequently (to Allah)." (Kaf, 6-8)

"Do you not see that Allah sends down water from the cloud, then makes it go along in the earth in springs, then brings forth therewith herbage of various colors, then it withers so that you see it becoming yellow, then He makes it a thing crushed and broken into pieces? Most surely there is a reminder in this for the men of understanding." (az-Zumar, 21)

Water that remains on the earth's surface serves humans; it is consumed, used for cleaning and various other needs. It is thus prone to become polluted from time to time. But through a magnificent circular process, the Almighty continuously purifies it and serves it up again to serve human need.

Urging us to contemplate the water's journey of transformation, Mawlana Rumi says:

"*When divested of its purity, muddied and murky, water becomes disturbed and astounded, just like us, for having been dirtied on earth...It begins to cry from its depths and beseech the Almighty. Thereupon, the Almighty vaporizes the water and elevates it to the skies. Steering it to a variety of paths, He purifies it from top to bottom. Then He pours it back on Earth, sometimes as rain, sometimes as snow, and at times, as hail. Finally, He paves its path to the vast ocean.*"

Narrating in a compelling style a natural phenomenon we get to witness during every season of the year, Rumi then adds the following:

"*Approach the Almighty and purify your heart from all dirt, just like the water! Become thereby a rain; pour down abundance and mercy!*"

The harmonious journey the universe has been setting out on since its creation, its sublime order entwined with a profound wisdom and mystery, is, in any case, more than enough reason for one to acknowledge that it is all the work of One, Eternal Force.

Contemplating the Skies

One proof of the power and majesty of the Almighty lies in the Divine Sovereignty displayed on earth, in the skies and in the stars. Failing to contemplate the marvels of the skies deprives human understanding from a splendid exhibition of wisdom.

Compared to the skies, the Earth is like a drop in an ocean, even smaller. There is almost no chapter in the Holy Quran in which the grandeur of the skies is not given mention to. There are even many oaths made in the name of the skies:

"By the heaven, holding mansions of the stars"
(al-Buruj, 1)

"But nay! I swear by the falling of stars. And most surely it is a very great oath if you only knew..."
(al-Waqiah, 75-76)[8]

---

8   Also see, ad-Dhâriyât, 7; an-Najm, 1; at-Takwir, 15; at-Tarıq, 1; as-Shams, 1-2, 5.

The immensity of the universe, the separate motions of its objects and the distances separating them are given in gigantic figures that exceed the wildest imagination and the most penetrating comprehension. Scientists have even felt compelled to admit:

"The universe is more terrifying, startling and greater then we can possibly imagine, for the objects in space are distancing themselves from one another at frightening speed."[9]

Scientists estimate the radius of the universe as 14 trillion light years. The speed of light, as known, is approximately 300,000 km (186,411 mph) per hour.

The Galaxies

There are some hundred billion galaxies in the universe visible to state-of-the-art telescopes. That makes the galaxy a colossal community of spatial bodies that each harbors well nigh a billion stars, including their raw material and residues.[10] The Milky Way, which is home to the solar system, is simply one galaxy among these.

---

9   Yûsuf al-Hajj, *Mawsûatu'l-I'cazi'l-Ilmi*, p. 413.
10 http://www.biltek.tubitak.gov.tr, Evren/Evrenin Yapıtaşları Gökadalar, (Accessed, 06.12.2005).

Communities of hundreds or thousand galaxies are called clusters. In turn, communities made up of galaxy groups are called galaxy super-clusters.[11]

Our Milky Way galaxy and the some 30 galaxies near us constitute the local galaxy cluster. The Virgo Cluster, a near cluster which stands at a distance of approximately 65 million light years, includes an estimated 2000 galaxies. A single super-cluster, it should be known, lies amid tens of galaxy clusters, boasting a circumference of a 100 million light years.[12]

Another aspect exhibiting Divine Splendor throughout space is the collision of galaxies. Galaxies collide on a frequent basis. If their orbits cross paths or if they have gained enough proximity their mass gravity attracts them closer to each other. No matter how many billions of stars galaxies may have, owing to the enormous distance separating them, stars pass by each other during the collision without coming into contact. The impact of the collision, however, causes the gases and dust, from which stars are made of, to converge in certain spots, stimulating the formation of stars. Observed, for that reason, is an escalation in the formation of new stars in galaxies that have undergone a collision. According to estimations, a col-

---

11 http://www.biltek.tubitak.gov.tr, Evren/Gökbilim Sözlüğü, (Accessed, 06.12.2005).

12 http://www.biltek.tubitak.gov.tr, Evren/Evrenin Yapıtaşları/Gökadalar/Gökada Kümeleri, (Accessed, 06.12.2005).

lision of a similar kind looms between the Milky Way and her neighbor Andromeda.[13] The two galaxies are approaching one another at a speed of nearly 500,000 km's (310,685 mph) per hour. Remembering they are separated by a distance of 2.2 million light years, a collision is imminent in around 3 billion years.[14]

There are approximately 200 billion stars in the Milky Way, just one of which is the Sun. The Milky Way has a circumference of 100,000 light years. Orbiting at a pace of 630 km per second (391 mps), it proceeds at a speed of 900,000 kph (559234 mph) towards the Star Vega.

The Hercules Cluster is made up of 100 small galaxies and lies at a distance of 650 million light years from Earth.

The Solar System

Lying amid the Milky Way, the Solar System has a circumference of 12 billion km (7,566,454,306 miles). The sun, located at a distance of 30,000 light years from the center of the Milky Way, is believed to be around 4.5 to 5 billion years old.

---

13 http://www.biltek.tubitak.gov.tr,   Evren/Evrenin   Yapıtaşları/ Gökadalar/Çarpışan Gökadalar, (Accessed, 15.12.2005); http:// www.biltek.tubitak.gov.tr/haberler/gokbilim/99-08-4.pdf

14 http://www.newsandevents.utoronto.ca/bin/000414b.asp; http:// www.biltek.tubitak.gov.tr/haberler/gokbilim/2000-05-3.pdf

The Sun transforms 564 million tons of hydrogen to 560 million tons of helium at each second. In the process, 4 million tons of gas radiates forth as rays of energy. In terms of lost mass, the Sun loses 4 million tons of mass per second and 240 million tons per minute. Considering the sun has been consistently consuming energy at this speed for the past 3 billion years, it means that until now, it has lost 400 billion × million of mass. Still, even a massive amount like that is equivalent only to about 1/5000 of the Sun's current mass.

The temperature of the Sun's surface is 6000 degrees C° (10,832 F). The heat of its core, on the other hand, reaches 20 million degrees C°. While the Sun's temperature increases constantly, so does it circumference. It is therefore considered a possibility that the ever-growing the Sun could one day explode and spell an end to the planets closest to it, in Mercury, Venus, Earth and Mars.

Exactly 324,529 times greater than Earth, the Sun has a mass of 2×10^{27} tons, that is a billion times a billion times a billion, multiplied twice, and a gigantic radius of 700,000 km, or 434.969 miles.[15]

---

15 See,http://www.physics.metu.edu.tr/~ecevit/bilinen_evren_gercekleri.ppt, (Accessed: 21. 06. 2007); http://gokyuzu.org (Accessed: 21.06.2007); http://www.ozaltin.8k.com/NN/2.htm. (Accessed: 16.10.2004); Yûsuf al-Hajj, *Mawsûatu'l-I'cazi'l-Ilmi,*, p. 413-417; Akram Ahmed İdrîs, *al-Falak wa't-Tıbb Amama Azameti'l-Qur'ân*, 19-112; Prof. Dr. Osman Çakmak, *Bir Çekirdekti Kâinat*, p. 66.

The Holy Quran reminds:

"Blessed is He Who made the constellations in the heavens and made therein a lamp and a shining moon." (al-Furqan, 61)

The Skies are Constantly Expanding

Allah, glory unto Him, states that He constantly expands the flawlessly created skies. The verse declares:

"And the heaven, We raised it high with power, and most surely We are the makers of things ample." (ad-Dhariyat, 47)

In 1929, scientists discovered that nebula[16] constantly travel further away from our galaxy, a finding later used as a basis for the theory that space is undergoing constant expansion.[17] According to this theory, doubtless one of the most significant turning points in 20th century space research, galaxies are increasingly moving away from each other in proportion with the accumulated distance.[18]

Applying this theory to the objects in space in 1950, scientists proceeded to calculate the speed with

---

16 Nebulas are the massive white spots, apart from stars, found in space, given the name due their resemblance of whitish clouds.

17 Celâl Kırca, *Kur'ân-ı Kerîm'de Fen Bilimleri, p.* 165; an-Najjâr, *as-Samâ*, p. 82-93; Faruk Yılmaz, *Kâinâtın Yaratılışı*, p. 64-67, 255-258.

18 Şakir Kocabaş, *Kur'ân'da Yaratılış*, Istanbul 2004, p. 19.

which galaxies travel away from each other. While a galaxy 10 million light years away from our own cuts loose at a speed of 250 km's per second, the breakaway speed of a galaxy 10 billion light years away is 250,000 km's per second.[19]

That the universe, the enormity of which is spoken of here, is ever-growing in dimension without ever remaining the same, goes to show the impossibility of perfectly comprehending the splendor of the Almighty.

Beautifully expressed is the feeling of awe that envelops one upon contemplation of these countless exhibitions of Divine Majesty:

> *Grand You are Lord, grand, so grand,*
> *Greatness itself to You is a strand!*
>
> (Ali Haydar Bey)

Constantly expanding this colossal universe, Allah, glory onto Him, will eventually roll it up, just like a scribe rolls up a piece of paper.[20] Again, when the time comes, He will transform Earth to an earth of another kind, and the skies to skies of another sort.[21] This entails the creation of a new universe, signaling the beginning of a new life.[22]

---

19 Prof. Dr. Osman Çakmak, *Bir Çekirdekti Kâinat*, p. 28.

20 al-Anbiya, 104.

21 Ibrâhîm, 48.

22 See, an-Najjâr, as-Samâ, p. 82, 105-106, 187-194; http://www.biltek.tubitak.gov.tr, Evren/Evrenin Kaderi/Kapalı Evren.

The Seven Heavens

In the Holy Quran, the Almighty also makes mention of seven heavens or levels of skies. Presuming what has been mentioned up until now pertains to the first level, how are human reason and comprehension expected to bear the mysteries of the others?

Allah, glory unto Him, asserts:

"Who created the seven heavens one above another; you see no incongruity in the creation of the Beneficent Allah; then look again, can you see any disorder? Then turn back the eye again and again; your look shall come back to you confused while it is fatigued. And certainly We have adorned this lower heaven with lamps and We have made these missiles for the devils, and We have prepared for them the chastisement of burning." (al-Mulk, 3-5)

Now, lift your head and turn your gaze to the skies! Reflect on the innumerable objects in space, faltering not even for a split second in their orbit amid this grand order, each loaded with an underlying mystery and wisdom in its movement.

If the Earth did not rotate on its axis, one side of it would constantly be bright, while the other side doomed to perpetual darkness. There would have been no way of separating the hours of work from the hours of rest.

There is also inherent wisdom in the fact that it takes 24 hours for Earth to rotate once around its axis. Were it to take longer, Earth would have been something like Mercury, where the difference between daily and nightly warmth exceeds 1000 C° (1,832 F). Excess heat would have scorched the Earth in those long days, leaving only for a menacing cold come the evening, freezing everything in its wake.

With these in mind, take note of how the Almighty has blanketed the day with night and rendered the former a time to work, while the latter a time to rest. Think of the manifestations of Divine Power and Mercy in their relentless pursuit of each other!

Again, had the Earth not rotated around the Sun with a tilt of 23 degrees and 27 minutes, there would not have been the four seasons so vital for life. Furthermore, had the Earth not been given this tilt, water evaporating from the oceans would have surged north and south, turning continents into daunting icebergs.

If the moon, say, was 50,000 miles further away from where it is now, the tides would have been so enormous that the continents would have been deluged twice on a daily basis. Even the mighty mountains would have eroded to utter annihilation, in almost the blink of an eye.[23]

23 See, *İlim-Ahlâk-İman*, prepared by, M. Rahmi Balaban, Diyanet

So therefore, do not be stuck in awe of the sky simply for the sake of its immensity and the myriad of stars it boasts. Instead, proceed to reflect on its Creator and how He has fashioned and ordered it all! How is it that the Almighty holds those massive stars together without a visible pillar or peg?

Just think of the Sun and the Moon; do they ever breakdown? Is there ever a time when they are sent to repair? While traveling in their predestined orbits do any of the countless objects in space step out of their Divine course and have accidents?

It is a Grave Sin to Abandon Contemplation

How amazing it is that man is infatuated upon seeing an ostentatious, embellished palace. The sight never leaves his mind, as he keeps on spreading the news of its beauty for the rest of his life. But in spite of constantly seeing the grand Divine masterpiece of art that is the universe, he shrinks back from thoroughly reflecting on it and shies away from making an adequate mention of it. He takes no notice of it and carries on, like it is an ordinary thing. Little is he aware that the palace he admires so much is but a tiny particle of Earth, which in turn is one of the smallest specks of the grand universe...

Publishing, Ankara, p. 187.

A person oblivious to contemplating Divine Power resembles the ant in the below parable:

An ant builds a nest in a king's palace, which is surrounded by high walls, built on a solid foundation, decorated by the most exquisite furniture and swarming with servants. When encountering its friends upon making its way out of its nest, the ant speaks to them about nothing but its nest, the crumbs it gathers and how it stocks them for the morrow. The ant is utterly and almost hopelessly remote from the thought of the magnificent palace in which it roams and the power, splendor and sovereignty of the king. Its ignorance is all the more compounded by the fact that he is completely unmindful of those who live there.

An ignorant man is also unmindful of the Almighty's divine masterpieces of art, the angels and the righteous person living in His dominion.

There is no way that an ant can become aware of a palace and the beauties it boasts. But through contemplation and imagination, we humans can journey through many realms. In a humble return for the countless blessings the Almighty has endowed him with, a person can come to terms with his nothingness and vulnerability, and prostrate in gratitude. Only a 'human' can do this; or in other words, only those who do this can carry the honor of humanness. Indeed, humanity has a natural predisposition and ability for

43

contemplation. Gradually laying waste to this potential by not putting it to use is to betray Divine trust and to bid farewell to one of man's most defining attributes.

The great Mawlana Rumi provides the following parable to describe those who roam on the display of eternal mysteries and wisdom that is Earth with an idle heart and respond to the glaring Divine messages radiating forth from creation with so little as a dim-witted expression.

"*An ox one day came to Baghdad and strolled around town from tip to toe. But amid all the beautiful sights, tastes and masterpieces, only some melon and watermelon peels dumped on the side of the road caught its attention. After all, befitting the gaze of an ox or a donkey is either hay scattered on a road, or weed and grass growing from its fringes.*" (Mathnawi, v.4, couplet: 2377-2329)

It is said that a certain man during the time of Musa –upon him peace- had worshiped persistently for thirty years; such that a cloud had even begun to shade him during his times of worship, owing to his piety. But there came a day when the cloud did not make its appearance, leaving the man to worship in the sun. He went to his mother to see if she might know the reason.

"You must have committed a sin", she commented.

"No", he responded. "I do not believe I have!"

"Did you not gaze at the skies, the flowers? Were you kept back from contemplating the splendor of Allah despite seeing them?" she asked.

"Yes", the man then confessed. "I failed to contemplate in spite of seeing the wonders around me."

"Are you looking for a greater sin than that?" his mother then said. "You must repent immediately!"

A believer of right mind must therefore never neglect the duty to contemplate.

The more a person learns of the magnificence of the Almighty's art and the more he contemplates it, the more his wisdom of the Almighty's Glory and Majesty and his proximity to the Truth will be.

Ali –Allah be well-pleased with him- has said, "Expanding knowledge of the Quran with some knowledge of astronomy enables one to grow in faith and certainty", after which he quoted the following verse:

"Most surely in the variation of the night and the day, and what Allah has created in the heavens and the earth, there are signs for a people who guard (against evil)." (Yunus, 6)

Every single being created by the Almighty, serves a specific purpose within the Divine order. Until now, mankind has been able to gain acquaintance with only a few of these purposes. Wisdom unseen and as yet not comprehended are multitudes infinitely greater in number than compared to those thought to have been understood.

If we know what sound is, it is because we have receptive organs like ears. If we know what color is, it is all thanks to our eyes. Who knows of the many Divine manifestations in this infinite realm of being of which we have absolutely no clue, simply because we are deprived of the receptive organs to sense them.[24]

Restrained by a limited power of reason, how can man be able to perfectly comprehend Allah, glory unto Him, when he cannot even completely grasp the entire creatures and their specific characteristics? Muslim scholars, who were able come to terms with just an infinitesimal glimpse of the Almighty's Splendor and the manifestations of His attributes, felt compelled to admit, in awe and dazzle:

---

24 The universe, according to Muslim scholars, consists of substances and accidents. Substances are material entities. Accidents, on the other hand, are the perceptible qualities of a material entity. Color and smell, for instance, are accidents perceptible only through the subsistence of a material being. As mentioned above, color would not have been perceived had there been no such thing as eyesight, and smell it were not for smelling. As we are to begin a life of a unique character in the Hereafter, presuming we will then begin perceive accidents of an entirely distinct nature is as conceivable as considering many other accidents to exist, here on Earth, that lie beyond our perception.

"To understand Him is to understand He cannot be comprehended."

This is because created beings contain no reflection or manifestation of the Almighty's essential reality. Everything created by Allah, glory unto Him, is constituted by the combinations of Divine attributes. The fact that there has not been created a single space that can endure an essential manifestation of the Almighty is proven by the Divine response "لَنْ تَرَينِى / You can never see Me" [25] given to Musa –upon him peace- upon his adamant request to see the Almighty, as a consequence of which he ended up passing out. It is for that very reason that, let alone seeing the Almighty's essential reality, man is limited by an insufficiency to even comprehend the reality of His attributes.

Elegantly depicting this is the late Necip Fâzıl:

The atoms in revel, bedecked, festive,

And a light all around, a light all around,

An architecture entwined, the self entwined,

I identify you Lord, the Famous Unidentified!

The Atmosphere

The air that envelops the Earth holds many secrets and is underlain with numerous wisdoms. The clouds

---

that suddenly appear in the sky, the wind that breezes through the air, sometimes light sometimes in a burst, lightings that emit a tremendous sound, the pelting rain, the falling snow; each is a fabulous manifestation that occurs in line with a magnificent measure.

The Holy Quran summons man to contemplate such manifestations rampant between the Earth and the sky and to behold the proofs that verify the Power of the Almighty, stating:

"Most surely in the creation of the heavens and the earth and the alternation of the night and the day, and the ships that run in the sea with that which profits men, and the water that Allah sends down from the cloud, then gives life with it to the earth after its death and spreads in it all (kinds of) animals, and the changing of the winds and the clouds made subservient between the heaven and the earth, there are signs for a people who understand." (al-Baqara, 164)

The atmosphere, which compassionately embraces our Earth, is one of the most splendid orders of the Almighty in alluding to His boundless mercy for human beings. It is made up of 77% nitrogen, 21% oxygen and 1% of a combination of carbon dioxide, argon and other gases. So easily flammable is oxygen that it is estimated that each increase of a hundredth of oxygen in excess of the 21% spoken of, would increase the probability of a lighting strike induced bushfire by around 70%. An oxygen ratio in excess of 25%, on the other hand, would be more than enough to turn an overwhelming majority of the vegetables we consume to ash.

On another note, despite the constant use of oxygen and carbon dioxide, their ratios in the air are maintained. If it only were humans and animals that inhabited the Earth, they would have used up all the oxygen in the air and turned it into carbon dioxide, and in swift time, they would have been poisoned through inhaling carbon dioxide, which would have increased in an inverse proportion to the decreasing oxygen. But the Power who created the universe also created vegetation. And by giving it an ability to process carbon dioxide and turn it into oxygen, He has endowed the universe with a magnificent balance and a life that never ceases.

The Earth's crust has been set with such a delicate measure that had it been just a little thicker, it would have absorbed all carbon dioxide and oxygen, leading to the end of all vegetation.[26]

Oxygen is a vital need for the biochemical functions our bodies constantly perform at every moment. We ceaselessly inhale air through our lungs and then exhale the very same air. That an appropriate density of oxygen in the atmosphere is needed to accom-

49

26 See, *İlim-Ahlâk-İman*, prepared by: M. Rahmi Balaban, p. 187.

modate this process of inhaling-exhaling shows that coincidence can not play a hand in maintaining this delicate ratio. Allah, glory unto Him, who has created our bodies in a way that requires a constant need for oxygen, has abundantly blessed us with our most vital, primary need. Not only has He made oxygen easily accessible, He has also placed it in the air in the most perfect ratio. Each simple breath we take is in fact a complex and meaningful exercise and an enormous Divine gift.

When aboard a state-of-the-art airplane, we hear an announcement right before it takes flight, advising us to "Wear the oxygen masks that will automatically deploy in case of a drop in pressure in high altitude."

But in everyday life, none of us carry the slightest apprehension that, the amount of oxygen in the air will rise to, say, 25% or plummet to 18% by tomorrow and anxiously rush to buy an oxygen mask. A believer or not, every single person leads a life of utmost dependence on the Divine Order. Life would have been unbearable if one was aware of each and every life threatening factor surrounding him.

The air is also like a mirror enlightening our surroundings. Light cannot radiate forth without making contact with matter. A light that crashes into a particle spreads itself around, like a firecracker, in the forms of heat and light. As there are no particles like molecules or atoms in the void of space outside of the atmosphere, they remain in darkness, despite them receiving the light of the Sun just the same.

The Moon, for instance, deprived of an atmosphere, has no layer of gas that can disperse the incoming light of the Sun and enlighten its surroundings. For that reason, whereas the surface of the Moon is bright, the surface above always remains in the dark despite it being inundated by a rain of light.

These wonderful manifestations are clear proofs that the Earth has been created in a way to accommodate human life and according to an all-important purpose. Together with being a grand blessing of the Almighty to His servants, this delicate balance which makes life possible is at the same time a proof of His existence and endless power. That each being in the universe moves in accordance with a set Divine program and that everything we encounter discloses an inner plan, measure and order necessitates the existence of a Power who plans, orders and measures this tremendous balance.

This makes the atheist claim that life and the universe for that matter have come to be and exist through sheer coincidence, a ridiculous nonsense.

İsmail Fennî Ertuğrul (1855-1946) illustrates this fact by way of the following analogy:

"Stumbling upon a measure and order at any given place, reason necessarily infers the existence of an ordering and measuring power.

Suppose you have a garden. You had the gardener consecutively plant many saplings around it. You turn up there one day to see that some of the saplings have been knocked down here and there, haphazardly. You ask the gardener for an explanation and he tells you that they were knocked down by a sudden storm. You will accept that answer. But you turn up there another day and this time see that the saplings have been knocked down in a pattern; you see, for instance, the fifth sapling in each line knocked to the ground while the previous four have been left in tact and you observe this pattern all around the garden. You, again, ask for an explanation and the gardener tells you, once again, that the storm is to blame. Will you believe that? Certainly, you will not. You will instead blame it on someone's malicious intent. Even though the first case could be explained through coincidence, the second can not; for this time both measure and calculation have come into the picture."[27]

No person of their right mind could dispute the fact that the universe maintains its existence through meticulous calculation and a most delicate balance.

27 *İman Hakikatleri Etrafında Suallere Cevaplar*, p. 21-22, Sebil Publishing, Istanbul, 1978.

Below are just some instances of this Divine balance:

Air Pressure

The gases that comprise the atmosphere apply a pressure of approximately 1 kg to a 1 cm square area, or 14.22 pounds per square inch. That is to say, the human body is under the constant pressure of 15 tons of weight. But Allah, glory unto Him, has balanced that out magnificently, too. Whatever amount of pressure there may be outside, our bodies contain the same amount of outward moving pressure. This drastic difference in air pressure is the very reason behind the illnesses and nasal bleeding experienced by some who ascend to higher elevation. Astronauts, who traverse beyond the atmosphere, on the other hand, can only travel wearing uniforms with inbuilt air pressure.

The Cold-Heat Harmony

With their capacity to retain high heat, carbon dioxide and vapor molecules adequately dispersed in the air enable the maintenance of a perfect harmony. Absorbing some of the rays of sunlight that come during the day, these molecules prevent an excess increase of heat. When night falls and the Sun withdraws its rays, the heat absorbed during the day is withheld by these molecules in the air, just like a hothouse, and is not released into the void of space. Because it does not have a protective roof of this kind, the Moon, for instance, is scorched by excess heat during the day and is under the grip of a blistering cold at night.

The Winds

In terms of its purposes with regard to heat, pressure, level of moisture and many other activities that take place therein, the atmosphere is divided into different layers. The troposphere, the first of these layers, is through which rain, snow and winds occur. The layer extends to almost 16 km's (10 miles) to the sky from above ground level and its temperature gradually decreases all the way to -56°C (-74 F). Founded in this layer of the atmosphere is a flawless cyclical system.

As the Earth's axis is a fraction tilted, it is not only the equatorial region that receives the rays of the Sun in a straight trajectory. This enables the distribution of heat to tropical regions. Consequent upon higher temperatures in these regions, a high amount of heat is stored; and the storage of this heat enables the maintenance of the required force and energy for winds.

Millions of tons of water vaporized from the seas and oceans mount the gentle air. From there, they are delivered by winds to lands in need of water. As a result of this cyclical motion, rainfall is not reserved only for wet regions, but, through a perfectly executed plan, each and every region receives its due share of rainfall.

The immaculate motion of the atmosphere enables the transfer of heat. With help from the north to south motion of the low and high pressure systems and the strong currents, the cold air of the northern latitudes makes its way down south, while the southern heat makes its way up north.

That the Sun provides different parts of Earth with various intensities of heat enables the masses of air in the atmosphere to heat up in different levels. Hot air, compliant with the Divine command it is given, rises immediately. Constituted that way are active sources of air, known as low pressure centers in warm climates and as high pressure centers is cool climates. As a result, the tiny particles of air begin to move in the form of a wind, through which moisture, heat, intensity and energy found in the atmosphere, as well as pollens that reproduce plants, are shifted to their required places.

The Holy Quran declares:

"And We send the winds fertilizing, then send down water from the cloud so We give it to you to drink of, nor is it you who store it up." (al-Hijr, 22)

Winds, just like the rest of creation in the universe, comply, in absolute obedience, with the Almighty's sovereignty. It is a means of mercy when our Lord commands it to be so, yet also a manifestation of a destructive wrath when, again, our Lord decrees.

A vivid illustration of this fact is the below verse, depicting how the Ad Tribe was annihilated by a vigorous gale:

"For We sent against them a furious wind, on a Day of violent Disaster. Plucking out men as if they were roots of palm-trees torn up (from the ground)" (al-Qamar, 19-20)

The Other Benefits of Air

As well as carrying on its gentle shoulders millions of tons of water, the air also lifts airplanes boarded with hundreds of passengers. It distributes light and heat. It also brings, to our hearing, sounds of hundreds of different wavelengths, of which mobile phones are perhaps the most noteworthy example.

On the other hand, air presents our sense of smell with various types of fragrances without mixing them together. If it were not for the atmosphere, neither would we have been able to make ourselves audible to the person right by our side, nor flick on the light switch with the hope of seeing what lies in front of us. Circulating through our lungs, air moreover performs a vital task. By all these, it reminds believers with a knack for contemplation of the infinite glory, power and mercy of Allah, glory unto Him.

A Divine Filter

The layer above the troposphere that reaches a height of 50 km (31 miles) from ground level is called the stratosphere. The stratosphere blocks out dangerous rays of excess energy from the Earth. Found here is the ozone layer. An oxygen molecule consisting of a triad of atoms, the ozone filters the harmful aspects of the Sun's rays.

Ultraviolet rays emitted by the Sun decrease growth in plants, cause skin cancer human beings, damage the eye and increase the risk of catching a number of contagious diseases. What the stratosphere does is that it catches the ultraviolet rays that come from the Sun and reflects them back, and at once, turns oxygen to ozone through a superbly balanced chemical reaction.

In fact, so dangerous a gas is ozone that inhaling 1/200 grams of it is enough to kill a person. But just look at the mercy of the Almighty that He has made a filter out of such a layer of poison and put it to use in maintaining the climactic balance and in preventing a harm that would have had fatal consequences for human beings.

The Guarded Canopy

The layer that extends to 80 km, (49.7 miles) above ground level and which is considered the middle layer of the atmosphere is the mesosphere, serving firm as a shield against pelting meteors.

Passing the obstacles of Jupiter, Saturn and the Moon, meteors come under the force of the Earth's gravity and enter the atmosphere at an incredible speed. What is commonly referred to as a shooting star is actually a meteor which comes into contact with the atmosphere and is burned to dust in the mesosphere. Had there not been a protective layer of the kind enveloping Earth, or if the current layer was a fraction thinner, millions of meteors would have fallen on Earth and wreaked destruction, punching countless holes on its surface just like that of the Moon. But the boundless mercy of Allah, glory unto Him, turns these giant cannons bound for Earth into dust before they ever make contact with its surface. Then, each particle of this dust turns into the nucleus of a tiny raindrop.

The formation of clouds requires fine particles that are a combination of both earth and space. On top of that, these particles are required to reach the highest atmospheric level. The moist winds that breeze their way into there apply an intensity on the nuclei and form a cloud particle. According to a physical and mathematical plan, the cloud particles, in turn, become tiny drops of rain, which will then fall once again on earth.

Long before anything about the atmosphere had been discovered, the Almighty, the Owner of the Earth and skies, had said:

"And We have made the skies a guarded canopy and (yet) they turn aside from its signs." (al-Anbiya, 32)

Radio Waves

The atmospheric layer that begins from 500 km (310 miles) above ground level and reaches an elevation of 1000 km is called the ionosphere. There, the atoms and molecules are not uncharged but ionized, that is either by receiving or emitting electrons, they are charged with electricity. As a result of these atoms becoming ionized through absorbing the high energy rays of the Sun, the heat in the layer can at times reach 2000°C. For the atmosphere, the ionosphere is like a mirror made up of ions. Virtually hitting this mirror are the electromagnetic waves of radio and wireless transmitters that rise to space, some of which are then reflected back on Earth. The reflected waves then reach every single corner of Earth, making it possible to follow radio and wireless broadcasts everywhere with relative ease.

As can be seen, Allah, glory unto Him, has rendered Earth, a massive body sailing at a rapid speed in the dark void of space, a home abounding in life, set moreover to an ideal heat. Dominated by a pleasantly warm climate, not even a single waft breezing through Earth is without wisdom; not even a single leaf drops of its own accord, without reason.

Each created thing, from the smallest to the largest, is a portrait of the pattern of lessons and a Divine masterpiece.

The Almighty says:

"Do you not see that Allah has made what is in the heavens and what is in the earth subservient to you, and made complete to you His favors outwardly and inwardly? And among men is he who disputes in respect of Allah though having no knowledge nor guidance, nor a book giving light." (Luqman, 20) [28]

How blissful it is for those who can read the wisdom and truth laden lines of the book of universe, understand them and plumb to the depths of contemplation![29]

---

28 Also see, al-Jathiya, 13.

60

29 See, Prof. Dr. Osman Çakmak, *Bir Çekirdekti Kâinat,* Istanbul 2005, p. 118-131.

Clouds, Rain and Snow

Just think of the clouds, giant vessels sailing in the skies. One of the functions of clouds is to prevent the Earth from being exposed to excess heat. When temperatures rise, water becomes vaporized at a faster rate, generating more clouds. The rays of the Sun are then mirrored back towards the direction whence they came, preserving the balance of heat on Earth.

Allah, the Most Compassionate, sends the winds as harbingers of rain. The winds then, with Divine Command, move the mountain like clouds and steer them to their destined places. The Almighty, who distributes clouds in the skies as He wishes and clusters them around one another, then extracts raindrops from out of them, through which He enables the growth of various fruits on Earth. He reminds us that this will be the manner in which the dead will be resurrected, wanting human beings to take note of this grand portrait of wisdom.[30]

The Almighty showers His mercy upon whom He wills. Delighted especially upon the glimpse of rain are those hit by a severe drought. Their despair immediately turns to hope.[31] For the Almighty is He "...who sends down the rain after they have despaired,

---

30 See, al-Arâf, 57; Fâtır, 9.
31 See, ar-Rûm, 48.

61

and He unfolds His mercy; and He is the Guardian, the Praised One." (as-Shura, 28)

The Almighty at times turns drought and at others rain or hail into means of punishment, penalizing His rebellious servants, striking whom He wills and protecting whom He spares.[32]

In other words, the Almighty aligns the relation between the skies and Earth in line with human behavior and their own inner world.

Rain is sent down by the Almighty in drops so that each remains separate in its own course without mingling with one another. Each drop of rain falls in its destined trajectory, without swaying the slightest bit. It neither comes late, nor does the raindrop next in line rush and overtake the drop beneath it. If entire humans and *jinn* were to join forces in making a single drop of rain or if they were simply to attempt to count the number of raindrops that fell in a single village at just one instant, they would not be able to. Only their Creator knows their exact number.

There is also an immeasurable wisdom in the icy, frozen drops of hail and in the snowflakes which fall like fine cotton, both of which are made up of fine water.

Who raises the drops of rain and snow that fall onto the ground to the highest branches of trees?

32 See, an-Nûr, 43.

Indeed, water is distributed around every single inch of a leaf but it is unseen. Through their capillary veins, each speck of the leaf and concurrently the whole tree receives its fair share of water.

How is it that water, which is supposed to flow on a downward course, able to make its way all the way up to the top?[33]

If raindrops were to fall in compliance with the law of gravity, each drop would have struck Earth at the speed of a flying bullet. And that would have meant living beings would have suffered instant death at the hands of these bullet-like drops. Yet, each raindrops falls onto the ground at a consistent speed, slowly, without causing the least hurt or harm.

Shaped according to a specified measure, water then takes the shape of tiny raindrops. Then through the lifting force of the air and the fluidity of the drops themselves, the force of gravity is balanced out, enabling the drops to hit the ground at a constant speed.

These truths alone would suffice for those who gaze with wisdom to appreciate just how magnificent the Divine order and harmony, effective throughout Earth in which we live, is. No less clearly would they

---

33 See, Imam Ghazzali, *Ihyâ*, VI, 67-68.

see the infinite knowledge, power and wisdom of the Almighty by such observation.

Contemplating the Ground

Pious servants are steeped in contemplation. They become acquainted with the language of blooming flowers, chirping birds and trees that yield fruit. They mirror onto their spiritual lives the elegance and beauty they see. They gain an elegance of spirit like flowers and generosity like trees abounding in fruits. These are the lucky people Allah, glory unto Him, praises in the Holy Quran.

The Almighty has decked out the Earth's surface in the best manner imaginable and has made it hospitable to human existence. Placing paths and passages thereon, He has mad the ground suitable and mild to travel on.

The Holy Quran states:

"Who made the earth a resting place for you and the sky a canopy and (Who) sends down rain from the cloud then brings forth with it subsistence for you of the fruits; therefore do not set up rivals to Allah while you know." (al-Baqara, 22)

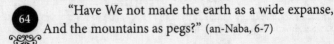

"Have We not made the earth as a wide expanse, And the mountains as pegs?" (an-Naba, 6-7)

"He it is Who made the earth smooth for you, therefore go about in the spacious sides thereof, and eat of His sustenance, and to Him is the return after death." (al-Mulk, 15)

Allah, glory unto Him, has spoken of the ground in His Sacred Book so that humans could delicately reflect on the wisdom underlying it.

Above ground is for the living, while below ground is for the dead. The Almighty says:

"Have We not made the earth to draw together to itself, the living and the dead..." (al-Mursalat, 25-26)

Now, look carefully at the ground when parched; it looks all but dead! Yet, once met with water from the skies, it vibrantly comes to life and regains its green. It grows multicolored plants. From the depths of its bosom emerge various forms of life. Then take note of how the Almighty has reinforced the ground with colossal mountains! Just look at how He has stored reserves of water underneath them? How does He then burst out springs from these and form vast rivers on Earth? Just how does He raise sweet and pure water forth from dry rock and murky mud? How is it that this water gives life to all things? Through water, how has Allah, glory unto Him, raised from the ground wheat, grapes, clovers, olives, dates, pomegranates and countless others? Each has a different shape, color, taste and aroma; to each a distinct beauty, a distinct pleasure…Some are superior to others in terms of nutrition. But all are watered by the very same water and emerge from the very same soil.[34]

Plants

Once a seed falls to the ground and is touched by the soil's moisture, it begins to develop, as a result of which its lower and upper parts crack open. From its upper part emerges the tree, which develops higher above the ground, while from its lower part comes the root, regally spread out deep under the soil. This is an amazing spectacle; for although the seed is of a single nature and is under the affect of a single influence, it brings forth one distinct part that grows upward and another that becomes entrenched further beneath the ground. It is astounding that a single entity can give birth to two opposing elements. This, we know, must be through the will and governing of One Creator, who exudes wisdom in all His acts.

One part of the tree that springs forth from this seed becomes wood, and another leaves. Further, another part smiles in the form of flowers which then further develop to yield fruits, generating certain vitamins of benefit to the human body.

34 See, Imam Ghazzali, *Ihyâ*, VI, 63.

Again, a single fruit possesses numerous characteristics. For instance, whereas the seed of a grape is cold and dry, its fleshy part is warm and juicy. That a fruit develops various characteristics from a single seed, despite each of these being exposed to the same influences, is undoubtedly the working of an infinitely powerful and wise Creator.

Furthermore, Allah, glory unto Him, has rendered flora a natural pharmacy for the healing of many diseases. Some plants are cures, sources of nutrition; they reinvigorate the body. While some revive, others, being poisonous, kill. Once consumed, a plant mutates to become another element. Many plants purify the blood. Many others give life and energy. Others provide calm and put one to sleep…

What a cause of wonder it is that through plants water and carbonic acids are transformed to sugar and wood and that oxygen is released for organisms to breathe.

There is hence not a single leaf or weed that buds out from the ground that does not carry loads of benefit for human beings; such that man does not even have the power to grasp them all at their core.

An assortment of colors, scents, tastes and leaves of distinct shapes which the seemingly ordinary weeds manage to garner from the depth of earth, are absolute wonders no chemist could manage to replicate.

The harmony and order prevalent during the growth of plants is a distinct manifestation of Divine Majesty. A plane tree, for instance, produces millions of seeds each year. To allow them to scatter to their surroundings, these seeds have transparent parachutes of feather; and with the aid of blowing winds they are ushered to places extremely remote. If each seed given off by a single plane tree was to end up developing into a tree, the whole world would have come under a plane tree invasion. In other words, the vast Earth would have been too small for only a single species of tree. This example can be extended to other beings as well.

In fact, years ago in Australia, they began using a species of kakitos to build hedges. But because there was no native insect in Australia hostile to the kakitos, the plant began to spread infectiously. A rapid growth that sent the locals to despair saw the kakitos end up covering an area as big as England, in length and width. Wreaking destruction on their lands and settlement, it eventually forced the local townspeople out of their homes, who gradually left a trail of ghost towns in their wake.

After rummaging the Earth from head to toe, scientists discovered a species of insect that lived only off the kakitos and consumed nothing else; an insect that developed in rapid speed and moreover had no known faunal or floral enemies in Australia. As antici-pated, the insect overpowered the entire kakitos in short time. Today, the kakitos are reserved to only a small area and are far from posing a threat. As for the hoards of insects imported to tackle the destructive plant, there remains only enough to keep the pressure on what now is a scarce amount of kakitos.[35]

This goes to show the existence of a somewhat mystifying and almost inexplicable yet at the same time a harmonious ecological balance effective throughout the universe. No sound mind could therefore chal-lenge the existence of a Power who prevents some species of plants and animals from increasing in excess and plaguing the Earth.

Again, what cause for wonder it is that millions of distinct plants and fruits emerge from the compound of soil! Our Lord, the *Razzaq*, the Absolute Provider, pre-pares different feasts for beings of different species…

A human being, for instance, cannot consume a majority of what a sheep eats, and vice -versa. Provisions are therefore distributed among creation according to a delicate balance. The below verse, displaying the Divine Power behind providing and distributing provisions to creation, is thought-provoking indeed:

69

35 *İlim-Ahlâk-İman,* prepared by, M. Rahmi Balaban, p. 190.

"And how many a living creature that does not carry its sustenance: Allah sustains it and yourselves; and He is the Hearing, the Knowing." (al-Ankabut, 60)

When one thinks of it, how great a manifestation of Divine Mercy it is that living beings provide mutual means for each others' survival, to the point where a bird feeds another injured bird by carrying morsels to its beak.

There exists a profound lesson in the fact that countless Divine feasts have been held since the beginning of the world without break and without neglecting to feed a single living being, and that this still continues as we speak. If we pause here for a moment and think… Three-quarters of Earth's surface is covered with water. A majority of the remaining quarter is comprised by deserts or rocky areas unsuited for the growth of plants. Only a portion of what remains is soil. But just how mighty the power of Allah, glory unto Him, is that through a ceaseless metamorphosis, He renders soil the source of nourishment for all living beings on the land!

The Vast Seas

Water covers three-thirds of Earth's surface entire. Because of this, neither can the freezing colds of the North and South Poles nor the scorching tropical heat can take Earth in their grip. The Earth's surface, warmed up by the rays of the Sun during the day, distributes this heat all around, like a radiator. As for the seas, despite receiving millions of calories of heat from the Sun, they can warm up only to a certain degree; but once warmed up they do not lose their heat easily. So, the Earth's seas regulate climates and act as a thermostat moderating against excessive heat or cold; hence the reason why they are of greater mass compared to land. By virtue of vaporization, they moreover satisfy the need lands stand in for water. Lesser seas would have meant lesser vaporization and that would have resulted in a drought fierce enough to turn the entire land on Earth to desert.

No less are the characteristics of maritime beings to those of land. Pearls, corals and other adornments and especially the fresh seafood acquired from the depths of seas are of particular importance to human beings.

Water

The survival of all beings on Earth depends on water. A person, unable to find water despite desperately needing to, would doubtless not blink an eye in surrendering all the treasures of Earth just to have one precious sip. Again, he would not think twice about relinquishing all of Earth's treasures just to release the consumed water from his body, if he was unable to. Man is cause for wonder! Just how does he make such a big deal of gold and silver while remaining oblivious to the enormity of the blessings placed by the Almighty within just a single sip of water?[36]

It would not take long for a person, who contemplates these underlying wisdoms as is worthy of their nature, to realize that all beings on Earth depend on the protection and aid of a Creator of infinite knowledge and power just to survive. He would come to terms with the fact that he lives under miraculously perfect conditions, in a virtual wonderland, he herself would have been unable to maintain. Neither reason nor conscience would then be blind enough to have the nerve to rebel against Allah, glory unto Him, the Creator and the Regulator of the Universe.

Underlying Wisdoms in the Animal Kingdom

One ought to look carefully at the birds fluttering in the skies, animals both domesticated and wild and the tiny, barely visible insects; for they possess such peculiarities that it is impossible not to stand in awe of the splendor, power and wisdom of the Almighty.

36 See, Imam Ghazzali, *Ihyâ*, VI, 65-66.

Just how has the Creator placed such incredible appendages on those tiny, hardly perceptible insects? And how to they flawlessly carry out their functions without faltering? Even a complete insight into the features they simply possess stands beyond the capability of human comprehension.

If man was to gaze carefully at animals, their diverse shapes and appearances and then reflect on what they provide of their skin, fur, meat and milk for man's comfort, he would no doubt become aware of the boundless blessings and mercy of the Almighty. Allah, glory unto Him, has given each of them a distinct skin to protect them from the cold, thick nails to safeguard their feet and has covered for all the needs they may have in the best, most aesthetic manner conceivable.

For example, parading in bodies adorned with the most beautiful, exquisite of patterns despite having a lifespan of a mere fortnight, butterflies reveal many mysteries through their body language; just one of the infinite Divine wonders presented to the gazing eye, the comprehending mind and especially the sensitive heart...

The Holy Quran summons us to observe the camel and reflect on how it has been created:

"Will they not then consider the camels, how they are created? And the heaven, how it is reared aloft? And the mountains, how they are firmly fixed? And the earth, how it is made a vast expanse? Therefore do remind, for you are only a reminder." (al-Ghashiya, 17-21)

That means that manifestations of Divine splendor beckon in an observation of the structure of animals and other organisms.

The Almighty has endowed all living beings with such characteristics that they produce different products despite feeding off the same food. For instance, if a cattle or sheep were to eat the green leaves of a mulberry, they would produce meat, milk and skin or wool. A silkworm on the other hand, a tiny bug, weaves silk from the very same leaves. Similarly, the ability of a bee to generate honey from pollen is absolutely beyond human power.

While a single animal is able to turn grass into meat and milk, human beings, the most perfect of creation, cannot emulate this feat even using tons of grass just in hope of producing a mere drop of milk, even if they were to set up the most state-of-the-art laboratories for the purpose.

The Almighty declares:

"And most surely there is a lesson for you in the cattle: We give you to drink of what is in their bellies, from between the feces and the blood, pure milk, easy and agreeable to swallow for those who drink." (an-Nahl, 66)

The Honeybee

Allah, glory unto Him, states:

"And your Lord revealed to the bee saying: Make hives in the mountains and in the trees and in what they build: Then eat of all the fruits and walk in the ways of your Lord submissively. There comes forth from within it a beverage of many colors, in which there is healing for men; most surely there is a sign in this for a people who reflect." (an-Nahl, 68-69)

The Prophet –upon him blessings and peace- has said:

"*A Believer is like a honeybee. He eats what is clean, he produces what is clean, he settles on clean places and he neither breaks nor harms where he settles.*" (Ahmed, II, 199; Hakim, I, 147)

Mentioning the traits of a Believer, the Prophet –upon him blessings and peace-, at the same time, hints at the beauties of a honeybee and its underlying wisdom.

Huseyin Kashifi comments:

"Contemplative believers know that Allah, the Omniscient and Omnipotent, has created the frail honeybee upon numerous underlying wisdom.

The honeybee obeys and never strays of the path.

It eats the sweet and sour fruits it comes across and gives sweet honey in return.

It is so pious that it does not eat anything but what is pure.

It is so obedient that it never leaves the Almighty's command.

It is so loyal that it travels to places remote only to return to its home of origin.

It is so clean that it does not perch upon and eat what is dirty.

It is such a craftsman that even if the entire architects and engineers were to join forces, they would not be able to imitate what it produces.

There…just as there are curative properties in the honey they produce for diseases of the body, there is, in contemplating their states a cure for ignorance, the disease of the heart."

The Marvel of Instinct

In the following, İsmail Fennî Ertuğrul highlights how animals lead their lives within a Divine program called the subconscious mind or instinct:

"Animals know through instinct without ever being taught of the essentials needed to maintain their survival, the continuation of their offspring and the food that is good for them. Birds build wonderful nests. Migrant birds come together on a specific day before setting out. Before dying, instead of killing the other bugs that are to become food for its babies waiting to hatch out of their eggs, some insects injure their glands so as to make them unable to crawl and then place the injured bugs by the side of the eggs. Yet, how amazing it is that once developed these very insects begin to live off foods of other kinds. Bees possess the ability to determine the gender of larvae by changing their foods. In this way the bees can make a queen out of a larva should the hive lose its leader through an accident of some sort..."[37]

Again, how astounding it is that once a hornet overpowers a grasshopper, it digs a hole in the ground. It then stings the grasshopper in such a spot that the grasshopper does not die though it loses consciousness. Placed in the hole in the ground, the grasshopper is henceforth like conserved meat. Soon after this, the hornet lays her eggs by the side of the hole and the newborns find the fresh meat they need to consume by their side the moment they enter the world. As for the hornet, she flies to a remote place, away from the newborns, to die. There is no way that such mysterious behavior can be explained through terms like adapta-

---

37 *İman Hakikatleri Etrafında Suallere Cevaplar*, p. 58-59.

tion and learning. They have been given this instinctual knowledge by the Almighty.[38]

After spending years in the sea, a salmon returns to its native waters, the river. What's more, it comes back to the very place it was born, the shore where the stream flows into the river.

Who has endowed the salmon with the instinct to return to its place of birth? If you were to put a salmon in another stream that flows into the same river, immediately realizing that it is in the wrong place, it would turn back and make its way back to its stream of origin, swimming against the flow to get to its place of birth.

It is even more difficult to make out the mystery of the eel. When about to hatch, these amazing creatures come from all the lakes and rivers across the world and make their way towards pits located near the Bermuda Islands[39], where they lay their eggs and die. The eels of Europe, too, traverse a distance of thousands of miles across the vast ocean and arrive at the same place. Without further ado, the newborn eels, which supposedly do not know anything other than that they have opened their eyes in boundless waters, set out from those pits and swim relentlessly, up until

---

38 See, *İlim-Ahlâk-İman*, prepared by: M. Rahmi Balaban, p. 189.

39 The Bermudas are a chain of islands in the Atlantic, off the north coast of the Caribbean, east of the United States.

they ultimately reach the shores where their parents had once come from. The eels do not stop there; they proceed to reach the river or lake where their parents had dwelled in. Up until now, there has never been a sighting of an American eel in European waters, and vice-versa. What's more, owing to the greater distance they are required to travel compared to other species of eels, Allah, glory unto Him, has extended the lifespan of the European eel by about a year!

Now, what is the origin of such a strong feeling of direction?[40]

These amazing traits of animals show that neither their lives nor their behavior are based on sheer coincidence and that, much rather, they all take place within a plan and program sketched out by the Power who has created them.

It stands as one of the clearest proofs of the existence, power, splendor and sovereignty of Our Lord that even animals are governed by a higher consciousness. By exhibiting such proofs to the judgment of mankind, Our Lord exposes those who are ready to acknowledge the Truth and submit to it, as opposed to those who will stubbornly turn a blind eye on the miraculous manifestations staring at him in the face. The verse indeed declares:

40 *İlim-Ahlâk-İman*, prepared by: M. Rahmi Balaban, p. 188-189.

"Surely Allah is not ashamed to set forth any parable- (that of) a gnat or any thing above that; then as for those who believe, they know that it is the truth from their Lord, and as for those who disbelieve, they say: What is it that Allah means by this parable: He causes many to err by it and many He leads aright by it! But He does not cause to err by it (any) except the transgressors" (al-Baqara, 26)

Creation in Pairs

Reserving singleness to Himself alone, Allah, glory unto Him, has created all beings in twos. The Holy Quran reveals:

"And of everything We have created pairs that you may be mindful." (ad-Dhariyat, 49)

"He created the heavens without pillars as you see them, and put mountains upon the earth lest it might convulse with you, and He spread in it animals of every kind; and We sent down water from the cloud, then caused to grow therein (vegetation) of every noble kind." (Luqman, 10)

Dual creation, of which science has only recently become aware, was informed by the verse of the Quran revealed 14 centuries ago, presented humankind as a gift of insight.

Delicately prepared beyond the most innovative thoughts and wildest imaginations of human beings, like the most exquisite bride's chamber, our universe has been subjected to a specific and incredible marital law, according to the particular characteristics of each and every element, from the cells of plants and animals to the mysterious protons and electrons of atoms that dwell harmoniously in matter. And this opens up for us a magnificent horizon for contemplation.

Contemplating the Blessings of the Almighty

The greatest favor Allah, glory unto Him, has bestowed upon us is that, among the entire possible range of creation, we have been created as human beings and have come into the world in a Muslim environment. Of even further greatness is that we have been subjected to the Holy Quran and have been made members of the followers of the Prophet –upon him blessings and peace-.

For us, the Blessed Prophet –upon him blessings and peace- is the most perfect example of the Holy Quran personified. Teaching us the Book and wisdom, he makes our inner worlds crystal-clear. Fully comprehending just these favors alone would be enough make us fall prostrate in gratitude, without lifting our heads for even a mere second.

81

Of course, the Almighty's favors are not limited to these. Like a virtual cloudburst, many of His blessings pour down upon us, His servants, at each moment. The Prophet –upon him blessings and peace- states:

"Allah has said, 'Provide, so that I provide for you'. The treasures of Allah are vast. What He provides for entire creation does not reduce His treasure in any way. He provides ceaselessly, day and night. Think of what Allah has provided since the day He created the heavens and earth! They have not reduced anything from His Sovereignty." (Bukhari, Tafsir, 11/2, Tawhid, 22)

Required by these blessings are their contemplation and inferring through them the existence of their Creator, conducive to a thankfulness for His Power and Generosity.

Omar ibn Abdulaziz –may Allah have mercy on him- remarks:

"There is beauty in remembering Allah in conversation. But contemplating the blessings of Allah, now that is the most virtuous of deeds." (Abu Nuaym, Hilya, V, 314; Imam Ghazzali, Ihya, VI, 45)

Ingratitude or a lack of due appreciation is to neglect giving thanks for these blessings and to squander the lavishly, in a manner dictated by the ego. This state of mind distances one from the Almighty, their ultimate source.

Thankfulness is threefold:

1. Thankfulness of the heart: To think about the blessing.

2. Thankfulness of the tongue: To utter praises of the Allah, glory unto Him, over the blessing.

3. Thankfulness of the limbs: To give the blessing's due in proportion, at least, with the enjoyment acquired.

It has been said on the other hand that 'to each blessing, a thanks of its kind'; that is, whatever it may be that the Almighty has blessed us with, we ought to extend it those in need. So states the verse:

"And seek by means of what Allah has given you the future abode, and do not neglect your portion of this world, and do good (to others) as Allah has done good to you, and do not seek to make mischief in the land, surely Allah does not love the mischief-makers." (al-Qasas, 77)

Contemplating at Every Opportunity

Ziya Pasha writes:

A wisdom of a thousand lessons read in every page,
Of the universe, o Lord, how beautiful a stage!

In what could be taken as an elucidation of the above couplet, the great Muslim scholar Sufyan ibn Uyayna –may Allah have mercy on him- used to frequently repeat the below saying, originally belonging to a poet:

"If contemplative, man takes a lesson from everything." (Imam Ghazzali, Ihya, VI, 45)

This must be the logic behind the Arabic proverb, "So many things to take a lesson from, yet so few are those who do."

Each Particle Explains the Almighty

Once one is able to learn how to read the book of universe through contemplation, every single particle around him begins to instill in him the majesty of Allah, glory unto Him, and bring him closer to His knowledge. Fuzuli articulates this beautifully:

If a wise is able to grasp the revelation Divine,

Each particle for him becomes a Jibril come-to-life

Allah, glory unto Him, declares:

"But nay! I swear by that which you see, and that which you do not see. Most surely, it is the Word brought by an honored Messenger." (al-Haqqa, 38-40)

One of the wisdoms underlying the vows taken in the Holy Quran is to draw attention to a particular lesson, benefit of and insight into the object on which

84

the vow has been taken. The servant is thereby summoned to gain a depth of spiritual feeling through an understanding of that splendor.

Thus all beings, both visible and invisible, evidence the power and lordship of Allah, glory unto Him. Countless wisdoms beckon in their thought and reflection.

The wisdom acquired and mysteries solved as a result of the strengthening of our ability to contemplate and sense through the verve of the Quran will be just as magnificent as the grandeur a tiny plane seed gains through becoming a grand tree in fertile soil.

The Almighty declares:

"Most surely in the heavens and the earth there are signs for the believers. And in your (own) creation and in what He spreads abroad of animals there are signs for a people that are sure. And (in) the variation of the night and the day, and (in) what Allah sends down of sustenance from the cloud, then gives life thereby to the earth after its death, and (in) the changing of the winds, there are signs for a people who understand." (al-Jathiya, 3-5)

Getting hearts and minds to focus on such material for contemplation alluded to by the Holy Quran will deliver one to the climes of *taqwa*. Just as flowers depend on water, air, soil and light to exist, granting contemplation a desired level depends on attaching it to piety.

The Almighty desires His servants to be people of delicate thought; inquiring human beings of understanding. Each Muslim should therefore turn to contemplation, at every given opportunity, with an ardent feeling of worship. The words of Rabia –may Allah have mercy on her soul-, the wife of Ahmed ibn Hawari, provide splendid examples in relation:

"Whenever I hear the *adhan*, I am reminded of the crier of Judgment Day…

"Whenever I see snowfall, it is like I see books of deeds drifting about in the sky…

"I am reminded of Resurrection the moment I see a pack of swarming grasshoppers…"

It is reported that Caliph Harun ar-Rashid once went to a bath, where the bath attendant accidentally poured boiling water over him. Suffering major burns on his scalded body and in agonizing pain, the Caliph rushed outside and gave away thousands in charity, commenting:

"I cannot stand the heat of hot water today… How will I be if I am destined for hellfire in the Hereafter?"

The Prophet –upon him blessings and peace-, taking a lesson from everything he witnessed, used to turn to the Lord in thanks and seek His refuge. We, too, ought to perceive Divine splendor in everything we see and seek to acquire the spiritual food to sustain the inner world of our hearts and minds. Wherever a Muslim may look, be it the Sun, the Moon, the atmosphere, his own creation, his ancestors or children, he must read the Divine messages communicated through them with the eye of the heart. By virtue of reflecting on his origin and destination, on how he is able to survive, by whom he is given a particular shape and form, a specific brand and span of life; and through acknowledging that neither life itself nor the universe is ever detached wisdom, that nothing has been created in vain and most importantly that man himself has not been left unaided and alone, he must constantly be aware of Divine power and majesty.

Why has the Almighty created the Universe?

Allah, glory unto Him, says:

"And We did not create the heavens and the earth and what is between them in vain. We did not create them both but with the truth, but most of them do not know." (ad-Dukhan, 38-39)

Contemplating the universe must grant one an appreciation of the will of the Almighty and of the fact that everything, presented to the use of man, has been created with a purpose. Through this, one must reflect on his responsibilities towards the Creator and not neglect his duties of servanthood. Remaining insensitive and ingrate to the enormous favors and blessings of the Almighty, is a undoubtedly a woeful ignorance that does not, in any way, befit the honor and dignity of being human.

Man must not forget he will be called into account for all the blessings received; so states the Almighty:

"Then on that day you shall most certainly be questioned about the joy you indulged in!" (at-Takathur, 8)

We are therefore eternally indebted to our Lord for all the blessings that surround us, both for those of which we are aware and unaware. How wonderful are those hearts of wisdom which, fully conscious of this debt, strive to put deeds of gratitude into practice!

CONTEMPLATION OF MAN

Just to think that the ground which we walk is filled with the bodies of billions of deceased human beings to have lived until now; bodies now completely turned to dust, like billions of shadows piled upon one another…Tomorrow, we too are bound to glide into this dense shadow. From there, an eternal life will begin; a journey to the never-ending. In that case, let's stop awhile and think: What wise mind would trade a moment for eternity?

CONTEMPLATION OF MAN

The Magnificent Subtleties of Creation

Allah, glory unto Him, states:

وَفِي الْأَرْضِ اٰيَاتٌ لِلْمُوقِنِينَ.
وَفِي اَنْفُسِكُمْ اَفَلَا تُبْصِرُونَ

"And in the earth there are signs for those who are sure; and in your own souls (too); will you not then see?" (ad-Dhariyat, 20-21)

So magnificently has the Almighty created man, that even the lauded science and technology of our age, despite its numerous discoveries, has fallen short of comprehensively making out the wonderful mystery that is the human being. The Quran states:

"O man! What has beguiled you from your Lord, the Gracious one, Who created you, then made you complete, then made you proportionate? Into whatever form He pleased He constituted you..." (al-Infitar, 6-8)

Reminding him of their past, Allah, glory unto Him, urges human beings to reflect on their creation; such that although made the most honorable among entire creation owing to an exceptional design, they were created in the first place from a somewhat unappealing and unsightly, watery substance.[41] How absurd it is then for man to take confidence from a temporary, vulnerable existence that is in fact tantamount to nothing, and rebel against his Lord, the eternally Powerful and Wise, who made a magnificent being from a tiny drop of liquid!

The stages of human creation, of which medicine has only recently become aware, are depicted in the Quran in the following:[42]

---

41 See, Abasa, 17-22; ar-Rûm, 20; al-Qiyâmah, 36-38; al-Mursalât, 20-22; Yâsîn, 77; al-Insân, 2.

42 The Quran has been reinforced with each scientific discovery over the past 1400 years. That a Book, presented to humankind through an unlettered Prophet, should touch upon laws effective throughout the universe and thousands of phenomena, the reflections of these laws, and not be disproven by as little as a single discovery, stands as an incontestable proof of its Divine origin. Simply put, the Quran is always at the forefront of science and scientific discoveries always support it, following in its wake.

Many Western intellectuals, prudent enough to lay anti-Islamic prejudice aside, have been able to draw a connection between discoveries made only recently in our times and their references in the *ayat* of the Holy Quran revealed some 1400 years ago, and have subsequently opted for the path of guidance, in utter admiration and

"And certainly We created man of an extract of clay, Then We made him a small seed in a firm resting-place. Then We made the seed a clot, then We made the clot a lump of flesh, then We made (in) the lump of flesh bones, then We clothed the bones with flesh, then We caused it to grow into another creation, so blessed be Allah, the best of the creators. Then after that you will most surely die. Then surely on the day of resurrection you shall be raised." (al-Muminun, 12-16)

Just like his creation, man's organs also invite him to contemplation through a language of their own. As vast objects for our contemplation, our eyes, ears, hands, feet, brains, hearts and in short our entire organs virtually call out to us, urging:

Look carefully at how the Almighty has regulated the limbs, made up of muscles, nerves and veins, and put them all together to form an incredible, harmonious system! He has made the head round and opened up thereon ears, eyes, a mouth, a nose and other inlets…He has created the hands and feet long, divided their tips into fingers and toes and them into phalanges. As for the internal organs such as the heart,

---

awe. One of them is the French embryologist Prof. Maurice Bucaille, who became Muslim following a similar thread. Of particular importance are his *The Bible, the Quran and Science* and *Moses and the Pharaoh*, which we encourage our readers to pick up.

stomach, lung, liver, intestines, spleen and womb, He has fashioned them in the most perfect way imaginable. Not one of them is futile and detached from the rest; each serves a crucial function, created in a manner most suitable to carry its specific function out. What's more, each organ is divided into internal components. The eye, for instance, has layers, each of which has a distinct quality and shape. Should any one of those layers break down or lose one of its qualities, the eye loses its entire power of vision.

The Bones

The formation of bones is awe-inspiring. How is that they have been made so hard and resilient by the Almighty when created from a mere drop of sperm? How are they then, as the skeleton, turned into the buttress of the body, so balanced and sturdy? And how are they then measured into distinct shapes, in a host of sizes and varying densities?

Neither is man made up of a single piece of bone. Bones are attached to one another through flexible joints, each with a shape compliant with the movement it is meant to make. So wonderful is the greasing mechanism of these joints that attempts to explain it through the three recognized types of mechanical greasing have proven fruitless.

Let's consider for a moment the difficulties we would encounter in life if a single joint in our body was to break down!

Had Allah, glory unto Him, created a bone more in our bodies than the amount there already is, that bone would have been a cause for agonizing discomfort, something needing to be surgically removed. In contrast, had there been a bone less, we would have been required to exert an enormous amount of effort to make up for its loss; and in most circumstances, our efforts would have been of little avail.

Let's imagine we were not able to use just one thumb. How immense an obstacle would that have proven to be?

Some teeth are flat, suitable for grinding. Others are pointed and sharp, ideal for cutting into and dividing food.

To move the bones, the Almighty has created muscles. The amount and shape of each muscle varies according to its specific location in the body. The eye, too, comprises many muscles. Only a simple malfunction of one has a detrimental effect on the entire eye.

These marvels are just those that are visible. There are also spiritual qualities imperceptible to sensory experience, like temperament, character, personality and conscience, which are even of a more astounding nature.

The wonders of the human body are the Almighty's art devised from a single drop of water. Upon seeing a beautiful painting, one tends to admire the painter's skill, art and genius. The painter's reputation is suddenly blown out of proportion. Yet, far from creating something out of nothing, all that the painter does is assemble some paint and a brush and reflect onto a canvas his impressions of sensible things, all of which are created by the Almighty in the first place.

In that case, seeing that even a painter's work attracts admiration, should not we contemplate the nature of the admiration we ought to nurture towards the wonder that is the human being, a unique masterpiece of art created, by the Absolute Artist, from a mere drop of liquid?

The Limbs

The structure of the ears, the benefit of the nose, the function of the tongue and the distinct manner in which it utters each letter, the teeth that adorn the oral cavity and their pearl-like wonderful design, the sensitive structure of the vocal chords…That the voice of each person is different from another, so much so that the blind recognize people simply from their voices…

The hair, beard, eyebrows and lashes…The stomach, liver, kidneys and veins…Underlain by a supreme intelligence and wisdom and working harmoniously with each other, each truly merits a lengthy reflection.

Our kidneys are a small piece of meat; they yet discern the poisonous from the nonpoisonous, sending the poisonous out of the body and returning the nonpoisonous thereto. Is it that the kidneys have a mind of their own or have access to computers or perhaps laboratories for medical analysis? We all know the troubles we are put through when this tiny organ begins to malfunction. Machines of enormous sizes are unable to fully perform what that small, 50 grams of meat does with ease.

Now, let's look at our hands. They have been made long so that they can reach out to the things desired. With a flat palm, the hand has been given five fingers, each with three phalanges. Four fingers stand to one side and the thumb to another. The thumb can run to the help of the remaining four fingers. If every human being, past and present, was to come together and ingeniously try to give the hand a better shape than what it already it has, they truly would not be able to.

If man was to lose a seemingly unimportant part of his body, like perhaps a fingernail, he would find himself the most helpless among all creation upon feeling the urge to scratch. If he were to ask the help of another person to scratch that severe itch, it would take numerous attempts of trial and error for the person to find that itching spot. Yet, one's own hand never finds any difficulty in locating that spot and scratching it, even when deep asleep.

The seemingly simple motions we carry out with our arms, hands and fingers in fact demand a highly complex and calculated effort. To think that the limb motions of the high-tech robots today still lag incomparably behind those of human limbs, it would be reckless to remain indifferent to the eternal power and wisdom the Almighty exhibits in the human body, day in day out.

Poetically expressed below is the fact that man, like the rest of creation, constantly pronounces through its own language the Absolute Artist, to eyes that can see and ears that can hear:

Witness to the existence of my Creator, is the existence of me

Other certain proofs are redundant, though there indeed may '*...*

(Şinâsî)

The Compassion and Mercy of the Almighty

Just look at the mercy and compassion of Allah, glory unto Him, that He postpones the full surfacing of teeth to two years after birth. In the first two years, babies are not able to receive nourishment in the fullest sense of the term except by being breastfed. They therefore do not need teeth during that period. Fully developed teeth during this period would have been a great cause of pain for breastfeeding mothers.

As the child develops so does his need for nourishment and there soon comes a time when milk alone is no longer enough to fulfill that need. Arising at this time is a strong need to digest certain foods and with that comes the need to chew and swallow. The full development of teeth in children is hence neither too early nor too late. They develop exactly at the right time. Were they to develop earlier, they would prevent proper breastfeeding. That Allah, glory unto Him, not only thrusts forth those hard bones from out of soft gums but also makes them surface at exactly the right time, is indeed cause for wonder.

The Almighty has moreover imparted parents with an exceptional feeling of compassion to look after the child. Who would have borne a baby's brunt had not the Almighty placed in the parents' heart a drop of His own mercy?

The human body presents an incredible object for contemplation. It is an indisputable witness to the existence of the Creator. But one entirely ignorant of this clear fact is constantly preoccupied with the desires of his ego. In attending to such desires, even animals stand on the same level as human beings. The ability that separates humans from animals and what grants them the credit of being the most honorable of creation is the wisdom acquired through gazing at the wonders of the skies and earth with a perceptive eye and contemplating the Divine works of art glaring throughout the universe, as well as human beings. As one grows deeper in this wisdom, he is raised to the level of angels, even higher, shortlisted to be resurrected in a state loved by the Almighty, amid the prophets and the righteous. This honor and privilege is remote from those enchained by their lusts, even more bewildered than animals.[43]

The Face and Fingerprints

One day, someone commented next to Omar –Allah be well-pleased with him-, "Chess truly amazes me. Even though a chess board is only a meter in length and width, a person could perhaps make a million different types of moves on it, without one resembling the other!"

"There is something even more amazing", replied Omar -Allah be well-pleased with him-. "The length

43 See, Imam Ghazzali, *Ihyâ*, VI, 58-62.

and width of a face is a mere hand span. To add to it, the location of the eyebrows, the eyes, the nose and the mouth always remain the same. Still, you would not find any two people, in East and West, who have the exact same appearance. How great the glory, majesty and wisdom of Allah is that He displays boundless differences on a little piece of skin!" (Râzî, *Tafsîr*, IV, 179-180 [al-Baqara, 164])

Drawing attention to this wisdom, the poet says:

Who is the Mastermind to have drawn this face?

Will not anyone face the mirror and ask?

(Necip Fâzıl)

Of even greater magnificence are man's fingerprints. Today, there are computers and doors programmed to have fingerprints as security codes. Each person carries different and unique fingerprints. Even the fingerprints on the fingers of a single hand are different from one another.

It was only towards the end of the 19th century that fingerprints were discovered to carry different patterns in each person, like barcodes, after which they were begun to be utilized for the purpose of identifying people, especially in the legal and criminal sphere. Today, there is a science called dermatoglyphics, reserved exclusively to the study of fingerprints.

Endowing human beings with this unique characteristic, Allah, glory unto Him, has moreover hinted at this wonder in the verses of the Holy Quran revealed some 1400 years ago, declaring that when Resurrection comes to pass, even the fingerprints are to be rearranged in the exact manner they were during life. The verse states:

"Does man think that We shall not gather his bones? Yea! We are able to make complete his very fingertips." (al-Qiyamah, 3-4)

The Holy Quran, as seen, continually leads the way and science only follows in its wake in confirmation.

Similar to fingerprints, the eyes also vary from person to person. Becoming prevalent in everyday life is the use of devices, from computers to doors that recognize its users not from old fashioned codes but from the specific qualities of their retinas.

Majestic is Allah, glory unto Him, who creates infinity of variety in an area even smaller than 1 cm^2.

The Marvel of the Gene

Recent discoveries in genetics show that each person carries another kind of code exclusive to himself. What's more, so tiny are these genes that even the entire genes of every single living being on Earth would not be able to fill up something as small as a tailor's thimble.

Invisible even through a microscope, these genes settle in the cells of every living organism and give them their characteristics. In this sense, a thimble might seem too small to be able to hold each individual characteristic of the over 6 billion human beings there are in the world today; yet the evidence in support leaves no room for doubt.

How does, then, this tiny thing called the gene keep hold of the characteristics of every single living organism of who knows what amount? How is it that it can safeguard in an infinitesimally small area every single attribute of a given organism, even all the way to her psychological characteristics?

The fact that millions of atoms trapped in a single gene, too small to see even with the aid of a microscope, can virtually govern life on Earth, can only be through the discretion of a boundlessly Wise Creator. Here, there is not the slightest room for theory.[44]

Drawing attention to this, the Almighty declares:

"And when your Lord brought forth from the children of Adam, from their backs, their descendants, and made them bear witness against their own souls: Am I not your Lord? They said: Yes! we bear witness.

---

44 See, *İlim-Ahlâk-İman*, prepared by: M. Rahmi Balaban, p. 189-190.

Lest you should say on the day of resurrection: Surely we were heedless of this." (al-Araf, 172)

These and alike manifestations of Divine power and art, which have been discovered only recently, leave reason speechless. Inspired by such feelings was Ziya Pasha, who as early as the 19th century, wrote:

I glorify He whose art makes minds meek,

And whose might leaves the wise weak...

Who operates the Factory that is the Human Body?

Man must appreciate the fact that all beings, in the skies and on earth and in the sea, including him, depend on the Almighty every moment. On the simplest level, he must see:

Nearly all the activities within our bodies take place independently of our will. In this manner do our heartbeats, our breathing, the actions of all our other organs take place, including the inner workings within our cells and the mutual aid and communication that run frenetically between them. Who knows of the amount of malfunctions we would have caused if only the activities of one of these perfectly functioning organs or even the hundreds of types of biochemical reactions that occur within a single cell were left to our administering and control for only a day?[45]

45   See, Şâkir Kocabaş, *Kur'ân'da Yaratılış*, p. 115.

How enormous a lesson there is in the fact that, on the one hand, we see a 10 ton elephant succumb to the command of a 10 year old child while on the other, as an expression of the sheer weakness of man, a tiny virus, invisible to the naked eye, bring down many an imposing man of strength!

We therefore must never ascribe to ourselves the strength given to us by the Almighty; we must never give way to arrogance and must always be reminding ourselves of the True Owner of strength. We must retreat to a constant state of gratitude, acknowledging that we are not even specks of dust next to the Divine Power. We must always seek refuge in the Almighty.

Here, we have only briefly touched upon some of the many instances of Divine power and wisdom so abundantly manifested in human beings. Sparing time to reflect on man is bound to expose many more mysteries and wisdom Allah, glory unto Him, has placed therein. If a book was to be written for each cell of the human body, it would surely be an appropriate undertaking.

Why was Man Created?

What is the true purpose of man, created in the best possible fashion as an honorable being and endowed with countless blessings of the Divine? What is expected of him? What are his responsibilities?

Allah, glory unto Him, asserts:

"What! Did you then think that We had created you in vain and that you shall not be returned to Us?" (al-Muminun, 115)

"And I have not created the jinn and the men except that they should serve Me." (ad-Dhariyat, 56)

Man must give thanks, in thousands, for each cell he has in his body, through deeds of worship, charity, enjoining goodness and patience, just to name a few. Each blessing comes with a price and each necessitates an expression of thanks.

The Prophet –upon him blessings and peace- says:

"*A charity a day is required for each joint man has. Helping a person mount his ride or placing his load upon it is charity. A kind word is charity. Every step taken on the way to the mosque for ritual prayer is charity. Giving directions, too, is charity.*" (Bukhari, Jihad, 72. See, Muslim, Zakat, 56)

"*A charity is required each day for each of your joints and bones. Every tasbih is charity. Every hamd is charity. Every tahlil is charity. Every takbir is charity. Advising with the good is charity. Preventing from evil is charity. Two rakat of ritual prayer offered at midmorn-*

ing covers for all of these." (Muslim, Musafirin, 84, Zakat, 56. See, Bukhari, Sulh, 11, Jihad, 72, 128)

Other reports include *"adjudicating justly between two people"* and *"removing from the street things that bother passers by"*. (See, Bukhari, Sulh, 11, Jihad, 72, 128; Muslim, Zakat, 56)

The need to strive towards becoming a worthy servant of the Almighty is hence obvious. Making the most of each moment through deeds of worship and goodness and preparing for the life eternal in the best way possible is, moreover, essential.

Solving the Mystery of Death

Muhammad ibn Kab al-Qurazi recounts:

"I had once met Omar ibn Abdulaziz in Medina. Back then he was a young man, quite handsome and wealthy, too. Years later when he became Caliph, I went to see him. After getting permission to go in next to him, I made my way through. Seeing him, however, I was stunned and I could not help but stare at him, astounded.

'Why are you looking at me like that, Muhammad?' he asked.

'You have gone pale, your body looks worn out, you have lost most of your hair and what remains of it is gray', I responded. 'Seeing you in this condition, Caliph, I could little hide my surprise.'

'Who knows then how great your surprise would be Muhammad, if you were to see me three days after I was placed in my grave' said he. 'Ants will have taken my eyes out of their sockets and they will have dribbled onto my cheeks; and my nose and mouth will have been filled with pus. It is really then that you will not recognize me and express a surprise greater than you can imagine!'" (Hakim, IV, 300/7706)

Above anything else, each person must contemplate his end: how is he to breathe his last, what will he encounter in the grave and what will his rank be in the Hereafter? These are the greatest mysteries lying in front of human beings; grasping the secret to the journey from the crib to the coffin and the wisdom underlying existence in this world and subsequent passage to the Hereafter. Each of us must make every effort in life to solve this riddle and thereby achieve eternal bliss.

One must first of all contemplate mortality, for it is an indisputable fact that:

"All that is on earth will perish." (ar-Rahman, 26)

There will come a day with no tomorrow; a day unknown to all of us. Allah, glory unto Him, states:

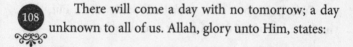

"And the agony of death will come in truth; that is what you were trying to escape. And the trumpet shall be blown; that is the day of the threatening." (Qaf, 19-20)

Everyone enters this life through one door, the mother's womb, and lives out this life, a steeplechase that is run in a flurry of either spiritual or egoistical feelings. After passing through this narrow corridor, through the gate of the grave, each person finally makes their passage to the life of eternity.

The world, like a house with two doors, has been filled with and emptied of countless human beings, from the time of Adem –upon him peace- until today. Where are they now? Where will we be a short while later? Unknown…But one thing is for certain. Death has knocked on the doors of both the oppressors and the oppressed, sinners and saints; and now they stand waiting for the beginning of eternal life, Judgment Day.

Just to think that the ground which we walk on is filled with the bodies of billions of deceased human beings to have lived until now; bodies now completely turned to dust, like billions of shadows piled upon one another…Tomorrow, we too are bound to glide into this dense shadow. From there, an eternal life will begin; a journey to the never-ending. In that case, let us each stop awhile and

109

think: What person in their right mind would trade a moment for eternity?

In the Quran, the Almighty declares:

"On the day that they see it, it will be as though they had not tarried but the latter part of a day or the early part of it," (an-Naziat, 46), informing us just how short this life is compared to the life of everlasting.

Echoing this truth is the following couplet, abbreviating the essence of worldly life:

Delicate is life, rapid, like the blink of an eye,

A bird taking flight, we heard not, yet it went by...

(Âşık Paşa)

Could there be anything more incredibly foolish than ruinously laying waste to the treasure of this earthly life like it is forever?

Contemplating Death

The Prophet –upon him blessings and peace– used to command a frequent remembrance of death, discouraging us against being lost in worldly affairs.[46] He would say, "*A cause for wonder is he who only strives*

46 See, Tirmidhi, Zuhd, 4; Nasâî, Janaiz, 3.

for the deceitful life of the world, despite having belief in the life of eternity." (Qudai, Shihab'ul-Akhbar, n. 383)

The thought of the impending time of complete separation from the world, after which one will be left face to face with what he or she had done in life, good and bad, and receive her or his rewards or punishment in full, distances one from sin and temptation, and brings one closer to deeds of goodness. Contemplating ones death, in other words, is a means to gaining greater conscience, straightening up one's life and working towards bettering one's condition in the life of eternity. The Prophet –upon him blessings and peace- says:

"Remember death frequently; for remembrance of death purifies one from sins and renders him indifferent to the world. If you think of death while rich, it will protect you from the disasters of wealth. If you think of it when poor, it will enable you to become satisfied with your life." (Suyuti, Jami'us-Saghir, I, 47)

Again, encouraging the remembrance of death, the Prophet –upon him blessings and peace- said:

"I had forbidden you from visiting graves. But now you may, for visiting graves will remind you of the Hereafter." (Tirmidhi, Janaiz, 60; Muslim, Janaiz, 106)

"Remember death and the decaying of bodies and

bones after death. He who desires the Hereafter deserts the dazzle of the world." (Tirmidhi, Qiyamah, 24)

"*Allah loves he who often remembers death.*" (Haythami, X, 325)

"Who is the cleverest Believer?" a Companion once asked the Prophet –upon him blessings and peace-, who replied:

"*He who frequently remembers death and prepares for what's to come in the best possible way...It is they who are truly clever.*" (Ibn Majah, Zuhd, 31)

The Companions' Contemplation of Death

Abu Bakr –Allah be well-pleased with him- once said during a sermon:

"Where are the handsome, the beautiful, who were once admired by everyone? Where are the young, gallant men of self-importance? Where are those kings who surrounded the grandiose towns they set up with high walls? Where are the invincible heroes of the battlefields? Time has eaten them away and made them level with earth. They have all been buried in the darkness of their graves. Hasten to come to your senses before it is too late and start preparing for beyond death! Save yourselves, save yourselves!" (Ibn'ul-Jawzi, Zamm'ul-Hawa, p. 668; Nadrat'un-Naim, III, 960)

Aisha –Allah be well-pleased with her- explains:

"I once thought of hellfire and began to cry. Seeing me in tears, the Messenger of Allah –blessings and peace upon him- asked, '*What is wrong, Aisha?*'

'I was reminded of hellfire, so I cried', I replied. 'Will you prophets remember your family members on the Day of Judgment?' I then asked.

'*There are three places where nobody will remember anyone. Before finding out whether the scale of deeds (mizan) will weigh in heavy or light; before knowing from which way the book of deeds will come, from the left, right or from behind, up until saying, 'Here; read my book' (al-Haqqa, 19); and when the Bridge of Sirat is set up, suspended above Hellfire. On both sides of the bridge, there are many hooks and hard thorns. With them, Allah catches whom He wills from among creation and throws them into Hellfire. A person cannot think of anyone else until he finds out whether he will be spared from these hooks or not.*"
(Hakim, IV, 622/8722)

Usayd ibn Khudayr –Allah be well-pleased with him-, of the most virtuous Companions, used to repeatedly say:

'Had I been able to always sustain the state of mind that overtook me in either one of these three moments, I surely would have been Paradise bound: While reading the Quran or listening to someone read it, listening to the talks of the Messenger of Allah –upon him blessings and peace- and upon seeing a funeral. Yes indeed…whenever I see a funeral, I feel like it is me experiencing the things the deceased is going through, taken to where the deceased is being taken." (Hakim, III, 326/5260)

The Benefits of Reflecting on Death

As stated in the *hadith* "**Death is sufficient advice**"[47], there are many lessons awaiting the thinking mind in the phenomenon of death.

Excess love of the passing pleasures of the world, and desire for fame and fortune are symptoms of spiritual disease. Envy, conceit, hypocrisy and lust are nothing but products of the love of the world. One of the most decisive remedies in protecting oneself from such malicious habits and spiritual shortcomings lies in the contemplation of death, the grave and events of the Afterlife.

Defeating the ego, becoming free of its damaging dominance and thereby purging the love of the world from the heart is the main objective of *tasawwuf*.

114

47 Haythami, *Majmau'z-Zawâid*, Beirut1988, X, 308.

Contemplation of death has therefore been an implemented method in many a *tariqah*, where the disciple spares five to ten minutes during his daily *wird* to reflect on death.

The Ottoman tendency to establish graveyards in town centers, by roads and in the courtyards of mosques, was only to provide an incentive for contemplating death. A Western traveler who picked up on this could not help but say, "Turks live with their dead."

Preparing for the Hereafter by frequently remembering death and brushing aside the desires of the ego will help one avoid the agonizing remorse that may come with the final breath. The Almighty informs that a person, who during the throes of death suddenly comes to his senses as if waking up from a dream, is bound to plea, in deep remorse:

"My Lord! Why did You not respite me to a near term, so that I should have given alms and been among the doers of good deeds?" (al-Munafiqun, 10)

To avoid going through this tragic ordeal of remorse, we therefore need to open our eyes while we still have the time and begin to prepare for the impending life of eternity before the opportunity is forever lost.

Hasan Basri –Allah have mercy on his soul- had

attended a funeral. Following the burial, he asked the man next to him:

"Do you think this person is right now wishing to return to the world to increase his good deeds, prayers and repentance over his sins?"

"Of course he is" assuredly replied the man.

"Then what is stopping us from thinking like him?" responded Hasan Basri. (Ibn'ul-Jawzi, al-Hasan'ul-Basri)

Preparing for the Tremor of Death

Hasan Basri –Allah have mercy on him- says:

"There are two nights and two days, the likes of which have never before been seen or heard. The first of these nights is the first night you spend in the grave with the dead. You had never before stayed with them. The second of these nights is the night whose morning breaks with the Hereafter. A day without a night is then to begin. As for the days, the first is when an emissary of Allah comes and tells you whether He is pleased with you or not, whether you are destined for Paradise or for Hell. The second day is when you shall receive your book of deeds, from your right or left, and then be taken to the presence of Allah." (See, Ibn'ul-Jawzi, az-Zahr'ul-Fatih, p. 25; Abu'l-Faraj Abdurrahman, Ahwal'ul-Qubur, p. 154)

Death is the greatest tribulation for man, the most terrible trial; but even worse than death is to live oblivious to death, to put it completely out of the mind and to fail to offer appropriate deeds for its preparation. Intelligent is the one who prepares for death before it comes knocking and cleans his or her soul of immorality.

Sheik Sadi says:

"You will become earth in the end, brother; so before you do, seek to become humble like earth."

Omar –Allah be well-pleased with him- has said:

"Call yourselves to account before you are called to account. Adorn yourselves with righteous deeds before the greatest tribunal! The tribunal in the Hereafter of one who used to call himself to account during life, will surely be comfortable." (Tirmidhi, Qiyamah, 25/2459)

As our mortal bodies are placed in the grave, our children and wealth will remain behind. Only our deeds will accompany us as we lay buried in the depth of earth. There, our bodies will turn to soil, together with our shrouds, leaving nothing behind but our good deeds.

Imam Ghazzali –Allah have mercy on his soul- says:

"Only three things remain with a person at the moment of death.

1) Purity of the heart, that is a heart purified of the dirt of the world. Allah states:

$$قَدْ اَفْلَحَ مَنْ زَكّٰيهَا$$

'He will indeed be successful who purifies it...' (as-Shams, 9)

2) Familiarity with the remembrance of Allah, glory unto Him, who says:

$$اَلَا بِذِكْرِ اللّٰهِ تَطْمَئِنُّ الْقُلُوبُ$$

'...Now surely by Allah's remembrance are the hearts set at rest.' (ar-Rad, 28)

3) Love of Allah, glory unto Him. Again, He declares:

$$قُلْ اِنْ كُنْتُمْ تُحِبُّونَ اللّٰهَ فَاتَّبِعُونِي يُحْبِبْكُمُ اللّٰهُ$$
$$وَيَغْفِرْ لَكُمْ ذُنُوبَكُمْ وَاللّٰهُ غَفُورٌ رَحِيمٌ$$

'Say: If you love Allah, then follow me; Allah will then love you and forgive your faults. And Allah is Forgiving, Merciful.' (Al-i Imran, 31)

Purifying the heart is possible only through *marifah*, knowing Allah, glory unto Him, in the heart. *Marifah*, in turn, is acquired through being constantly

118

occupied in *dhikr* and contemplation. These three qualities are thus saviors." (Ruh'ul-Bayan, XI, 274)

If a person is able to make adequate preparation for 'tomorrow', death starts to assume a beautiful shape; he soon finds himself no longer afraid of it.

Bishr ibn Harith –Allah have mercy on him- in fact asserts, "What a wonderful station the grave is for he who obeys Allah."[48]

Similar words of wisdom come from Mawlana Rumi -Allah have mercy on him:

"The color of death, son, is in the eye of the beholder. To those who hate death without sparing a thought that it is death that unites one with the Lord and are hostile to it, death appears as a terrifying enemy. To the friends of death, death comes as a friend.

O the soul who flees in dread from death! If you want to hear the truth of the matter, you are not really afraid of death; you are but afraid of yourself.

For it is not the face of death that you behold in the mirror in horror; it is your own ugly face. Your spirit is like a tree. Death is a leaf on that tree. And every leaf belongs to the species of the tree it stems from…"

---

48 The Commission, *Nadratu'n-Naîm,* III, 963; Abu'l-Faraj Abdurrahman, *Ahwâlu'l-Qubûr,* p. 155.

In short, our death and experiences of the grave, set to continue until Resurrection, will take shape according to the way we lived and the deeds we offered. It is for that reason that Allah, glory unto Him, explains to us the gist of both the life of the world and that of eternity on numerous occasions in the Holy Quran. Encouraging us to consider how the world will ultimately come to an end in due course, He urges us to remain aloof from its dazzle and deceit. He wants us to consciously turn instead to the life eternal, a life approaching by the minute that shall never cease.

It is therefore necessary for a person to sincerely repent from all of ones sins before death and make amends for his or her shortcomings in complying with the commands and prohibitions of the Almighty. Again, he must restore the rights to all those whose rights he may have infringed on; that is, before breathing his last, he must seek the pardon of people he may have verbally or physically assaulted, slandered, backbitten or acted with malicious intent, and be cleared of all personal debts, be they physical or spiritual.

An ignorant person may rejoice over having infringed on the rights of others; he may misread his corruption for joy. But there is simply no telling how bottomless his remorse will be on the day when the scales of justice are set and it is said to him, "You are a helpless, low and deprived man in ruin. Here, you may no longer restore any rights or seek the forgiveness of anyone."

As his death approached, Abdulmalik ibn Marwan, the Umayyad Caliph, saw a launderer in the outskirts of Damascus wrapping the clothes around his hand and thrashing them against a washing rock. Heaving an agonizing sigh upon suddenly remembering the terrifying tribunal of the Hereafter, the Caliph lamented:

"If only I too was a launderer! If only I earned my daily feed with my hands and did not have any say in worldly affairs!" (Ghazzali, Ihya, VI, 114)

Together with preparing for the tremor of death, it is also essential not to lose hope in the mercy of Allah, glory unto Him.

Uqba al-Bazzar recounts:

"Viewing a funeral procession, a Bedouin standing next to me, who was looking on at the coffin, commented, 'Congratulations…you have all the joy in the world!'

'Why are you congratulating him?' I asked.

'How can I not congratulate a person being taken into custody by an Eternally Generous Custodian, whose treatment of His guests is splendid and mercy boundless!'

It was as if I had never before heard words so beautiful." (Abu'l-Faraj, Abdurrahman, Ahwal'ul-Qubur, p. 155)

CONTEMPLATION IN THE QURAN

For believers of heart, the Holy Quran is a majestic gateway to the depths of the realm of contemplation, a vast horizon of reflection. It is the language of the heavens and earth. With its words of wisdom, spirit's only food, it is an endless treasure of inspiration, a miracle of eloquence given to human beings.

Thousands of books written in the Islamic world over the past 1400 years have had the aim of understanding and delving into the depths of one 'Book' and gaining a closer acquaintance with one 'Man' and becoming annihilated in his person.

CONTEMPLATION IN THE QURAN

Humans are naturally predisposed towards contemplation. But we need a guide to steer our minds out of the narrow straits of the ego and turn its direction to the truth and good. The most dependable guide is the Holy Quran, the Almighty's word, and its embodiment and physical clarification, the Blessed Prophet –upon him blessings and peace-.

For believers of heart, the Holy Quran is a majestic gateway to the depths of the realm of contemplation, a vast horizon of reflection. It is the language of the heavens and earth. With the words of wisdom it provides, spirit's only food, it is an endless treasure of inspiration, a miracle of eloquence given to human beings.

The Holy Quran is the elucidation of man and the universe. The universe, man and the Quran are three interconnected planes that shed perfect light on each other. A person steeped in the Quran starts to read the Divine blessing both in himself and in the universe and begins to turn the pages of the book of wisdom. Many Divine secrets become manifest to him, many windows open up in his heart to beyond.

The remedy to curb the desires of the ego that push humanity onto the path of destruction is in the Quran; it is also the cure for moral depravity that renders man lower than beasts and the measure for preventing feelings of justice from turning into uncompromising oppression. In short, the most potent medicine for happiness, for which human beings stand in need under all circumstances, is only in the Holy Quran.

Allah taught the Holy Quran

The Holy Quran is the greatest gift to humankind from the Almighty's own presence. It states:

"The Beneficent. Taught the Quran. He created man. Taught him the mode of expression." (ar-Rahman, 1-4)

Teaching the Holy Quran as an enormous manifestation of His eternal mercy, the Almighty has thereby provided human beings access to much wisdom and the answer to many mysteries. Humanity is therefore required to learn the Quran and first develop ones inner world, then strive towards becoming the Quran come-to-life with all ones actions and behavior and finally toil to communicate it to the rest of humankind in the most effective manner.

All Books are for *One Book*

Thousands of books written in the Islamic world over the past 1400 years have been for the aim of understanding and plumbing the depths of one 'Book' and gaining a closer acquaintance with one 'Man' and becoming less like ones self, and more like his person. If all the trees in the world were to serve as pens and the seas as ink, it would still be impossible to enumerate the wisdoms and truths contained in the Holy Quran.[49] Within it are the codes of all knowledge and wisdom, as well as the keys to happiness in life both in this world and in the Hereafter.

The Holy Quran always leads the way, while the sciences follow in its wake. Each scientific discovery confirms and sheds light on the truths of the Quran.

Allah, glory unto Him, declares:

"We will soon show them Our signs in the Universe and in their own souls, until it will become quite clear to them that it is the truth. Is it not sufficient as regards your Lord that He is a witness over all things?" (Fussilat, 53)

49   See, Luqmân, 27.

Continuing research into the Quran will continue to manifest its hidden miracles anew. The Prophet –upon him blessings and peace- has in fact informed that scholars can never have enough of reading the Quran, that it never loses its freshness in spite of continuous recital and that its aspects which reduce man to speechless admiration are inexhaustible.[50]

Reading the Quran Contemplatively

Muslim scholars have defined the purpose of reciting the Holy Quran as contemplating its meaning, inner wisdom and then acting in accordance with what it demands.

For the stimulation of thought, there is nothing better than reading the Quran, since it is the word of the Almighty who infinitely knows the intricacies of the human condition. In other words, the Holy Quran holds a mirror to each person, enabling him to recognize himself just the way he is. Every Muslim must therefore frequently recite the Quran and reflect on what it exactly is that the Almighty requests with each verse.

Since each word of the Quran comprises immeasurable secrets, a contemplative read of a single verse

50 See, Tirmidhi, Fadâilu'l-Quran, 14; Dârimî, Fadâilu'l-Quran, 1.

in this manner is preferable to a careless read of the Quran entire. Only a purified heart and a refined soul gained through delicate contemplation, high morals and righteous deeds can grant one access to the truth of those mysteries.

Allah, glory unto Him, states:

"A *surah* (chapter) which We have revealed and made obligatory and in which We have revealed clear communications that you may be mindful." (an-Nur, 1)

"A Book We have revealed to you abounding in good that they may ponder over its verses, and that those endowed with understanding may be mindful." (Sad, 29)

"Do they not then reflect on the Quran or are there locks on the hearts?" (Muhammad, 24)

The Blessed Prophet –upon him blessings and peace- was once asked about the best tone of voice and manner of recitation (*qiraah*) for reading the Quran.

"The recitation by he, whose voice, upon hearing it, makes you feel he fears Allah", he replied. (Darimi, Fadail'ul-Quran, 34)

Reading the Quran is one of the foremost activities exposed to the whispers of Shaytan, for a person who reads the Quran and reflects on its promises, warnings, clear signs and explanations will offer righteous deeds with greater enthusiasm. He will refrain from the impermissible and the doubtful with greater dedication. As reading the Quran is among the most virtuous of all the righteous deeds, Shaytan leaves no stone unturned in trying to keep people away from the Word of Allah, glory unto Him. It has therefore been commanded to seek refuge in the Almighty before beginning to read the Quran, by saying « أَعُوذُ بِاللهِ مِنَ الشَّيْطَانِ الرَّجِيمِ ». As the verse declares:

"So when you recite the Quran, seek refuge with Allah from the accursed Shaytan." (an-Nahl, 98)

How did the Prophet of Allah read the Quran?

The Prophet –upon him blessings and peace- used to recite the Holy Quran slowly, with a depth of feeling. He would contemplate the meanings of each verse, immediately putting into practice their commands. Upon reciting a verse commanding to glorify (*tasbih*) the Almighty, he would say *subhan'Allah*, negating the Creator of all deficiencies. Upon reciting a verse suggesting prayer, he would pray the Almighty. Reading a verse speaking of seeking refuge in the Almighty, seek refuge is what he would do.[51]

At times he would focus on single verse so intently that he would pray and contemplate it until daybreak.

51 See, Muslim, Musâfirîn, 203; Nasâî, Qıyâmu'l-Layl, 25/1662.

Abu Dharr –Allah be well-pleased with him- recounts:

"The Messenger of Allah –upon him blessings and peace- once kept on repeating the following verse at ritual prayer until morning:

اِنْ تُعَذِّبْهُمْ فَاِنَّهُمْ عِبَادُكَ وَاِنْ تَغْفِرْ لَهُمْ

فَاِنَّكَ اَنْتَ الْعَزِيزُ الْحَكِيمُ

'Should You punish them, then surely they are Your servants; and should You forgive them, then surely You are the Mighty, the Wise.' (al-Maida, 118)"
(Nasai, Iftitah, 79; Ahmed, V, 156)

The Blessed Prophet –upon him blessings and peace-, after reading the above verse, once added the following:

"My Lord! Surely they have led many men astray; then whoever follows me, he is surely of me, and whoever disobeys me, You surely are Forgiving, Merciful."
(Ibrahim, 36)

Immediately afterward, he lifted his hands aloft and began pleading, "My Allah…My followers, my followers!" shedding tears at the same time.

Allah, glory unto Him, thereupon commanded Jibril –upon him peace- to, "Go and ask why Muhammad is crying, so humans know the reason, although Your Lord of course knows why he is."

131

Jibril –upon him peace- returned, informing the Almighty that His Messenger was crying over concerns for his followers. Allah, glory unto Him, then once again commanded the Archangel to, "Go to Muhammad and give him Our glad tidings that 'We shall please him regarding his followers and never distress him." (Muslim, Iman, 346)

Such was the Prophet's –upon him blessings and peace- compassion and keenness for his followers. We need to thoroughly reflect on the above and honestly assess our degree of love for the Prophet –upon him blessings and peace- and how much we are able to practice his *sunnah* as a testimony of that love.

Abdullah ibn Masud –Allah be well-pleased with him- narrates:

"One day the Messenger of Allah –upon him blessings and peace- asked me, 'Can you read me some Quran?'

'How can I read you some Quran when it is you to whom the Quran is revealed?' I responded.

'I like hearing the Quran from others, too' said the Messenger of Allah (peace be upon him). Thereupon I began reciting chapter an-Nisa. When I came to the verse that says:

'How will it be, then, when We bring from every people a witness and bring you as a witness against these?' (an-Nisa, 41), he said:

'That will suffice for now...'

When I fixed my eyes on him, I saw tears flowing freely from both his eyes." (Bukhari, Tafsir, 4/9; Muslim, Musafirin, 247)

Aisha –Allah be well-pleased with her- recounts a scene that provides a glimpse of the Prophet's –upon him blessings and peace- sensitivity of heart and depth of contemplation:

"One night, the Messenger of Allah –upon him blessings and peace- said to me, 'If you allow me, Aisha, I wish to spend the night worshiping my Lord.'

'I would surely love to be with you', I said, 'but would love even more anything that makes you happy.'

He then got up, took a thorough ablution and began his ritual prayer. He was crying...So much that it soaked his clothes, beard and even the ground on which he fell prostrate. Still in that condition, Bilal came to call him to the ritual prayer of *fajr*. Seeing him overflowing with tears, Bilal wondered:

'Why do you cry, Messenger of Allah, when Allah has forgiven your past and future sins?'

'Shouldn't I be a thankful servant to his Lord?' replied he. 'Such verses were revealed to me this evening that shame on him who reads them without contemplating.' He then disclosed the revelation:

'Most surely in the creation of the heavens and the earth and the alternation of the night and the day there are signs for men who understand. Those who remember Allah standing and sitting and lying on their sides and reflect on the creation of the heavens and the earth: Our Lord! You have not created this in vain! Glory be to You; save us then from the chastisement of the fire!' (Ali Imran, 190-191)" (Ibn Hibban, Sahih, II, 386; Alusi, Ruh'ul-Maani, IV, 157)

The night in which these verses were revealed, the Prophet –upon him blessings and peace- shed tears of pearl until daybreak, as if to make the stars in the sky jealous. Tears shed by believers when contemplating the manifestations of Divine Might and Splendor will, with the blessing of the Almighty, adorn passing nights, radiate the dark grave and reappear as dews in the gardens of Paradise.

In expression of the necessity and rewards of reading the Quran in a thoughtful and inquiring manner, the Blessed Prophet (peace be upon him) has said:

"If a group of people gather in a house among the houses of Allah, read the book of Allah and talk about

it amongst each other, serenity will descend onto them, they will be encompassed with mercy and be surrounded by angels. And Allah, glory unto Him, will mention those people in His presence." (Muslim, Dhikr, 38; Abu Dawud, Witr, 14/1455; Tirmidhi, Qiraah, 10/2945)

"One who completes reading the entire Quran in less than three days cannot properly understand it and properly contemplate on it." (Abu Dawud, Witr, 8/1390; Tirmidhi, Qiraah, 11/2949; Darimi, Salat, 173)

"Recite the Quran in a way that it will hold you back from evil! If it does not hold you back from evil, then you have not really read it." (Ahmed ibn Hanbal, Zuhd, p. 401/1649)

The Companions' Reading of the Quran

The Companions put all their focus on contemplation in order to understand the Holy Quran and meditating on the Word of Allah, glory unto Him, they read it in a way conducive to practice.

A perfect example of this, are the words of Omar –Allah be well-pleased with him-:

"I completed chapter al-Baqara in twelve years and sacrificed a camel in gratitude." (Qurtubi, I, 40)

Similarly, Abdullah, the son of Omar –Allah be well-pleased with both- is reported to have studied chapter al-Baqara for an entire eight years, in order to put its commands to practice. (Muwatta, Quran, 11)

They read the Quran, properly learning each of its commands and prohibitions in the process. A depth of contemplation on each verse of the Quran made it possible to put each into practice. (Kattani, Taratib, II, 191)

A man once went to Zayd ibn Thabit –Allah be well-pleased with him- and asked him his opinion regarding a complete reading of the Quran in a single week. "It would be good" replied the Companion, adding:

"But I take greater enjoyment from completing the Quran in fifteen days, or even twenty. If you ask why, it is because that way I can thoroughly reflect on the Quran and better understand its meanings." (Muwatta, Quran, 4; Ibn Abdilbarr, Istidhkar, Beirut, 2000, II, 477)

Abdullah ibn Masud -Allah be well-pleased with him- says:

"Whoever seeks knowledge should contemplate on the meanings of the Quran, focus on its interpretation and recital; for Quran contains the knowledge of both past and future." (Haythami, VII, 165; Bayhaki, Shuab, II, 331)

A Bedouin had once heard the Blessed Prophet –upon him blessings and peace- recite:

"So he who has done an atom's weight of good shall see it. And he who has done an atom's weight of evil shall see it." (az-Zilzal, 7-8)

"The weight of a grain, Messenger of Allah?" he asked, astounded.

"*Yes*", responded the Prophet –upon him blessings and peace-. Suddenly growing pale, the Bedouin began to moan, lamenting, "Then shame on me for my faults!" which he repeated many times, repeating the verse of the Quran to himself over and over, he then left the scene.

From behind him, the Blessed Prophet –upon him blessings and peace- commented, "*Faith has trickled into his heart!*" (Suyuti, ad-Durr'ul-Mansur, VIII, 595)

The Righteous' Reading of the Quran

Fudayl ibn Iyad –Allah have mercy on him- had said, "The Quran was revealed to be practiced. But humans have only adopted its reading as practice."

"How does one put the Quran into practice?" he was then asked.

"By accepting what it declares as permissible and impermissible, putting them to practice, complying with its commands, avoiding its prohibitions and pausing to think over its awe-inspiring expressions."

137

(Khatib al-Baghdadi, Iqtida'ul-Ilm'il-Amala, p. 76)

Even a single verse of the Holy Quran is comprised of a vast array of meanings. Imam Shafii –Allah have mercy on him- in fact says:

"Just chapter al-Asr would suffice if people were able to adequately contemplate and reflect upon it." (Ibn Kathir, Tafsir, 'al-Asr')

Asmai, a great Muslim scholar, recalls the following account with regard to contemplating on the Quran:

"A Bedouin had turned up next to Caliph Hisham ibn Abdulmalik. 'Give me some advice', the Caliph said upon which the man, directing the Caliph's thoughts to the Quran, said:

'The Quran suffices as an adviser. I seek refuge in Allah from the expelled Shaytan. In the name of Allah, the Compassionate and the Merciful:

'Woe to the defrauders! Who, when they take the measure (of their dues) from men take it fully! But when they measure out to others or weigh out for them, they are deficient. Do not these think that they shall be raised again? For a mighty day; the day on which men shall stand before the Lord of the worlds...' (al-Muttaffifin, 1-6)'

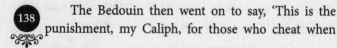

The Bedouin then went on to say, 'This is the punishment, my Caliph, for those who cheat when scaling and measuring for others. It is for you to esti-mate the punishment for those who completely seize others' possessions!'" (Ibn Abdirabbih, *Bedevî Arapların Özdeyiş ve Âdetleri,* Istanbul 2004, p. 57)

The famous Ottoman scholar Muhammed Hadimi states:

"The only way to be saved from all kinds of troubles, tribulations and misfortunes lies in embrac-ing the Quran and actualizing it in life. Persist in deeds of worship, especially in reading the Quran slowly and contemplatively, with discretion, which is among the best of deeds! Reading the Quran in such manner is like speaking with Allah, glory unto Him." (See, Hadimi, Majmuat'ur-Rasail, p. 112, 194, 200)

Examples for Contemplation in the Holy Quran

Contemplating the Knowledge of Allah, glory unto Him

In many a verse, the Holy Quran touches upon the infinite knowledge of Allah, glory unto Him, and invites human beings to contemplation. Stated in one such verse:

"And with Him are the keys of the unseen trea-sures - none knows them but He; and He knows what is in the land and the sea, and there falls not a leaf but He knows it, nor a grain in the darkness of the earth, nor anything green nor dry but (it is all) in a clear book." (al-Anam, 59)

Upon hearing the above verse, a believer should pause and think: There are so many treasures which are unknown, the keys of which are with the Almighty only; never before opened, not yet existent and ever out of reach of human comprehension. Nobody except for Allah, glory unto Him, knows about them. Together with possessing an infinite knowledge of these mysteries of the unknown, the Almighty also has knowledge of every single being, up to their minute details. Never does a leaf fall outside the Almighty's knowledge, who knows when and where it fell and how many times it turned in the air before it actually hit the ground.

The Almighty knows when a grain that has fallen to the earth is to flourish and by whom it will be eaten. All that is seen or unseen, felt or unfelt, large or small, known or hidden, every event that has happened or is waiting to happen are within the knowledge of Allah, glory unto Him, with all their complexities.[52]

Reading the above verse allows one's imagination to spread its wings. It opens new horizons and unseen

52 See, Muhammed Hamdi Yazır, *Hak Dîni*, III, 1947; Abû Hayyân, IV, 145-146, (al-Anam, 59).

realms; it wanders in the unknown corners of the land, into the bottomless depths of seas. With every experience, the mind beholds the knowledge and art of Allah, glory unto Him, in every corner of the vastness of space and beyond the visible universe. It gazes at the countless number of leaves that fall off from each and every tree on Earth, fully aware that the Almighty is seeing one leaf dropping here and another falling there. It appreciates that not a single grain, no matter how deeply hidden in the ground it may be, can elude Divine Sight and that every single particle, be it wet or dry, moves according to His command.

This journey through life fills the mind almost to the point of being overwhelmed, with awe. It is an expedition to the frontiers of time, to the most distant horizons of space, to the depths of worlds, known and unknown. The distance to be covered by the journey is tremendously long, the area immeasurably vast. If truth be told, the imagination is utterly helpless in perfectly invoking this area; for it is beyond measure. Still, this perfect scene has thoroughly, yet flawlessly, been depicted in the above verse in just a few words. (Sayyid Qutub, Fi Zilal, II, 1111-1113, al-Anam, 59)

As one continues to contemplate on the Holy Quran in this manner, he begins to realize a glimpse of the Almighty's knowledge and power. One detached from contemplation, on the other hand, continues to be dragged relentlessly in the ego's torrent, deprived of Divine wisdoms, and majesty, hidden and yet there for all to see.

Sadi Shirazi says:

"For persons of wisdom, each leaf of a green tree is a book of Divine wisdom. As for the ignorant, all the trees do not add up to a single leaf."

In another verse, the Almighty avows:

"He knows that which goes down into the earth and that which comes out of it, and that which comes down from the heaven and that which goes up to it; and He is the Merciful, the Forgiving." (Saba, 2)

With a read of the above verse, the vision of innumerable objects, motions and shapes rush into the mind. It is even impossible for the imagination to accommodate all these visions. Even identifying and counting a split second portion of the phenomena alluded to in the above verse is out of the question. If all of humankind was to come together for this task and devote their entire lives for its accomplishment, in the end they would be left exhausted as they came to terms, in resignation, with their sheer helplessness in counting the number of objects raised to the skies and the number of those that tumble down in a single moment.

What exactly are those things that make their way into the ground? What sorts of seeds fall into the Earth's bosom? What kinds of species of bugs, insects and animals abide under ground? Who knows of the amount of water, gas molecules and radioactive rays that infiltrate the seemingly endless soil? Indeed, many things crawl their way underground; all with the command and permission of Allah, glory unto Him…

On the other hand, what kinds of things make their way out of the ground? How many plants sprout forth? The Holy Quran declares:

"Do they not see the earth, how many of every noble kind We have caused to grow in it?" (as-Shuara, 7)

"That We pour down the water, pouring it down in abundance. Then We cleave the earth, cleaving it asunder. Then We cause to grow therein the grain. And grapes and clover. And the olive and the palm. And thick gardens. And fruits and herbage. A provision for you and for your cattle…" (Abasa, 25-32; also see Qaf, 7-11)

Again, are the springs not without number? How many a volcano erupts, spilling forth its lava? How many varieties of gas are vaporized? How many an insect creeps out onto the surface of Earth from its hidden nest? How astounding it is that when fallen snow covers the entire ground, countless beings seek refuge in the bosom of the earth and, by Divine protection, remain there safe and sound for weeks or months. The Almighty has made earth a virtual cradle for their well being. When the snow eventually melts, we never see piles of corpses belonging to those insects. They make their way above the surface of earth like nothing happened and once again resume their existence as before.

Again, if we pause for a moment and think of the forces, angelic and spiritual, as well as voices and prayers which rise to the skies…Many things, perceptible and imperceptible, living and nonliving, human beings know very little of, with the remainder entirely outside the limits of their knowledge.

What comes down from the skies, one wonders? Raindrops, meteors, flaming and illuminating rays on the one hand, arrows of destiny, predestined decisions and breezes of Divine mercy on the other. Some are inclusive of all beings, while others are wafts of mercy exclusive only to some.

All of these take place in the blink of an eye. Could human understanding grasp such happenings, occurring worldwide in a split second? A myriad of life spans would not be enough to count these happenings. Yet, the infinite Divine knowledge, which immeasurably goes beyond human cognition, recognizing no limit whatsoever on the way, encompasses all these happenings, whenever and wherever they may take place. It is therefore necessary to always bear in mind that every heartbeat, with its hidden intentions, is under the surveillance of Allah, glory unto Him. (See, Sayyid Qutub, Fi Zilal, V, 2891-2892, Saba, 2-3)

Chapter al-Waqia

We know that it is vital to deeply reflect on each verse of the Holy Quran. But here, we will only focus on some verses from the chapter al-Waqia, an-Naml and ar-Rum as cases in point.

The Almighty begins chapter al-Waqia by depicting the dread of the Day of Judgment, a day in which some will be elevated and others debased. After having been called into account, human beings are to be separated into three groups.

Then with a spellbindingly eloquent depiction, the Almighty explains the blessings that will be given to the servants, who led the way in life in all things good, and the righteous who received their book of deeds from the right side. This is followed by an illustration of the sad and horrid punishment that will be inflicted on those who receive their book of deeds from the left. By depicting hair-raising scenes of torment, the Almighty thereby deters His servants from committing sins. To steer clear of falling into this lamentable state, He then warns His servants by inviting them to contemplation, stating:

The Creation of Mankind

"We have created you, why do you not then assent? Have you considered the seed? Is it you that create it or are We the creator?" (al-Waqia, 57-59)

What a tremendous work of Divine art it is that from a mere speck of water the intricately detailed yet harmoniously organized human body is formed.

Death and Resurrection

"We have ordained death among you and We are not to be overcome. In order that We may bring in your place the likes of you and make you grow into what you know not." (al-Waqia, 60-61)

This is the reality of death, the inevitable from which nobody can run. If the Almighty wills, He could destroy the deniers all at once and generate a brand new batch of people.

"And certainly you know the first growth, why do you not then mind?" (al-Waqia, 62)

Having perfectly created human beings once already, the Almighty doubtless has the power to recreate them. It is vital to contemplate on this fact and prepare for the resurrection, the inescapable rebirth after death.

Seeds and Plants

"Have you considered what you sow? Is it you that cause it to grow, or are We the causer of growth? If We pleased, We should have certainly made it broken down into pieces, then would you begin to lament: 'Surely we are burdened with debt; nay - we are deprived!" (al-Waqia, 63-67)

We must look at the surrounding crops, trees and other plants with a perceptive eye and admiringly gaze at the Almighty's blessings and inimitable art of creation. Without the working of Allah, glory unto Him, all efforts of human beings count for nothing; we could not even grow a single weed.

Let us imagine, for a moment, that all the greenery around us suddenly dried out. How bleak would our lives would be then!

Fresh Water

"Have you considered the water which you drink? Is it you that send it down from the clouds, or are We the sender? If We pleased, We would have made it salty; why do you not then give thanks?" (al-Waqia, 68-70)

Fresh water brought down by the clouds is an enormous treat of the Almighty. Had it been bitter, nobody could have been able to sweeten it. Or if there was a severe drought…who would have had the power to gather the clouds together and make them to spill a single drop of rain?

Fire

"Have you considered the fire which you strike? Is it you that produce the trees for it, or are We the producer? We have made it a reminder and an advantage for the wayfarers of the desert." (al-Waqia, 71-73)

Worthy of reflection is the question of who it is that created fire, which is of tremendous use for humanity, and trees, which are its fuel?

Just look at the might of Allah, glory unto Him, that He produces fire from green trees! And let's consider the nature of fire. How does it produce light and heat as it burns?

Travelers in the desert seek refuge in fire, from the cold and dark of night. For them, fire is an indispensable means of heating, cooking and light. Fire is no doubt an essential need for all human beings also. Living without fire is almost impossible. Fire, as remarkable as it is, is therefore also an essential need, much like earth, water and air. The Prophet –upon him blessings and peace- has said:

"Muslims are partners in three things: Water, greenery and fire." (Abu Dawud, Buyu', 60/3477)

Gazing at fire, on the other, ought to remind us of Hellfire. How significant it is that standing under us is a giant layer of magma, an incredible ocean of flames, while over us is the Sun, a great ball of fire. No amount of thanks we give to our Lord for granting us a pleasant life amid a two raging fires could possibly be enough!

In return for all these blessings, one must frequently glorify (*tasbih*) the Almighty:

"Therefore glorify the name of your Lord, the Great." (al-Waqia, 74)

Our tongues should be occupied with the Quran and enjoining the good. That is its *tasbih*.

Our hearts should give thanks, immersed in a depth of feeling. That is its *tasbih*.

Our bodies, too, should continue their *tasbih* through voluntary prayers, fasts and deeds of goodness.

Stars or Revelation

"But nay! I swear by the falling of stars; and most surely it is a very great oath if you only knew!" (al-Waqia, 75-76)

The infinity of Divine Splendor...The Almighty directs our contemplation to infinity.

Space is virtually a sea without a pillar, a boundless ocean...

These verses draw attention to dawn, which begins after the stars disappear from sight, and to deeds of worship offered by believers at night.

Again, vowed upon in these verses are the revelations given to the Blessed Prophet –upon him blessings and peace-. Each revelation would consist in one or more verse or it would be an entire chapter, for which reason each revelation has also been called *najm* or a star.

The Holy Quran

"Most surely it is an honored Quran. In a book that is protected. None shall touch it save the purified ones." (al-Waqia, 77-79)

It is necessary to show great respect towards the Holy Quran. Even touching the outer cover of the Quran without ablution is considered impermissible. Unless a person has ablution, he or she may not hold the Quran even if it be with the tip of her clothing. It is a grave ignorance to behave in a disrespectful manner towards the Holy Quran, as it is:

"A revelation by the Lord of the worlds. Do you then hold this announcement in contempt? And to give (it) the lie you make your means of subsistence." (al-Waqia, 80-82)

That we have been made subjects to the Holy Quran is one of the greatest blessings we have been given. Giving due thanks to this blessing requires us to appreciate its worth and conduct our lives accordingly.

Death

"Why is it not then that when it (soul) comes up to the throat…and you at that time look on." (al-Waqia, 83-84)

When the time comes and, with the Almighty's command, death arrives, man can not do anything to turn it away.

"And We are nearer to it than you, but you do not see. Then why is it not- if you are not held under authority. That you send it (not) back-- if you are truthful?" (al-Waqia, 85-87)

Such is the might of Allah, glory unto him and the helplessness of man…Humankind in all its entirety is bound to succumb and surrender to Divine Decree, willingly or unwillingly. At that moment of truth, conceited oppressors who spent their lives rebelling against Divine Command will not be able to do so much as to raise their voices. Relieved of the countless drapes of ignorance veiling his understanding, man will finally see and fully realize at that moment, once and for all, that it is to Allah, glory unto Him, that true sovereignty belongs.

Awaiting the Deceased is One of Three Situations

"Then if he is one of those drawn nigh (to Allah). Then happiness and bounty and a garden of bliss. And if he is one of those on the right hand. Then peace to you from those on the right hand. And if he is one of the rejecters, the erring ones. He shall have an entertainment of boiling water; and burning in hell." (al-Waqia, 88-94)

Nonbelievers and corrupt Muslims are included in that final group.

"Most surely this is a certain truth." (al-Waqia, 95)

Seeking Refuge in the Almighty

"Therefore glorify the name of your Lord, the Great." (al-Waqia, 96)

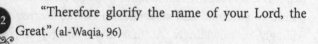

Chapter an-Naml

This chapter begins by affirming that the Quran is sent by the Almighty, the infinitely Wise and Knowledgeable. The majesty of Allah, glory unto Him, is beyond measure and imagination. It says that the miracles and aids He grants his prophets are invincible. It goes on to give the good news that the sending of the Blessed Prophet –upon him blessings and peace- as the final messenger is means for a tremendous advance of humankind, touching upon the experiences of prophets Musa, Dawud, Sulayman, Salih and Lut –upon them all be peace- to make the case clear.

These historical accounts are proofs of the power and perfection of the Almighty. As the idolaters did not come around to believing them, the Almighty challenged them with more general proofs addressing their ability to understand:

"Nay, He Who created the heavens and the earth, and sent down for you water from the cloud; then We cause to grow thereby beautiful gardens; it is not possible for you that you should make the trees thereof to grow. Is there a god with Allah? Nay! They are people who deviate." (an-Naml, 60)

Immediately after reciting this verse, the Prophet –upon him blessings and peace- would say:

153

بَلِ اللهُ خَيْرٌ وَأَبْقَى وَأَحْكَمُ وَأَكْرَمُ وَأَجَلُّ

وَأَعْظَمُ مِمَّا يُشْرِكُونَ

"Nay; Allah the Almighty is (infinitely) better, longer-lasting, wiser, more generous and sublime, and greater than what they hold partners to Him." (Bayhaki, Shuab, II, 372)

Inviting us to a contemplation of beings and events, marks of Divine power, the chapter continues:

"Or, Who made the earth a resting place, made in it rivers, raised on it mountains and placed between the two seas a barrier? Is there a god with Allah? Nay! Most of them do not know! Or, Who answers the distressed one when he calls upon Him and removes the evil, and He will make you successors in the earth? Is there a god with Allah? Little is it that you mind! Or, Who guides you in utter darkness of the land and the sea, and Who sends the winds as good news before His mercy? Is there a god with Allah? Exalted by Allah above what they associate (with Him). Or, Who originates the creation, then reproduces it and Who gives you sustenance from the heaven and the earth? Is there a god With Allah? Say: Bring your proof if you are truthful." (an-Naml, 61-64)

Chapter ar-Rum

Allah, glory unto Him, again calls His servants to contemplation:

"Do they not reflect within themselves: Allah did not create the heavens and the earth and what is between them two but with truth, and (for) an appointed term? And most surely most of the people are deniers of the meeting of their Lord. Have they not travelled in the earth and seen how was the end of those before them? They were stronger than these in prowess, and dug up the earth, and built on it in greater abundance than these have built on it, and there came to them their messengers with clear arguments; so it was not beseeming for Allah that He should deal with them unjustly, but they dealt unjustly with their own souls. " (ar-Rum, 8-9)

A few verses later, proofs of the unity, infinite power and majesty of Allah, glory unto Him, are mentioned, one after another:

"He brings forth the living from the dead and brings forth the dead from the living, and gives life to the earth after its death, and thus shall you be brought forth. And one of His signs is that He created you from dust, then lo! You are mortals (who) scatter. And one of His signs is that He created mates for you from yourselves that you may find rest in them, and He put between you love and compassion; most surely there are signs in this for a people who reflect. And one of His signs is the creation of the heavens and the earth and the diversity of your tongues and colors; most surely there are signs in this for the learned. And one of His signs is your sleeping and your seeking of His grace by night and (by) day; most surely there are signs in this for a people who would hear. And one of His signs is that He shows you the lightning for fear and for hope, and sends down water from the clouds then gives life therewith to the earth after its death; most surely there are signs in this for a people who understand. And one of His signs is that the heaven and the earth subsist by His command, then when He calls you with a (single) call from out of the earth, lo! You come forth. And His is whosoever is in the heavens and the earth; all are obedient to Him." (ar-Rum, 19-26)

Neglecting the Contemplation of the Verses of the Quran

Categorizing His true servants, Allah, glory unto Him, states:

"And they who, when reminded of the communications of their Lord, do not fall down thereat deaf and blind." (al-Furqan, 73)

When they are read the Quran or advised with it, believers are all ears; they listen to it with their hearts, think about what they hear and obey what they are called to.

Stated in another verse:

"Those only are believers whose hearts become full of fear when Allah is mentioned, and when His communications are recited to them they increase them in faith, and in their Lord do they trust." (al-Anfal, 2)

In contrast, those who fail to reap their share of the Quran's inspiration, remain unaware of its signs and secrets, recoil from delving into the truth of its mysteries and are neglectful in sticking to its commands and prohibitions, are in a state of bitter loss.

The Almighty declares:

"I will turn away from My Revelations those who are unjustly proud in the earth; and if they see every sign they will not believe in It; and if they see the way of rectitude they do not take It for a way, and if they see the way of error. They take it for a way; this is because they rejected Our communications and were heedless of them." (al-Araf, 146)

The conceited who behave arrogantly towards others, feeling themselves all high and mighty, are unable to reflect on the meanings of the Quran and therefore cannot receive their share of its guiding light, as the Almighty has divested the hearts of oppressors of the opportunity to understand the wisdoms of the Quran and become acquainted with its manifestations of Divine Power. They are deprived of an unrivaled Divine treat, since it is not fitting for the Quran, a treasure of Divine wisdoms and mysteries, to dwell in such swamps of misery. It may only enter the hearts of the righteous, and for them, it becomes a guiding light.

The sad condition of those without the least share of righteousness is due to their lack of contemplating the Quran properly, as a result of which they are debauched by the extravagances of their egos. If they were to conscientiously reflect on the Quran and follow it, they would not find themselves left dumbfounded at the face of Divine commands. On the contrary, they would accept the truth and by adopting a good moral standard, they would begin to reap their share of Divine secrets and wisdoms; and as a result, the gates of eternal peace and happiness would become wide open for them.

Evident from what has been stated so far is that neglecting contemplation and consequently wasting the fortune of life is, for a believer, unthinkable. As a warning against not appreciating the precious value of time and wasting it, the Almighty proclaims:

"By the time. Most surely man is in loss. Except those who believe and do good and enjoin on each other truth, and enjoin on each other patience." (al-Asr, 1-3)

The look of a righteous believer must therefore be of depth and his silence ought to be of contemplation. He must especially gain depth in contemplating on the Divine truths spelt out in the Quran and strive towards acquiring knowledge of Allah. A believer, again, must perceive the Quran like a letter sent by the Almighty to His servants and embrace that eternal source of happiness with the enduring enthusiasm of faith.

Being in a Constant State of Muraqabah

Muraqabah means to inspect the inner world, to keep it under surveillance and to divert all attention to it. *Muraqabah* has been defined in *tasawwuf* as awaiting inspiration or spiritual enlightening, as well as protecting the heart from what is harmful, with the awareness that Allah, glory unto Him, sees one at every moment and peers into the heart. Simpler put, *muraqabah* is for one to turn to his inner world and constantly reflect on and call to account his own condition; and in that way to acquire an awakened heart

159

and the state of mind needed to properly seek refuge in the Almighty.

The Shortest Way to Allah

The realm of the heart, just like those that we see, provides boundless grounds for contemplation. The below parable by Mawlana Rumi –Allah have mercy on his soul- beautifully underlines the importance of *muraqabah*, the contemplation of that inner world:

"A Sufi went to an adorned garden, to raise his spirits and to thereby throw himself deep in contemplation. He became infatuated with the vibrant colors of the garden. Closing his eyes, he began his muraqabah and contemplation. An ignorant man passing by thought the Sufi was asleep. Astonished and upset, he scolded the Sufi:

'Why are you sleeping?' he asked. 'Open your eyes and stare at the vines, the booming trees and the greening grass! Gaze at the works of Allah's mercy!'

The Sufi replied:

'Know one thing very well, you ignorant man, that the heart is greatest work of Allah's mercy. The rest are like its shadow. A stream flows amid the trees. From its crystal water, you can see the reflection of trees on both sides. What is reflected on the stream is a dream garden. The real garden is in the heart, for the heart is the focus of Divine gaze. Its elegant and slender reflections are to be found in this worldly life, made of water and mud. Had the things in this world not been the reflection of the cypresses of the heart's joy, the Almighty would not have called this dream world the place of deception. It is said in the Quran:

'Every soul shall taste of death, and you shall only be paid fully your reward on the resurrection day; then whoever is removed far away from the fire and is made to enter the garden he indeed has attained the object; and the life of this world is nothing but a provision of vanities.' (Ali Imran, 185)

The ignorant who presume the world to be Paradise and exclaim 'here is Paradise!' are those fooled by the sparkle of the stream. Those who are left distant from the true gardens, who are the righteous servants of Allah, incline to that reverie and are deceived. A day will come when this slumber of ignorance will come to an end. The eyes will open, the truth shall be seen. But what is the worth of seeing that sight during the final breath? A great joy to he who has died before death and whose spirit has had a scent of the truth of this garden...'

Muraqabah forms a vital path to reaching the Almighty and acquiring knowledge, wisdom and keys to mysteries. It is one of the most precious and inspirational ways, in *tasawwuf*, of spiritual progression.

A Muslim who wishes to do *muraqabah* first prepares his heart to it, and sitting just like in ritual prayer, tilts his head forward towards his knees. Gathering his entire concentration, he then turns to the Almighty, and in that state of mind contemplates on the truth that, 'Allah constantly sees me all the time; He is with me at all times, closer to me than myself.' Consequently, the Divine light which encompasses all things begins to trickle into his heart.

The people of love esteem *muraqabah* as the shortest way to obtain closeness to Allah, glory unto Him. Turning to the Almighty with the heart is definitely more effective and important than turning to Him with the other parts of the body. Anyone can turn their hearts to the Lord at any given time, with ease, whereas moving other parts of the body to offer deeds of worship can become difficult with injury or old age.

Sufis say that "A calm breath of *muraqabah* for Allah is better than owning the treasures of Solomon."

As reported by the Prophet –upon him blessings and peace-, some people are to be shaded under the Throne on the Day of Judgment, a day in which there will be no other shade. One of such fortunate people will be those who remember Allah, glory unto Him, all alone in secluded places and shed tears of emotion.

(See, Bukhari, Adhan, 36; Muslim, Zakat, 91)

Achieving Muraqabah

Muraqabah is to reenact the consciousness of *ihsan* as is defined in the Jibril *Hadith*:

"Ihsan is to serve Allah as if you see Him. Even if you do not see Him, He surely sees you…" (Muslim, Iman, 1, 5; Bukhari, Iman, 37)

Achieving maturity in Islam and faith depends on acquiring that certain state of *ihsan*; and in order to live a life of *ihsan*, with an awareness of being under the Almighty's constant supervision, we need to run a self-assessment through *muraqabah* and get our acts together.

The fact that Allah, glory unto Him, is closer to us than ourselves needs to become embedded in our hearts as a steady conviction.

A person has effectively reached *ihsan* through *iman*, once his heart begins to pulsate with these feelings. Thereafter, he offers all good deeds with an inspired heart filled with spirituality, becoming immersed in the spiritual zest of contemplating on the Quran, the universe and humanity.

In order to read the entire Quran contemplatively, the disciples of *tasawwuf* first do an exercise of contemplation on certain verses. Chosen for this are verses which have a greater affect on the heart and reinforce more compellingly the sentiments of feeling the presence of the Almighty and His love. In the Naqshibandi Order, this process of throwing oneself deep into contemplating such verse is called *muraqabah*.

Muraqabah has four stages:

1. Muraqaba-i Ahadiyya (Contemplation of the Oneness of Allah)

Contemplated here is the chapter al-Ikhlas and the *ahadiyyah*, that is the oneness of Allah, glory unto Him, who, ascribed with the most perfect attributes, is free of all kinds of deficiencies. It is believed at this stage that inspiration begins to flow into the heart.

The meanings of the verses are to be pictured in the mind without, however, resorting to analogies or seeking to ascribe physical qualities to the Almighty. One only considers these attributes the Almighty is ascribed with. When the picture becomes vague, the verse is repeated and the contemplation begins anew. As this continues, a Believer's feelings of *ihsan* increase, as he begins to receive a share of knowledge of Allah.

What chapter al-Ikhlas essentially reminds us of is this: Allah, glory unto Him, is One and Unique. Unity is exclusive to Him alone.

The Almighty does not manifest His Essence in this world. He has the attribute of *mukhalafatun'lil-hawadis*, that is He does not resemble creation in any way. Whatever there is in the universe we may think of or imagine, the Essence of Allah, glory unto Him, is of greater distinctiveness and supremacy. Our Lord is transcendent; infinitely greater than however we may conceive Him, and of perfection the understanding cannot possibly imagine. As He has no resemblance or opposite, it is impossible to conceive His Essence.

The Almighty is *Samad*. He stands in need of nothing, whereas everyone and everything stand in need of Him. All forces in the universe belong to Him. Man ought to reflect on the might and majesty of Allah, glory unto Him, and coming to terms with his own weakness, must surrender his entire existence to his Creator. Shedding his ego, he must seek to become a precinct of the manifestation of the Almighty's attributes of beauty (*jamal*).

Ahadiyya, or Oneness, does not allow of any division, segregation into parts or any partnership. The Almighty has therefore not been born and has not begotten; there has never been anything equal to Him. He is not a father, a mother or a son as the Christian creed claims. Belief in the Unity of Allah, glory unto Him, does not permit any notion of partnership or birth, for what is born segregates and what segregates

165

is doomed to perish; it faces the same fate as what it begets. Begetting is an activity that belongs to mortals and pertains to the need of prolonging the human race. A need of this caliber would have been a deficiency for Allah, the One, the *Samad*, the Necessary Being, who is remote from all kinds of faults and flaws.

The heart, the center of contemplation and spirituality, must feel the manifestations and flows of Divine Majesty and Power deep inside and be in a ceaseless state of gratitude.

2. Muraqaba-i Maiyya (Contemplation of Divine Togetherness)

Deeply contemplated during this stage is the meaning of "He (Allah) is with you, wherever you may be…" (al-Hadid, 4). A person gains an understanding of whom he should accompany and this state of mind turns into a consciousness in the heart.

Humanity cannot, in any way, remain outside the knowledge and sovereignty of Allah, glory unto Him, even if one was to hide underground or in the deepest end of the ocean. Every beat of the heart, every breath taken, every object seen and every sound heard proves that the Almighty is constantly with His servants. When their times arrive, the Almighty in fact puts an end to their possession of these abilities as they breathe their last.

Allah, glory unto Him, pronounces:

"Do you not see that Allah knows whatever is in the heavens and whatever is in the earth? Nowhere is there a secret counsel between three persons but He is the fourth of them, nor between five but He is the sixth of them, nor less than that nor more but He is with them wheresoever they are; then He will inform them of what they did on the day of Resurrection: surely Allah is Cognizant of all things." (al-Mujadalah, 7)

The Almighty is man's dearest friend, closer to him than his closest kin and relatives; a presence which is apparent through His power as such and the work of His angels. Others can only know one's external conditions. Not only are they not helpful in each and every aspect, they are unable to solve many problems that may trouble one time and again. Allah, glory unto Him, on the other hand, intimately knows every condition one may find himself in and does as He wills, especially during the moment of death. It is then that one truly comes to terms with the fact that all along there has been no other closer to him than the Almighty. The Quran states:

"Why is it not then that when it (soul) comes up to the throat. And you at that time look on. And We are nearer to it than you, but you do not see." (al-Waqia, 83-85)

To those who forget the Almighty is with them at all times and those who lack this consciousness, the Almighty sends the following warning:

"They hide themselves from men and do not hide themselves from Allah, and He is with them when they meditate by night words which please Him not, and Allah encompasses what they do." (an-Nisa, 108)

One who is aware of being accompanied by Allah, glory unto Him, at all times and is conscious that all deeds are under Divine surveillance begins to mind what he or she does and thereby avoids temptation and committing evil.

3. Muraqaba-i Aqrabiyya (Contemplation of Divine Nearness)

"And certainly We created man, and We know what his mind suggests to him, and We are nearer to him than his life-vein," (Qaf, 16) is the verse contemplated at this level. As suggested by the word *aqrabiyya*, that is to say 'closeness', Allah, glory unto Him, is closer to us than ourselves. He knows our thoughts, intentions and feelings.

Things hidden even to angels entrusted with the duty of recording each and every word spoken, thoughts and decisions that come to the mind, even momentarily, are never secret to the Almighty, for it is He who has created thoughts, like everything else.[53] How can the Creator not know?

It is impossible for one, who properly reflects on this, not to shiver and call oneself to account! Envisioning this verse alone in the heart and the mind would be enough to instill the fear to prevent one from uttering a single word that would displease the Almighty; even from entertaining a malicious thought. This verse is truly sufficient to keep one steady on the path of righteousness and alert with the thought of an impending judgment in the Hereafter.

It is said in chapter al-Anfal that Allah, glory unto Him, enters between a person and his or her heart and regulates ones thoughts and desires if He wills.[54] The Almighty is closer to a person than his or her heart, and closer to and more commanding of the heart than the person is himself. So valid is the power of Allah, glory unto Him, that not only does He enter between a person

---

53 Allah, glory unto Him, manifests with the attribute *Khaliq*/Creator in the occurrence of both good and bad. When a person intends on committing a bad deed, the Almighty manifest His attribute as Creator and either allows the person to go through with the deed or prevents him from doing it. This is equally valid in good deeds, too. When a person intends on doing something good, the Almighty, again, manifests His attribute as creator, and either allows the person or prevents him. If prevented, the person still receives a reward for carrying a good intention. In short, it is Allah, glory unto Him, who creates good and evil, yet His pleasure always resides with the good.

54 See, al-Anfâl, 24.

and others, He also enters between the person and his or her own heart, depriving them, in as little as a moment, of the heartfelt desires he or she may have. Disrupting the will, He may turn a person towards the opposite direction, changing his or her opinions and preferences. When Allah, glory unto Him, therefore raises a curtain between one and his or her heart and invites him or her to death, it is impossible to ignore the call and put up a fight against the command. Human beings can thus never now what awaits them with their next breath. (See, Elmalılı M. Hamdi, IV, 2386-2387, [al-Enfal, 24)

Abu Musa al-Ashari –Allah be well-pleased with him- recounts:

"We were with the Messenger of Allah –upon him blessings and peace- during a journey. As we rose to the hills, we would call out, at the top of our voices, '*Allah-u Akbar! La ilaha ill-Allah*'. Thereupon the Messenger of Allah –upon him blessings and peace- said:

'*Do not force yourselves, Muslims, for you are not calling out to someone deaf or absent. Allah is always with you, closer to you than yourselves.*'" (Bukhari, Jihad, 131; Muslim, Dhikr, 44)

As understood by many verses of the Quran and *ahadith* of a similar nature, the Almighty wants His servants to seek closeness with Him, just as He is ever close to them. It is for that reason the Almighty says, "Prostrate and get closer!"[55]

A person who, through *muraqaba-i aqrabiyya*, realizes that even the thoughts that cross his mind are known to Allah, glory unto Him, not only tries to keep distant from wrongdoings, but also refrains from entertaining ill feelings and thoughts, striving to keep his intention honest and on a straight path.

As a result of this kind of contemplation, one grows feelings of deep love and closeness with the Almighty.

4. Muraqaba-i Muhabbah (Contemplation of Divine Love)

Contemplated at this stage is the verse "...He shall love them and they shall love Him", (al-Maida, 54), as a result of which the love of Allah, glory unto into him, grows in the heart. One, thereafter, perceives entire creation with love, simply for the sake of their Creator. The cat lying by the door, the dog strolling around and the green branch hanging down in the garden suddenly grow dear in one's eye. One feels jubilant, simply upon seeing a blooming flower, knowing that, too, is the blessing of the Almighty. People of this ilk

---

55   al-Alâq, 19.

always remain in a genuine state of gratitude. They never hurt anyone and are always quick to forgive others who hurt them, remembering the countless faults they themselves have in the sight of Allah, glory unto Him. How can I have the face to ask forgiveness from the Almighty for my numerous flaws, they say, if I am not even willing to forgive the slightest harm inflicted upon me?

Deserving the forgiveness of Allah, glory unto Him, by continually forgiving others is an indispensable trait of mature believers.

True victory is where a person forgives the cruelty inflicted upon him by another without the slightest ill-feeling.

Forgiving for the sake of Allah, glory unto Him, is one of the greatest manifestations of Divine love. Without efforts like this, any claim of loving the Almighty is just paying lip service.

By contemplating on the aforementioned verse during *muraqabah*, each believer receives an inspiration in proportion to their understanding, aptitude and sincerity. The believer continues to strive forth to rise to a level where he or she can read the entire Quran contemplatively.

Consequent upon sessions of *muraqabah*, a person directs one's inner world to the Almighty and keeps ones heart clean from being occupied with anything other than Allah, glory unto Him. The believer esteems the Almighty's command above everything else; his tongue becomes ever busy with Divine remembrance.

A loyal servant of the Almighty is like a child devoted to his toy. The child sleeps excited with the love of his toy and it is the first thing he thinks of and searches for when he wakes up. Such will be the exact case when one suddenly dies and wakes up, before long, from his grave to make his way to the plane of resurrection. One therefore needs to be careful of the kinds of concerns that cross and occupy the mind right before falling asleep. If it is Allah, glory unto Him, who dominates a person's thoughts in life, then his death as well as his resurrection will take place with Allah, glory unto Him, and according to His will and pleasure.

Stated in some sayings of the Prophet are the following:

"Humans will be resurrected on the Day of Judgment on the state upon which they had died." (Muslim, Jannat, 83)

"You shall die the way you live and shall be resurrected the way you die." (Munawi, Fayz'ul-Qadir, V, 663)

If a person's desire is actuated toward something other than Allah, glory unto Him, such is the way his death and resurrection will be; stranded without an aid on the Day of Judgment.

Exercising in *dhikr* and contemplation are essential in order to achieve a perfect state of *muraqabah*. The Blessed Prophet –upon him blessings and peace- says:

اِحْفَظِ اللّٰهَ تَجِدْهُ تِجَاهَكَ

"*Seek Allah so that you may find Him in front of you.*" (Ahmed, I, 293)

To fully benefit from *muraqabah*, contemplation and *dhikr*, it is necessary to observe their prerequisites and adopt their required manners, which includes looking out for the most peaceful moments for doing them and avoiding moments when the heart is under duress like, when hungry, angry or sleepy.

THE MANNER OF
CONTEMPLATING

All beings are mirrors of Divine
manifestation, held out to human
understanding and consciousness by
the Hand of Might. Sensing the wisdom and mysteries reflected forth
from this mirror, on the other hand,
depends on the purity of the mirror
of the heart.

THE MANNER OF CONTEMPLATING

The Manners of the Righteous' in Contemplating

Abu Bakr –Allah be well-pleased with him- one day found himself in deep contemplation, thinking about the Day of Judgment, the great tribunal, Paradise and Hell, the assembling of the angels in rows, the folding of the sun, the blacking out and consequent falling of the stars and the flinging of mountains. Overcome with fear, he afterwards said:

"If only I was a grass amid that greenery over there, soon to be eaten by a passing animal to perish!" Revealed thereupon to the Blessed Prophet –upon him blessings and peace- was the verse of the Quran:

"And for him who fears to stand before his Lord are two gardens." (ar-Rahman, 46) (Suyuti, Lubab'un-Nuqul, II, 146; Alusi, XXVII, 117)

Again, Abu Bakr –Allah be well-pleased with him- had once gone outside on a clear, sunny day. Looking at the bright sky, he was gazing around at nature, created by Allah, glory unto Him, for His servants, with a beauty almost beyond description. Meanwhile, he noticed a bird perched on a branch, chirping in a beautiful voice. Suddenly saddened, he let out a sigh. Looking at the bird with envy, he remarked:

"How fortunate you are…I swear I would have loved to have been in your position. You flutter about then perch on any tree you wish, eat away at its fruits and then take flight again. Neither is there a tribunal awaiting you, nor a punishment you ought to fear! By Allah, instead of being a human waiting to be called to account in the presence of my Lord, I would have preferred to have been a sapling by the road and have a camel chew me up and swallow me!" (Ibn Abi Shaybah, Musannaf, VIII, 144)

Ali –Allah be well-pleased with him- says:

"There is no benefit in worship without insight, in insight without piety and in a read of the Quran without contemplation." (Abu Nuaym, Hilya, I, 77)

The following words of wisdom are also from Ali –Allah be well-pleased with him-:

"No benefit is there in ritual prayer without concentration, in fasting accompanied by vain words and behavior, in a read of the Quran without contemplation, in knowledge without piety, in wealth without generosity, in brotherhood without protection, in a blessing that is not everlasting and in a prayer without sincerity." (Ibn Hajar, *Munabbihat*, p. 31)

Ali –Allah be well-pleased with him- used to perceive everything with a contemplative eye, reflecting lengthily on what he saw. From the fear of the Almighty, he would at times cry like an orphan, shiver like a man bedridden with fever. Being much fond of deeds of worship, he would persevere in acts of piety. He would eat only a little, but spend lots in the way of good. Esteeming Islam above anything else, he would say:

"Good lies entirely in four things: speech, silence, look and behavior. A speech outside the remembrance of Allah is vain. A silence devoid of contemplation is an error. A look without perception is ignorance. Behavior that does not direct one to worshiping Allah is foolish. May Allah have mercy on him whose speech is of Divine remembrance and good, whose silence is contemplation and whose behavior is of righteousness! People are always safe from their words and actions."[56]

56 Abû Nasr Sarrâj Tûsî, *al-Luma'* / *İslâm Tasavvufu*, trns. H. Kâmil Yılmaz, Istanbul 1996, p. 137-140.

In describing the genuine people of the Quran, Ibn Masud –Allah be well-pleased with him- says:

"When people speak to one another, a *hafiz*, who has memorized the Quran, should be recognized with his silence. The tears of a *hafiz* are of a distinct beauty. A *hafiz* ought to be dignified and display an excellent character through silence and contemplation…" (Abu Nuaym, *Hilyah*, I, 130)

When Umm Darda –Allah be well-pleased with her- was asked what deed Abu'd-Darda –Allah be well-pleased with him- regarded as most important, she replied:

"Being absorbed in self-correcting contemplation…" (Waqi bin Jarrah, Zuhd, p. 474)

Amr ibn Abdiqays, a notable of the *Tabiun* generation (the generation that saw the Companions without seeing the Prophet), has said:

"I heard this not from one or two Companions but many; they used to say:

'The shining of the light of faith or its increase is through contemplation.' (Ibn Kathir, I, 448, Suyuti, ad-Durr'ul-Mansur, II, 409, 'Ali Imran, 190')

Rabi ibn Haytham –Allah be well-pleased with him- was asked to describe a person of greater virtue than himself, to which he replied:

"He whose talk is *dhikr*, whose silence is contemplation and whose look is of perception..." (Ibn Hanbal, Zuhd, p. 334; Abu Nuaym, Hilyah, II, 106)

Abu Sulayman Darani says:

"Get your eyes used to crying and your heart to contemplation!"

"Being enslaved to the world is a veil between a person and the Hereafter, as well as a tremendous loss in the long run. Thinking of the Hereafter, on the other hand, gives birth to the light of wisdom in a person and revitalizes the heart." (Imam Ghazzali, Ihya, VI, 45)

Yusuf Hamadani states:

"Once a contemplative faith sets root in a person, righteous deeds follow. It is necessary to bring these two, contemplation and deeds, together in whichever way possible."[57]

Fudayl ibn Iyad states:

"Contemplation is like a mirror of Divine majesty and sovereignty; it manifests the good and the bad." (Imam Ghazzali, Ihya, VI, 44)

Muhammad ibn Abdullah has said:

"There are five kinds of contemplation:

---

57 Yusuf Hamadanî, *Rutbat'l-Hayât,* trns. Necdet Tosun, Istanbul, 2002, p. 60.

Contemplating the verses of Allah through which comes *marifah*. Contemplating the blessings of Allah from which comes love. Contemplating the promises and rewards of Allah from which comes desire. Contemplating the warnings and punishment of Allah from which comes fear. Contemplating the ungratefulness of humans in return for the benevolence of Allah from which come shame and repentance."

Compliant with the above are also the following words of wisdom:

"A lengthy contemplation is what combines everything good and right. Silence is peace. Getting carried away in what is vain is sorrow and an agonizing remorse. Whosoever remains enslaved to the desires of his ego, ignorant of the Hereafter, will put his own self to shame on the Day of Judgment and avidly desire to perish away." (Bayhaki, Shuab, VII, 417/10812; IV, 272/5070)

Flowing the River of Contemplation onto Fertile Soil

Allah, glory unto Him, has endowed every human being with the ability to grow in contemplation. In the depths of every person lies a roaring river of contemplation, ever flowing, relentless in its course. When not given direction and left on its own, it does not know where to flow as it passes through all kinds of courses, good and bad. Sometimes it perishes in arid deserts, while at other times it is dragged to an unknown fate, knowing little what the future holds in store, like driftwood caught up in a flood.

Spiritual finesse lies in directing the river of contemplation to fertile soil and growing abundant crops with it.

The Almighty sends the below warnings to those who do not utilize the gift of contemplating and sensing in line with His pleasure:

"Surely the vilest of animals, in Allah's sight, are the deaf, the dumb, who do not understand." (al-Anfal, 22)

"And certainly We have created for hell many of the jinn and the men; they have hearts with which they do not understand, and they have eyes with which they do not see, and they have ears with which they do not hear; they are as cattle, nay, they are even more bewildered; these are the heedless ones." (al-Araf, 179)

The heart is like a mirror blemished with ignorance and disbelief. Its garnish is to first believe in Allah, glory unto Him, and then turn to Him with love. At the most basic level, a person must think of answers to such questions like 'why are we were, on whose property do we live, who is it that sends our food and where are we going?' A life lost in the desires

183

of the ego without any concern for answers to such vital questions and a heart aloof from acknowledging the Real is destined for a pitiful end.

People of this kind turn a blind eye on things that display the Truth in the clearest and most comprehensible languages and never pause to reflect, for which reason they have been compared to beasts, cases in point in ignorance and in being gone astray. All their desires consist of is eating, drinking and satisfying their gluttonous pleasures of the flesh.

Allah, glory unto Him, states:

"Have you seen him who takes his low desires for his god? Will you then be a protector over him? Or do you think that most of them do hear or understand? They are nothing but as cattle; nay, they are further astray from the path." (al-Furqan, 43-44)

A righteous man says:

"Life is a display of Divine art for the wise and just consumption and lust for the fool."

Contemplation, from another vantage, is like a two edged sword; it can serve the good, as well as the bad. It can become a tool for the despicable ambitions of the ego, as well as the sublime purposes of the spirit. The Almighty cautions those who use their ability to contemplate for bad ends:

"And it is not for a soul to believe except by Allah's permission; and He casts uncleanness on those who will not understand." (Yunus, 100)

The disease of disbelief is the ugliest dirt that could smear a human being. One who does not busy his heart and mind with reflecting on the verses of the Quran, can never be purified of this dirt.

Minds nourished with the light of faith and led by the guidance of revelation find the way to come to know the Almighty, while those deprived of this are stranded on the way the to the Truth. This is the greatest delusion of those philosophers who somehow believe they can find the Truth without taking Divine revelation as basis. Minds remote from faith, in their books, can find a way to the Truth just the same.

Maximizing the ability to contemplate, on the other hand, requires keeping the mind and the heart distant from ineffectual activities that amount to nothing but wasting time. Thus declares the Holy Quran:

"And who keep aloof from what is vain." (al-Muminun, 3)

"And they who do not bear witness to what is false and when they pass by what is vain, they pass by nobly." (al-Furqan, 72)

185

The Prophet –upon him blessings and peace- says:

"*Abandoning useless activities is the mark of a good Muslim.*" (Tirmidhi, Zuhd, 11; Ibn Majah, Fitan, 12)

The most effective medicine for the diseases of the ego is to focus all thinking on things beneficial and to move away from all things that should not be of any concern. Contemplating on useless things opens the door to all kinds of evil and depravity. Those who busy their minds with useless thoughts miss out on the good, on what they really need.

Ibn'ul-Jawzi says:

"If constantly thinking over things that are licit (*mubah*) leaves the heart in the dark, you go and imagine the damage done by thinking over the illicit (*haram*)! If even musk can change the makeup of water and take away its cleansing character, imagine water licked by a dog! Hence, says an elder, 'He who makes a habit of doing things that are licit misses out on the taste of uniting with the Lord.'" (Bursawi, Ruh'ul-Bayan, 'al-Muminun, 51')

If one does not direct his powers to contemplate, represent and imagine to the good, Shaytan will direct it to the evil; and the person will consequently become unable to contemplate in a manner worthy of the Divine. Instead of benefiting from the gifts of the heart and reason endowed by the Almighty, he will only incur damage.

A Believer therefore must always have his thoughts occupied with the good, in the direction shown by the Quran and Sunnah.

Accompanying Contemplation with *Dhikr*

Yusuf Hamadani describes:

"The heart and *dhikr* are like a tree and water. The heart and contemplation, in contrast, are like a tree and its fruits. It would be a mistake to wait for the tree to flourish before watering it and expect it to yield fruits before its leaves grow and flowers blossom. It will never yield any fruits, no matter how much one desired. For the time is not to expect fruits from the tree, but to feed it and tidy up around it. One needs to water it, rid it of ivies and alien weeds and then wait for sunshine. Only when all these come together does the tree come alive and become adorned with luscious green leaves; and only then does it become right to expect its branches to yield fruits, for this means that the time has truly arrived." (Rutbat'ul-Hayat, p. 71)

Hasan Basri says:

"The intelligent continue getting themselves used to contemplating through *dhikr*, and *dhikr* through contemplating. In the end, they get their hearts to talk;

187

and when the heart does begin to talk, it only utters words of wisdom." (Imam Ghazzali, Ihya, VI, 46)

Dhikr and contemplation must never be separated. The most important thing about *dhikr* is to do it contemplatively and accompany it with a sense of awareness. According to Muhammad Parsa –Allah have mercy on him-, a prominent saint, "When saying '*La ilaha*' (There is no god…), one should think of the mortality of all creation and consider them as nothing; and distancing everything but Allah, glory unto Him, from the mind, clear all thoughts. The heart should be filled with the consciousness of being a slave only of Allah and no-one else. When saying '*ill-Allah*' (… except for Allah) one should think that the primordial existence of Allah, glory unto Him, is also eternal and that He is the only One to whom one can turn to with love. The Almighty's attributes of beauty (*jamali*) thereby begin to manifest in the heart."

Bahauddin Naqshband -Allah have mercy on him- says:

"The aim of *dhikr* is not just to repeat 'Allah' and 'La ilaha ill-Allah'. It is to go from causes to the Cause and realize that all blessings come from Him."

The truth of *dhikr*, in other words, is to enable one to rise from the swamp of ignorance to the horizons of witnessing the truth.

188

Mawlana Rumi –Allah have mercy on him- says:

"Allah, the One and Unique has given us permission to remember (dhikr) Him, saying اُذْكُرُوا اللّٰه: *Remember Allah!'. Seeing us ablaze in fire, He gave us light. A dhikr done only with the tongue and lips without feeling and contemplation is a deficient dream. A dhikr that comes from the bottom of an admiring heart is distilled of sentences and words."* (Mathnawi, v. 2, couplet: 1709, 1712)

In time, Divine love grows in a person who continues to remember the names and attributes of Allah, glory unto Him, contemplatively. The point is not to just repeat verbally the word 'Allah' but to place the love of 'the Word' in the heart, the center of comprehension.

Through *dhikr* and contemplation, one first reaches *muhabbatullah*, Divine love, and through *muhabbatullah* one proceeds to attain knowledge of Allah, that is a better understanding and knowledge of Divine names and attributes. As a result, Allah, glory unto Him, loves the person, too, and befriends him. Stated in a *hadith al-qudsi* is the following:

"The righteous from among my servants and the ones I love from among creation are those who remember me; and I mention them in return for their remembrance of Me." (Ahmed, III, 430)

Dhikr is considered threefold: with the tongue, the body and the heart. The *dhikr* of the tongue is to recall Allah, glory unto Him, with His names and attributes, glorify Him, read His word and pray to Him. The *dhikr* of the body is to busy each and every limb with what has been commanded and to keep it away from committing the wrong. As for the *dhikr* of the heart, exegete Elmalılı Hamdi Yazır comments:

"The *dhikr* of the heart is to remember Allah in a most sincere, heartfelt way, and that comes in three forms:

1) Thinking of the proofs that attest to the essence and attributes of Allah, glory unto Him, and searching for answers to doubts that may come to the heart about His sovereignty.

2) Contemplating on the rights Allah, glory unto Him, has over us and our duties of servanthood; thinking of His commands and prohibitions, their proofs and underlying wisdoms. Gaining insight into the commands and prohibitions and the consequences of adhering to them only increases tendency towards righteous deeds.

3) Contemplating on creation, both inner and outer, and the wisdoms underlying their existence in a way that allows one to realize that each particle acts as a mirror for the Divine realm. To eyes that properly

gaze at that mirror, the lights of that realm shine forth and just a glimmer of that zest consciously acquired in a split second is worth the entire world.

There is no end to *dhikr* carried out at this level. At this stage, one loses consciousness of himself and his surroundings; all consciousness is lost in the Real, to the point where not a speck remains from either the words of *dhikr* or the person doing *dhikr*. Only the object of the *dhikr*, that is the Real, is felt. Although there are plenty who talk about this level, those who are at it have no business with talking." (*Hak Dîni Kur'an Dili*, [el-Bakara, 152])

All beings are thus mirrors of Divine manifestations, held out to human understanding and consciousness by the Hand of Might. Sensing the wisdoms and mysteries reflected forth from this mirror depends on the purity of the mirror of the heart.

Dawn: The Most Precious Time for *Dhikr* and Contemplation

A lover frequently talks about the beloved. One who frequently talks about something begins to feel a greater affection for it. Love is measured by the degree of sacrifice shown for the beloved. Abandoning a pleasant sleep and a warm bed near dawn to seek refuge in Allah, glory unto Him, is one of the most supreme indications of such love.

It is worthy of note that Divine mercy and forgiveness overflows near dawn. Nightingales, inspired by this Divine abundance, tweet in the sweetest tunes and flowers that boom in multicolored tones, emit their most delicate scents. What a shame it would be for man to miss out on this feast of Divine mercy!

The most precious time of day is dawn, corresponding to the last third of night. Dawn marks a period where the mind is the most distant it can be from petty concerns, when the heart subsides to purity, a peaceful silence abounds all around and passing interests wane. This time is when Divine mercy descends and the Lord of the Universe is at His closest to His servant. Being so remote from petty concerns, the heart can then turn to the Almighty in the truest sense of the word, for which dawn is the most appropriate and fertile time to retreat to contemplation.

Allah, glory unto Him, states:

"O you wrapped up in garments! Rise to pray in the night except a little. Half of it, or lessen it a little. Or add to it, and recite the Quran in measure. Surely We will make to light upon you a weighty Word. Surely the rising by night is the firmest way to tread and the best corrective of speech. Surely you have in the day time a long occupation." (al-Muzzammil, 1-7)

As opposed to the heavenly serenity of dawn, daytime is a period when noise reigns, and which leads to a lapse in concentration. A person who does not make the most of the effective hours of night may not be able to attain to that spiritually inspiring enjoyment of turning to and worshiping the Almighty, amid all the distracting activities of daytime, as much as he can at dawn.

Dawn is a unique time made for worship, whereas daytime is a wonderful blessing given for serving the good and earning a living. A believer should only be with the Real at dawn, while amid the public, yet still with the Real, at day.

The Blessed Prophet –upon him blessings and peace- never abandoned offering ritual prayer, reciting the Quran, praying and contemplating at dawn, the richest and most inspiring time of night. Such that even when struck down with an illness that drained him of the strength to even allow him to stand up straight, he would still put his dawns to good use, even if it meant he had to be seated.[58]

The Blessed Prophet -upon him blessings and peace- would especially make the most of dawn to contemplate. He would remain standing, in tears, to the point where his feet would swell, and prostrate for hours on end.

58   See, Abû Dawud, Tatavvu', 18.

Imam Hasan ibn Rushayq says:

"There is no better key to open the locks of the ocean of contemplation and the gates of the Real than to wake up from sleep at dawn and engage in activities conducive to spiritual promotion. At that time, man is remote from external interests, worldly concerns and ambitions. The time is ripe for privacy with the Lord. The body has been rested and revived; it has come to its senses. Dawn is the time when the weather is at its most pleasant, the breeze is at its gentlest; it is the most appropriate time between day and night. *Light covers darkness at dawn*. It is a stark contrast at evening: darkness caves in on light." (See, Abu Ghuddah, *Zamanın Kıymeti* p. 86)

The Holy Quran pronounces:

"Those who forsake their beds to cry unto their Lord in fear and hope, and spend of that We have bestowed on them…" (as-Sajdah, 16)

Repenting for sins at dawn, becoming emotional from thinking of Divine punishment, remembering death, planning what to do in the name of good in the remaining days of life and contemplating on the Quran are among the righteous deeds treasured by Allah, glory unto Him.

To those who revive their dawns in the said manner and spend a life of charity, the Almighty promises the exceptional glad tidings below:

"No soul knows what is kept hid for them of joy, as a reward for what they used to do." (as-Sajdah, 17)

The Prophet -upon him blessings and peace- has interpreted this verse as follows:

"*Allah the Almighty has said 'For My righteous servants, I have prepared treats no eye has seen, no ear has heard, no mind has ever and can ever imagine!'*" (Bukhari, Bad'ul-Khalq, 8; Tafsir. 32/1; Tawhid, 35; Muslim, Jannah, 2-5)

Understood from here is that the awaiting treats of Paradise that have not yet been revealed are far greater than those that have. According some reports, not even angels and prophets have full insight into what they are.

CONCLUSION

Contemplation: The Key to the Truth and Salvation

Reaching the Truth is possible only through contemplation. How can a person who acts blind and deaf towards the glaring presence of Divine majesty find the right path? Not for no reason do they say, 'That which does not awaken feelings is not knowledge'.

The mindsets of nonbelievers who cannot come around to finding the Truth are described by Allah, glory unto Him, below:

"Surely you do not make the dead to hear, and you do not make the deaf to hear the call when they go back retreating." (an-Naml, 80)

A mind trained under Divine revelation, which assures security from coming under the grip of groundless fears, deliriums and desires, combined with an effort to emulate the heart thread of the Prophet

-upon him blessings and peace-, guides one to the truth and good. The Prophet's -upon him blessings and peace- all other miracles aside, just reflecting on his morals and life would suffice to convince one of his honesty and the goodness of everything to which he invited. As a result of this reflection and with Divine help, one is then saved from the clamp of the ego and the dead ends of reason.

The plight and remorse of those in Hellfire are depicted by the Almighty as follows:

"And they shall cry therein for help: O our Lord ! Take us out; we will do good deeds other than those which we used to do. Did We not preserve you alive long enough, so that he who would be mindful in it should mind? And there came to you the one who warns; therefore taste; because for the unjust, there is no helper." (Fatir, 37)

That means man can reach the truth and eternal salvation through two avenues:

1) By either finding righteous Muslims and surrendering himself to their dependable hands and obeying the Real through the inspiration and spirituality received from them;

2) Or by using his ability to contemplate and sense in the direction of the Quran and Sunnah to find the truth, to which he is to submit his ego. Not obeying

the *ahl'ul-haqiqah* and not training the mind and then following its unwavering lead is bound to conclude in a tragic end.

True Contemplation: Affirming the Necessary Existence

As expressed before, it is impossible for human beings to grasp the Essence of Allah, glory unto Him. The only means for knowledge open to humans are the five senses, reason and heart; yet all of their capabilities are limited. With limited means, there is simply no way of grasping the One who is Absolute, Primordial and Everlasting. Limited means only amounts to a limited understanding.

Engaging in activities that surpass man's capability, like thinking of the Almighty's Essence and seeking to solve the riddle and mystery of fate, has therefore been prohibited by the Quran and Sunnah. Just as failing to contemplate Divine realities is a an invitation for disaster, not knowing one's place and plunging into thoughts that exceed mortal capability can also lead one down the path of destruction.

It is for that reason that the Blessed Prophet –upon him blessings and peace- says:

"*Contemplate on Allah's creation and blessings but do not think about His Essence; for you can never*

estimate His Might as befits Him." (see, Daylami, II, 56; Haythami, I, 81; Bayhaki, Shuab, I, 136)

The great Ibn Arabi has said:

كُلُّ مَا خَطَرَ بِبَالِكَ وَاللهُ غَيْرُ ذٰلِكَ

"Whatever thought may pass your mind regarding Allah, He is something else."

Indeed, as taught by Islam and as has been aforementioned, one of the essential attributes of the Almighty is *mukhalafatu'n-lil-hawadith*, that is not to resemble anything of creation. That we ascribe to Him attributes like wise, just and many others in which human beings also partake, is secured from amounting to *shirk*, that is ascribing partners to the Almighty, thanks to our belief in Him being *mukhalafatu'n-lil-hawadith*.

In contrast to the impossibility of coming to an understanding of the essential reality of Allah, glory unto Him, it is indeed possible to come to an inner certainty of His Unity and Existence, based on the manifestations of His attributes in the universe and phenomena. That marks the boundaries of human grasp, which like that of all other creation, is limited. And that is sufficient in Divine Sight to be accepted as a *mu'min*, a believer. Muslim scholars have for that reason often said, "The peak of knowledge is the knowledge of Allah."

Human beings have an understanding that only enables them to move from the attribute to that which is attributed of, from the work to its creator, from the art to its artist and from the effect to its cause. By gazing at created beings, each of which is truly a work of art, humanity can come to an understanding of the majesty, splendor and mercy of the Almighty, to the extent of his aptitude. One may only take as much from the ocean that is the knowledge of Allah as is allowed by the capacity of his bucket.

Mawlana Rumi says:

"One day a desire awakened in me to see the light of Allah on men. It was as if I wanted to see the ocean in a drop, the Sun in a speck."

Reflecting on the attributes, acts and works of the Almighty with a pure heart and sincere intention would make it inconceivable for anyone to be a disbeliever. Disbelief only begins when intellectual activity stops and the sensitive balance of the heart is disturbed. It is impossible for one, whose predisposition of mind and heart is still in tact, to be led to disbelief; and given he or she has opened his or her eyes in a world of disbelief, the likelihood of her being led out of it is very high. A good example of this is Ibrahim –upon him peace- who, despite being born into an environment in which idolatry reigned, ultimately acknowledged the existence and unity of Allah, glory unto Him, simply by virtue of his intellectual and inner capabilities; an account of which the Quran gives plenty of mention.

Disbelief is therefore impossible for one who can think straight. Claiming something not to exist does not, in any way, settle a dispute. Strong proofs and clear evidences are required. What purpose does claiming something not to exist serve when the mystery of life, death and the universe remains to be solved? This is just like the case of those who are unaware that they are suffering from excruciating hunger, simply because their bodies are too frail to feel it. Being in denial of their hunger in fact only shows just how grave their illness really is. A person whose entire nervous system is paralyzed or who is sedated is never aware of a nail spiking his body or a knife cutting through his limbs like shredding paper. Those who bring diseases upon their spirits without being aware of it in the least are described by Allah, glory unto Him, as:

"Blind, deaf and dumb..."

The Almighty has placed in the predisposition of each human being both the need and the power to believe and the desire to search for the truth. Being oblivious to or detached from faith and the truth is therefore caused only by a spiritual blindness and deafness. Otherwise the spirit of a nonbeliever, too, is ready to understand or is at least at its threshold; but

201

this feature of his is suppressed from rising to the surface by a spiritual impairment by which he is struck, just like the vague dreams one cannot remember after waking up.

The human spirit is naturally inclined to belief, a need that meets us as early childhood, like a hunger urgently waiting to be satisfied. A child who sees her father offer ritual prayer, for instance, does not ask any question pertaining to the details of ritual prayer. Instead, she tries to learn the greatness of the Almighty; and upon trying to express this 'greatness' herself, she resorts to physical descriptions, as she is not yet able to understand it in abstract terms. She asks how many Allah's there are and curious of what awaits her after she dies, she eagerly asks questions to find out what kind of places Heaven and Hell are. She finds herself in a relentless search, for no other reason than that spiritual hunger is embedded in her predisposition. When this embedded aptitude rises to the surface, a person becomes a *mu'min*, a believer. When it is left incarcerated deep within consciousness, just like an encaged bird, it makes a person a nonbeliever. After long years in captivity, a bird forgets how to fly and cannot take flight, even if it were to be released; for its wings have become calcified. When the feeling of faith is held back from rising above consciousness, the ability to believe, too, in time, becomes blinded.

We must therefore seek to know Allah, glory unto Him, who created us out of nothing, to the best of opportunity and ability. To attain to wisdom and knowledge of Allah and thereby reach the Almighty, it is necessary we come to a correct understanding of His attributes and actions.

Had Allah, glory unto Him, infinitely Wise in all His acts, revealed first off to the Blessed Prophet –upon him blessings and peace- to 'Read in the name of your Lord, who has no kin or partner', it would have brought with it a ready made objection, reducing the possibility of guidance for minds inured to disbelief. But the Almighty instead began His Revelation with an emphasis on an indisputable attribute: the Creator – "Read in the name of your Lord Who created..." (al-Alaq, 1). Idolaters, who very well knew that idols were not creators of anything, then began coming to terms with the fact that it is Allah, glory unto Him, who is the real Lord, the only One deserving praise and thanks.

Baydavi, the prominent exegete, comments:

"The great Allah reminds in chapter al-Alaq that He delivered man from the lowest level to the highest. He thereby draws attention first to creation, an act that refers the mind back to the Almighty. Secondly, He underlines reading-writing, which refers the ability to hear the Almighty. In other words, He unites rational and narrative sciences."

The Almighty has rendered contemplation on His creation a means for disbelievers to receive the honor of faith. For believers, on the other hand, it serves as a means to increase the certainty of their belief.

All Things are in a State of Flux and Change

If truth be told, everything in the in the universe is subject to constant change, alternating from one appearance to another. In the mother's womb, for instance, a clot turns into a lump of flesh and that to flesh and bones. Change reigns over the vast array of every perceptible thing, from stars to planets, from minerals to plants, and so forth.

There is an enormous movement within a single atom. Electrons spin in a delicate dance, at a dizzying speed beyond the wildest imagination. The speed of protons and neutrons, on the other hand, being compressed in a lesser mass, revolve in an even more exhilarating speed of over 60,000 km per second. This gigantic speed makes them appear like the drops of a liquid boiling and frothing from immense heat.

The below couplet elegantly express how even a single particle is enough to highlight a link between the art and the Artist:

No need for the entire universe, to come to know You,
Enough proof is a single speck You made...

Remembering there are approximately 100 trillion atoms on a 1 millimeter square needle head will give us a better appreciation of the nature of the Might that sets all things in motion throughout the universe.

There is needed a Real Cause for all this change and motion to take place; and that is the Almighty Allah, the Supreme Creator. It is absolutely inconceivable for this awe-inspiring parade of events to be without a source or to stem from an unconscious cause.

Everything is Created with a Purpose

Evident is the fact that every single thing that exists in the universe has been created in line with a purpose. As expressed before:

-With rays coming from the Sun and reflecting from the Moon, organisms receive their light and flourish. Time comes to be with the Earth and Moon revolving around the Sun. Coming into being through the Earth revolving around its own axis are seasons, years, days and nights; and months as the Moon spins around the Earth.

-The air we constantly breathe infiltrates the lungs and cleans out the blood. Air is the most accessible, since it is the one thing our bodies stand in need of the most.

-Steering the clouds in front of them, winds take rain to where needed, fertilizing plants and trees, regulating heat and cleaning the air.

-The benefits of seas and oceans are, likewise, countless.

The importance of these benefits and the countless more we have not been able to mention in human life is glaring. A contemplative gaze upon these would be enough to reveal the enormous wisdom and purpose underlying every single creation. Supposing these to be merely a haphazard assortment of coincidence is simply to cancel all power of judgment and clear thinking. They are undoubtedly the workings of One Allah, glory unto Him, infinitely Wise, Powerful and Glorious.

Different Things are made from the Same Material

At their core, the seemingly different things we see around us are all the same. They are all made of matter. Different elements are but parts of the same content. Objects in space, for instance, are all made up from the very same matter, yet they each have a unique identity, position, density and life span. Some are cold, while others are extremely hot.

Plants and animals are made up of elements like nitrogen, carbon, oxygen and hydrogen, even though there is no connection between these elements and life, especially with characteristics like knowing, willing, power, hearing and seeing.

All these are Divine works of art. The diverse yet perfect range of organisms we see throughout the universe is the working of a Majestic Artist. It is inconceivable for a Being, who brings into existence so many works of masterpiece, to all of a sudden begin to resemble them. He is the *Wajib'ul-Wujud*, the Necessity of whose Existence comes from Himself.

In a word, it is really not difficult for a thinking person to find his Lord and admire Him. Through contemplation, a nonbeliever finds faith, while a believer perfects his or her faith and strides forth on the ladder of *marifatullah* and *muhabbah*.

The *Marifatullah* Road

Muslim theologians have said that the first obligation humankind is commanded with is to turn to a contemplation that will deliver them to a knowledge of Allah.

The most general and basic aim of the Holy Quran is to deliver minds and hearts from the invasion of every thought other than Allah, glory unto Him, and duly guide them to *marifatullah*.

Human beings were created to know and to serve the Almighty. There is no better way to fulfill this aim than *dhikr* and reflection. Worship is the essence of human life. *Dhikr*, on the other hand, is one of the best ways of worshipping Allah, glory unto Him. *Dhikr* and contemplation are like inseparable twins.

The most important thing for human beings is, without a doubt, attaining to eternal happiness and peace. Other desires should be trivial in comparison. By far, the most essential means of reaching everlasting happiness and peace is *marifah*.

Scientific knowledge is to grasp a given event with its causes and effects. *Marifah*, on the other hand, occurs with an additional understanding of Divine Will manifesting in that event. It is for that reason knowledge of Allah, glory unto Him, has been coined *marifatullah*, which is to understand the Almighty's existence as much as allowed by knowledge.

Tadhakkur (remembrance-thought) has therefore been given a priority of mention over *taqwa* (piety) in chapter al-Muminun, in verses 84 to 87. For it is through contemplation and spiritual sensing that humans acquire knowledge of worth, through which comes a recognition of Allah, glory unto Him, instill-ing one with an awareness of the need to become pious and abandon opposing His Will. No deed is of any worth without knowledge of Allah.

There is thus not a shadow of a doubt that the noblest knowledge is *marifatullah*. Junayd Baghdadi says:

"Had I known of a better knowledge under the sun than that which the students of *marifah* chase, I would not have dealt with anything else and striven relentlessly to acquire it."

Ibn Qayyim al-Jawziyya has similar words:

"In the Quran, Allah, glory unto Him, invites His servants to *marifatullah* through two ways:

1. By observing the things created by Allah, glory unto Him, and reflecting on them,

2. By contemplating and reflecting on the verses of the Holy Quran.

The first group consists of the Lord's observable signs, while the second consists of the visible, audible and thinkable." (Ibn Qayyim, Fawaid, p. 31-32)

Spiritually sensing and contemplating on these deliver one to an investigative faith (*al-iman'ut-tahqiqi*) and to the purpose of existence.

The poem says it beautifully:

209

The vast universe, a grand book of Allah, imposing,

Whichever letter you peer into, Allah is its meaning…

Contemplation Must Lead to Practice

To reach the truth through contemplation, *dhikr* and *muraqabah*, it is necessary to put all the knowledge one has learned to practice. However much one may think of Divine truths and the verses of the Holy Quran, his contemplation means nothing unless he properly practices what he learns; for practice is the external reflection of contemplating and spiritual sensing.

Imam Ghazzali says in this regard:

"Knowledge, the fruit of contemplation, is to acquire a state of mind (*hal*) and turn to doing good deeds. Once knowledge sets in the heart, the heart begins to undergo change. And when the heart undergoes change, so do the deeds executed by the limbs. Action therefore depends on the state of mind, the state of mind on knowledge and knowledge on contemplation. That means that contemplation is both the beginning and the key to all things good. True contemplation is that which delivers one from ugliness to beauty, from greed to abstinence and contentedness. This is the kind of contemplation that yields perception and piety." (Imam Ghazzali, Ihya, VI, 47)

Through a contemplating and sensing that is conducive to practice, man becomes cured from the disease of looking on at the marvels of the universe simplistically.

An ordinary man, who is impressed with man made paintings, which after all are based on an imitation of nature, can not feel the same way when gazing at the universe in connection with its Creator. Things that should evoke awe are, for him, just ordinary happenings.

The pious, whose hearts are purified, on the other hand, have no business in acclaiming paintings made by artists with an interest of acquiring fame, and instead turn their interest and acclaim to the Real Artist and His masterpiece. They enjoy the zest of beholding the Divine art embroidered in the innumerable wonders of nature. They gaze at the multicolored flowers and leaves of plants, the inexhaustible difference of color, smell and shape each tree has, the unique taste of each fruit, even though they all spring from the very same soil, and look on admiringly at the wonderful patterns on the wings of a butterfly and the incredibility of human creation. They lend an ear to the mysterious words expressed through the silent language (*lisan'ul-hal*) of Divine wonders like eyesight and understanding, seen by many as just ordinary happenings.

For such people, the entire universe is like a book waiting to be read. Having surpassed knowledge of the written, they eye the knowledge of the heart; just like Mawlana Rumi, who as a scholar buried in his books and minding his own business in the Saljuk Madrasa, was suddenly ignited by the enlightening call of an enamored, mystic dervish named Shams, and found himself ablaze in the fire of love...Reborn in the atmosphere of love, it was the same Mawlana in whose sight the value of written books dropped to where they rightly belong, as he began reading the mysterious patterns of the universe with his very own eye of the heart. It was only after this stage that the masterpiece that is the *Mathnawi*, a cry exposing the mysteries of the Quran, universe and man, came to be.

How great a joy for the true servants who, through a refined heart and a reason guided and enlightened by the light of faith, lead their lives in the climate of contemplating and spiritual sensing, and are able to attain to *marifatullah*!...

AFTERWORD

In our times, many people alienated from their own history and culture seek peace in personal development programs of Western origin or in courses of yoga and meditation derived from the Far East. Little are they aware that the real peace humans desperately seek is only to be found in *dhikr*, *tafakkur*, *tahassus* and *muraqabah*, strongly recommended by Islam as the keys of unlocking Divine wisdom and truth.

A contemplation matured through inner, spiritual sensing is the source of spiritual expansion and inner peace. Only a contemplation of such nature can deliver one to wisdom. The beginning of wisdom, on the other hand, is the fear of Allah, glory unto Him, coupled by feelings of piety and awe. Contemplation, in a word, carries a believer to the pleasure and love of the Almighty.

A person who duly reflects on the universe and the events that take place thereon seeks answers to questions like 'What is life?', 'Why was I created?', 'What is the truth behind these passing days?', 'Which path is it that leads to happiness?', 'What must I seek to be?', 'How must I live?', 'From where have I come and where am I headed?', and so forth. These thoughts detach him from the passing desires of the world and take him to the right path that leads to eternal happiness.

In this humble book, we have tried to convey only some of the mysteries, wisdoms and truths contained in the universe, man and the Holy Quran, with some help from contemporary scientific findings. Who knows of the amount of mysteries and underlying wisdoms that are set to become unraveled in the near future to shed further light on the infinity of Divine Might and Majesty?

What we have touched upon here are, moreover, just a few examples proportionate to the modest size of the book. We sincerely hope that our dear readers will *insha-Allah* be able to reenact that horizon of contemplation, which we have tried to expand upon in the light of those examples, within the realms of their own hearts, in a way that can encompass all beings and events; and thereby derive many a pearl of secret and wisdom from the vast ocean of *marifah*.

214

May Allah, glory unto Him, grant each of us a horizon for contemplation! May He resurrect our hearts by giving us the ability to read the underlying wisdoms of the Quran, universe and man with a perceptive eye! May He include all of us among His blissful servants who live a life of *muraqabah* and are delivered to *marifatullah*!

Amin!

CONTENTS

CONTENTS

I AM A JEW

Moshe Davis

MOWBRAYS
LONDON & OXFORD

© 1978 A.R. Mowbray & Co. Ltd.,
First published 1978 by A.R. Mowbray & Co. Ltd.,
Saint Thomas House, Becket Street, Oxford, OX1 1SJ

ISBN 0 246 66496 5

Typeset by Oxford Publishing Services,
The Studio, Stratford Street, Oxford.
Printed by Fletcher & Son Ltd, Norwich

CONTENTS

PREFACE

When I was invited by the BBC to broadcast a weekly series of "Reflections" over the World Service I readily accepted. I was instructed by my producer, Colin Semper, that I should be strongly personal, that I should present the story of my own particular pilgrimage through life, but also, through that story, I should try to convey a picture of the life, times, outlook and hopes of the Jew generally.

I attempted to complete the writing of the whole series before recording the first broadcast, because I wanted the sequence to be right and I wanted to feel that I had told the *whole* story. But the time it takes to write a short piece is long, and the broadcasts commenced when I was only part way to completion.

Reactions to the broadcasts as they unfolded helped to guide me. Some pieces came easily — they almost wrote themselves. They were among the better sections. Others were difficult and, I am afraid, showed their faults.

When offered the opportunity to commit these talks to print I was not so sure of the wisdom of accepting. For the spoken and the written word differ greatly. The former should be personal and intimate, and should appear spontaneous and immediate. [Hence it suffers from a suspicion that it may be ephemeral.] As speech is the primary form of communication, a talk does not always come across so well when set down as an essay.

But the chance is too tempting to miss. I have been able to incorporate answers to a number of questions which were raised after the broadcasts finished and to deal with further relevant issues. I have also been able to correct the sometimes erroneous conclusions drawn from the necessarily brief statements of the broadcasts. This book, therefore, is a considerably expanded version. The stitching-in of new material may, occasionally, be unskilfully managed. For this I apologise.

I have tried to retain in the written version the basic directness of the original talks, although I realise that the style may be criticized as simplistic and the message naive. To this I offer no defence.

I believe that religion *should* be presented in a clear, simple way, certainly initially. Most of us seek straightforward, unsophisticated basic statements. And Judaism has never been overly speculative. The blessings of the Old Testament are the realities of sun and rain; very much of the here and now.

Where there are ambiguities, these may be due to my own deficiencies of expression, but they may well reflect the simple fact that I *am* often confused, that I realise there remains far more to understand about

Judaism than I already know. My ignorance, on all matters, far exceeds my knowledge. [In this, I suspect I am not alone.]

Edmund Flegg once wrote a book entitled "Why I am a Jew". He tried to explain to his unborn grandson (who never was born — both of Flegg's sons were killed in World War II before they married) why he had returned to the Jewish faith. When I read his book many years ago, I gained much inspiration. The title of this present book was not of my choosing, but was simply suggested by the publishers, after they read the original scripts. Although I suspect they did not know of Flegg's book, their instinct was right. I would like to think that this book is a progression from the statement of Flegg. I dedicate it to my wife and also to my granddaughter — my first grandchild — born whilst I was writing this book.

I am particularly indebted to Colin Semper, whose guidance was always wise and whose gentle criticism was invariably helpful. Robin Denniston is equally deserving of my gratitude. His many perceptive comments on the original scripts, his encouragement, his questions and suggestions have enabled me to expand the scripts into a book. It would have been far, far poorer without him. Finally, I am also grateful to two secretaries — Norma Pearlman and Judy Lerner — who typed and retyped the scripts many times as my revisionary zeal caused me to redraft and recast.

Moshe Davis

PROLOGUE

The train due to leave at 5.22
Has just been cancelled.
Amongst its passengers would have been
The maintenance crew
For the oil tankers,
Which need to be serviced
In order to carry
The supply of fuel
To the Power Stations
Which have not been operating
Due to the lorry drivers' strike
(Just concluded)
Which caused the Power-cut
Which prevented the 5.22
From running.

WHAT WE ARE, WE ARE

"The sailors said to one another: 'Let's draw lots and find out who is to blame for getting us into this danger.' They did so, and Jonah's name was drawn. So they said to him: 'Now then, tell us! Are you to blame for this? What are you doing here? What country do you come from? What is your nationality?'

'I am a Hebrew', Jonah answered, 'I worship the Lord, the God of heaven, who made the land and the sea.' "

(The Book of Jonah)

My earliest childhood recollections are of jail — Walton Jail Liverpool, to be precise. I do not mean by this that I exhibited criminal tendencies at an early age. It is simply that my father served on the medical staff of the jail and, naturally, we lived nearby. So I made friends with prison-officers, and I often walked to the jail after tea to greet my father when he finished work.

As a small child, I looked up in awe at the huge, high walls. I was most impressed by the big, wooden, double gates, which opened only to admit the police Black Marias. I was not then aware of the human cargo they transported.

After entering through a small gate, set into the large doors, I went into a reception office on the right hand side. I was fascinated by the constant jangling of keys and I was particularly intrigued by the metal staircases and by the iron bars which covered every window, no matter how small. To me, as a child, there was no unfriendliness or harshness about these bars. They were simply further, unknown objects in a world where much was strange and where I knew so very little.

It took me a long time to realise that there was a whole, sad universe within the walls of the prison, inhabited by a group of people who could not emerge of their own free will. I occasionally saw them outside, in "working parties". Sometimes they would repair or decorate our home. I found them pleasant and friendly.

I suppose, then, it was from these very early days of impressionable childhood that I came to understand that the world is built on many levels, and is divided into many zones. Especially into "us" and "them", "known" and "unknown". I simply accepted that there were differences — some innate, some imposed and some assimilated.

It was against this background that I acquired a

better understanding of that division of the world which has affected me most in my lifetime. Not a division by class, colour, country or cloth, but a division into Jew and Gentile.

As a child, I was only dimly aware of the distinctions. I knew I had to go to Synagogue and to "Hebrew Classes" and most of my playmates did not. But that did not particularly worry me. I learned to play truant when it suited me, and then I would take the tram down to the Mersey and look at the ferries which crossed the river, travelling to the intriguing world which lay within my gaze, but beyond my reach.

I have always been amenable to differences. I like individuals to express their individuality. I have never regarded Jewish differences as bestowing special privileges upon the Jew, or reflecting discrimination upon the Gentile. I have always felt that we should express ourselves and our attitudes to God each in the ways of our own faith.

Judaism looks to all peoples as having their distinct characteristics and as being able to play their own special part in the advancement of society and mankind. This emphasis on the role and value of the individual has influenced the teachings of other religions, particularly Christianity.

Today Western Society seeks ways whereby the individual may attain fulfilment. Our concern for human rights is essentially to ensure that the State does not override the individual. Only if the very rights which society seeks to maintain would themselves be endangered, may individual freedom be curtailed. No one can claim that the right to free speech entitles him to shout "fire" in a crowded theatre.

I am against differences which others impose upon us, but I assert and defend the right of individuals to preserve their own way of life and to accept upon themselves special responsibilities. Differences, of circumstance and history, may lead us to undertake upon ourselves additional duties, may prompt our desire to be a 'light unto the nations', but we cannot claim any heavenly — or earthly — bonus in consequence.

Judaism believes that every individual is a unique creation of God, formed in his image, and each of us can and should make our own special contribution to life and to the betterment of the world. Each of us is a partner with God in the works of creation. Our talents, however limited they may be, should be exercised for the benefit of mankind, to hasten the coming of the Messiah.

An Eskimo demonstrates the physical ability of man to live, to survive, under the most difficult climatic and environmental conditions. I believe that the Jews collectively have shown by their experience that "not by might, nor by power, but by my spirit" is the cause of mankind advanced.

BUT JEWS WE ARE

"Now, therefore, O Lord our God, impose thine
   awe
upon all thy works, and thy dread upon all that
thou hast created; that all works may fear thee
and all creatures prostrate themselves before thee,
that they may all form a single band to do thy
will with a perfect heart, even as we know, O Lord
our God, that dominion is thine, strength is in
thy hand, and might in the right hand, and that
thy name is to be feared above all that thou
hast created."

                                    (The Prayers of the Solemn Days)

In the land of Israel, our Jewish family first started.
My forefathers — Abraham, Isaac and Jacob — lived
there amongst the other peoples of that land, and
inaugurated the group from which I am descended —
and to which I belong.

After the redemption from Egypt, my people lived
in the Land of Israel for over a thousand years.
During much of that time they were independent,
and in that Land of Israel, the prophets spoke and

gave their message, not only to me and to my fellow Jews, but to the whole of mankind.

During two thousand years of exile a small Jewish community — as many as the times and the authorities would allow — remained continuously within the Land, and Jews throughout the world, in all the lands of their dispersion, spoke of Zion, and prayed for the Return. To this day, not only on the anniversary of the destruction of the Temple, but at every wedding, at every celebration and at every bereavement, three times a day in each of our statutory prayers, and every time we give thanks to God for our food, we remember Zion. "If I forget you, O Jerusalem, let my right hand forget its cunning"; "Return in mercy to Jerusalem, your city"; "May our eyes see your return to Zion in mercy".

There was hardly a portion of the globe to which the exiled Jews did not wander. The Jewish community in Babylonia was inaugurated in the 6th Century BC and later reached further east into Afghanistan, India and China — and also northwards to Bokhara, Tashkent and Uzbekhistan. The Egyptian colony spread westwards to Morocco and then crossed into Iberia. Exiles to Rome reached the Rhine and North-West Europe by the first and second centuries. Shortly after the New World was discovered, Jews settled in South America and from there moved to North America. This emigrant thrust provided the resourcefulness, intelligence and subtlety which characterises the Jew throughout his history.

Jews were great travellers and tradesmen. They operated along the great trade routes as far as China and the chronicles of their travels make exciting reading. But the main waves of migration were initiated because Jewish communities were either totally expelled from a country or faced unendurable persecution. Over generations, few Jews died where they were born. Thus the medieval attacks, especially during the Crusades, prompted a migration of Jewry eastward to Germany, Poland and, later, to Russia. There, by the 18th Century, flourished a deeply devout community of six million Jews. These Jews, during the period from 1882 to 1914, fled in their hundreds of thousands from Czarist repression. They came to Britain (where a community had already been re-established under Cromwell) and especially to the USA, which now contains six million Jews.

In all of these far-flung lands, annually, on the ninth day of the month of Av, the anniversary of the destruction of the Temple in the year 70 AD, Jews sat on the ground, or on low stools — as a sign of mourning — and chanted the Lamentations of the Prophet Jeremiah. For me, as a child, this was always the saddest occasion of the year. I watched the tears flow down the faces of the elderly people. We recited the elegies that recalled not only the Babylonian and Roman oppression, but all the sorrows of the Jew since the Exile. They seemed real, immediate, and personal. In 20th Century England I shed my tears for the Ten Martyrs of 2nd Century Palestine.

Israel has always been close to the heart of the Jews. For us it is the Promised Land and the Land of Promise. It is the land to which we believe the Messiah will come who will redeem our people, and usher in an age of peace for all mankind — in that land and in all lands.

The Jewish concept of a Messiah has evolved over many centuries. The word itself, like the Greek 'Christos', means 'the anointed', and originally signified any priest or king ordained for office. Cyrus was termed "Messiah" on this basis.

Later the term referred only to the Messiah who was to come to redeem Israel from exile. (In fact, two Messiahs were envisaged, the son of Joseph and the son of David; carrying out, as it were, a two-stage operation for the Ten Tribes and for Judea.)

Messianic days are depicted as a time when Jews will not be in servitude; when, generally, no nation will have dominion over any other people. Only God will reign as king and ruler.

One Talmudic source envisages that this will be the *only* difference between our present condition and Messianic times. (The wolf lying down with the lamb is treated allegorically.) Others felt that there would be a super-natural element and that the very nature of man, the animal (and even of plant life) would change.

Maimonides, the great medieval Jewish philosopher, completely rules out any idea that the Jewish people will reign supreme or be especially elevated over other nations. Nor does he feel that the era will be a time of physical pleasures ("eating, drinking and making merry"), but simply that Jews will be entirely free to study Torah and wisdom, in order to merit the world-to-come. There will no longer be wars or famine, jealousy or competition. The basic physical requirements will be freely available for all. The entire concern of humanity will be to know God. "For the earth shall be full of knowledge of the Lord, as water covers the sea."

The Messiah himself is thought of as being a person of supreme ethical and intellectual attributes. One school firmly refutes the notion that he will perform miracles or change natural laws, or revive the dead. The Torah will not be abrogated or altered. The Messiah will conform to the Law, will persuade Israel to walk in the ways of the Torah, will rebuild the Temple, gather in the exiles and promote universal order and recognition of God. There is little support in Jewish thinking for a Messiah who will be "supernatural".

There may well be terrible days before the Messiah arrives. Elijah will be the forerunner. But the general picture is vague and warnings are issued against speculation as often this can lead to sin. Hence, calculations of "the end" (i.e. the coming of the Messiah) were discouraged. The Rabbis simply urged the people to have faith and believe in the coming of the

Messiah. This has become fundamental to Judaism and is one of the Thirteen Principles of Faith enumerated by Maimonides.

I do not look for an age when there will be a merging of religions, certainly not when all peoples will be Jewish. For two thousand years, Jews have ceased to proselytise. Partly our depressed state and subjection has dictated this; partly there has been a growing realisation and understanding that, even in a Messianic Age, there must be room for different approaches to God. We simply pray that: "And God shall be King over all the Earth. In that day, may God be One and His Name One". We do not envisage that this will require conformity of religious practice, beyond adherence to a basic ethical code, nor do we accept that this will involve total uniformity of religious belief, beyond acceptance of monotheism.

In one sense, however, and probably in the most meaningful sense, we have never ceased to proselytise; not towards belief in and formal conversion to Judaism, but towards a propagation and acceptance of Judaic aims, standards and ideals. We have aspired to be a: "Kingdom of Priests and a Holy Nation" in order that the values we cherish should be seen to be worthwhile. Whilst we have not been missionaries, we certainly have always felt that we have a mission. Insofar as we ourselves portray the fulfilment of that mission, or the striving towards its fulfilment, we "Sanctify the Name". If we fail, we are guilty of "Profaning God's Name." These are the two poles of the judgement that a Jew must make regarding his actions and the interpretation placed upon them by others, especially by non-Jews.

What we ultimately look towards is a time when we will universally recognise the futility of war and embrace the concept not only of the Rights of Man, but of the responsibilities of Man to Everyman, when we will *all* sanctify God's Name.

FAMILY AND FESTIVAL

"And Joseph arrived in Shechem and was wandering about in the country when a man saw him and asked him: 'What are you looking for?'

'I am looking for my brothers' ".

(The story of Joseph)

I spent my childhood and youth in the North of England, mainly in Leeds, which was then — and to a great extent still is now — an industrial town. I remember it was smokey and rather unattractive. There was a Jewish population of over 20,000, most of them engaged in tailoring. Originally located near the centre of the city, there was a graual migration of our community northwards towards Harrogate. New synagogues marked both geographical progress and growing affluence.

We lived as a closely-knit, warm-hearted community. Jews have a strong feeling of togetherness and seldom respect social distinctions, other than those achieved by scholarship, merit or personal-attainment. The "group" is protective and reassuring.

Jews seek out other Jews, and it is only in and through the family (and the extended family which is the community) that our religion, in both its spiritual and ethical aspects, finds its fullest and truest expression. Judaism can be practiced but inadequately by a castaway on a desert island.

My terrace-housed street was 90% Jewish. The primary school I attended was not a Jewish school, but almost all the pupils were Jewish, and so we had no problem with our religious holidays. We always finished early on a Friday afternoon, in order that we might reach home before sunset when the Sabbath commenced. The teachers, both Jewish and non-Jewish, helped to create for us a Jewish atmosphere, but one which was more ethnic than religious.

At break each morning, only an hour and a half after school had commenced, mothers of the younger children would come to the railings of the playground and push through baigels and sandwiches for their offsprings. The mother birds were feeding their chicks. This over-possessiveness and protectiveness, frequently criticised, derived in the main from the long period of Jewish history when anxieties were based on very real threats to the safety, indeed life, of any and every Jewish child.

There was a strong concentration on food. In the home of my paternal grandmother the table was always laid. Any visitor, at any time of the day, was expected to partake of food. A simple cup of tea was by no means considered an adequate expression of hospitality. Whenever I visited the home of relations and friends I expected, as a natural course of action, to sit down and consume however much food was placed in front of me. Fortunately I did not tend to fatness and so I was considered a well-mannered, sensible child, simply on my merits as a substantial eater. Those children who pecked at their food, who could not consume the goliath portions almost forced upon them, were regarded as somewhat rebellious and almost wilfully obstructive.

Food of course, represented security to the Jew. As children rescued from concentration camps, and subsequently well cared for, would yet steal food because it represented the warmth and security of their mother's milk, so in my childhood did the generation which had migrated from Russia and the deprivation suffered there regard food as the symbol of safety. It was wonderful for them to be in a land of both freedom and plenty.

We experienced only occasional friction, over and above the normal troubles that arise with any immigrant community, which we then constituted. When we went to synagogue classes in the evening, gentile youngsters would sometimes throw the odd stone to the accompaniment of the cry 'Go back to your own country', or, 'The Jews killed Christ'.

These incidents made little impression, and certainly left no dents, on the pattern of our protected life within the unwalled Ghetto. It was very much a Jewish world whose flavour — culinary, intellectual and spiritual — I suppose, was similar to that of the Eastern European "shtetl" at the end of the last century, villages which often had a majority of Jewish inhabitants and where the Jewish life style affected the pattern of the entire community.

We had no actual "Fidler on the Roof" in our neighbourhood and our homes and physical conditions were infinitely better, but the quality of life, the feeling of mutual dependence, the hesitance about the "outside world" and suspicion of its intentions, all of this resembled the villages in Russia, Poland and Rumania where Jewish life flourished for a thousand years.

For us, too, the Jewish home was the pivot of our existence. Indeed, the home more than the synagogue, has long been the centre of Jewish life and of the Jewish religion. It has been of far greater significance in shaping Jewish awareness and response than any other element in our society. It is far stronger than in other creeds and experiences.

Within the home we observed our festivals. Passover in the Spring was, for me, the highlight of all the festival celebrations, as much of its ceremony is related to children. This festival commemorates the emergence of the Jew from slavery in Egypt some three-and-a-half thousand years ago. It is by far the oldest event of its kind, continuously celebrated — and basically in the same form — since the Exodus well over three thousand years ago.

A collection of foods, displayed in a prescribed

pattern on the table, symbolises this festival of freedom. The unleavened bread recalls the haste of the Children of Israel, unable to wait for their bread to rise. We eat it for the eight days of Passover. Ordinary bread is banned.

Salt water is also placed on the table, in a dish. It represents the tears of our forefathers in bondage. Alongside it, a delightful mixture of apples, nuts, cinamon, and wine is the "mortar" with which were built the store cities of Pharoah. Bitter herbs, such as horseradish, which brings tears to our eyes when we eat it, recall in vivid form, the bitterness of slavery.

But a spirit of celebration dominates. Four glasses of wine are drunk at various stages during the recital of the Hagadah (Narration). In prose and verse — sometimes spoken, sometimes sung — we tell the evergreen story of the Exodus.

Special roles are allotted to the children. It is their great occasion of the year, especially for the youngest child present. He or she asks four questions about the foods and customs of the evening, which prompt the father to lead the telling of the narrative.

Our meal no longer features a roasted Paschal Lamb, for that ceased with the destruction of the Temple in 70 AD. The Passover meal, eaten by Jesus was the basis of the Eucharist.

Each Autumn, just before our New Year we would take the thick Festival Prayer Books out of the bookcase. I always wondered how we would manage to get through so many prayers. But there was really no need to worry. The synagogue I went to started Morning Service at 7.30 sharp.

The changed look inside the synagogue always roused my childhood curiosity and interest. A white silk curtain replaced the red velvet cover of the Ark. The Scrolls of the Law inside had white mantels placed over them, and the Cantor of the Congregation, standing on the platform in the centre, wore a long white robe. During the Service, the blowing of the Ram's horn, the prostrations which were made by the entire congregation, and the haunting music of the prayers excited my boyhood wonder.

However impressive Rosh Hasanah was, even greater was the impact on me of the Fast of Yom Kippur. I marvelled at the fortitude of my elders. Was it possible for anyone to go without food or drink for 25 hours? My fears seemed justified. In our synagogue we always had women who fainted during Kol Nidre — the Evening Service — just one hour after the Fast had begun. I was sure that this was because they were already feeling the pangs of hunger. I did not realise that this was simply due to the lack of air. Our synagogue did not believe in fresh air. Windows were always kept tightly closed.

I secretly enjoyed the spectacle of a good faint in the ladies' gallery and the diversion it created. Everyone would immediately crowd round and smelling salts were thrust forward. Indeed, even today, Yom Kippur, the Day of Atonement, conjures up for me the acrid whiff of smelling salts.

Rosh Hashana and Yom Kippur were by no means days of sadness. We celebrated them as "Good Days" — Yamin Tovim — and warmly wished our friends a happy New Year. Hope and faith were the keynotes.

After the New Year and the Fast of Atonement, we would celebrate the festival of Tabernacles. We built a little, wooden hut in our backyard and there ate all our meals. This festival served to remind us that much of what we cherished was impermanent. As the Children of Israel lived in makeshift huts during the forty years of their wandering in the wilderness, after the Exodus, so each year we did likewise, making our own pilgrimage through a life which is but one stage in the journey of eternity.

Most Jewish festivals relate both to our past history and to the cycle of nature. They convey a spiritual message in a pleasant, homely package. The play acting they often involve brings to life the inner teaching.

It would be hard to expect Jewish parents to be able to communicate to their children, to convey the abstract, philosophical teachings enshrined in the Festivals were it not for the drama of Passover evening or the quaintness of the Tabernacle. This, and the special foods of each festival — honey, unleavened bread, cheese-cake and so on — relay in fine form, the story of our people and the essence of our purpose. The Festivals have always excited me and, to this day, I look forward eagerly to their advent, each festival with its distinctive form and its special type of celebration.

At the centre of my home was the table. On this our festive meals were eaten, round it our family regularly met, beside it we sang our songs and Sabbath hymns, on top of it we placed our books when we studied. Jewish tradition maintains that the family table symbolises, and has replaced, the altar of old, found in the Temple of Jerusalem.

The regularity of the heartbeat of the home life and the stability of the family has moulded the character of the Jew and created the typical Jewish family life which for so long has been the pride of our faith. The strong anchorage thus provided has prevented juvenile delinquency and caused divorce to be a rare phenomenon and 'wife-battering' to be virtually unknown.

Unfortunately, this is not universally true today. Currently the nuclear family is the model. It is replacing the extended family of my youth. Possibly the reduction in the number of children — which is the case of most Jewish families today apart from the very orthodox — has diminished the sense of responsibility among the fewer family members. Previously, each child, except the youngest, looked after another smaller sibling. The parental role was thrust upon children at an early age. Although this reduced their hours of play and leisure, it gave them a feeling of real personal participation in shaping the destiny, and contributing directly to the welfare and even economy, of the family. They never had any doubts about their right to a place within the family. They knew they were wanted.

Now things have changed. Divorce is common, about one in six Jewish marriages end in divorce. Whilst that figure is better than the national average, it represents a sad deterioration from former standards. Juvenile delinquency is still low but no longer is it a rarity, and teenage drug problems do exist. Alcoholism does not generally afflict Jews, possibly because of the early exposure to wine as part of the Jewish ceremony in the home, which fits naturally into the pattern of living. Gambling is a problem possibly because of the feeling of insecurity which, even today, afflicts many Jews. Also, Jews are prepared to take risks, because material success, after all, is still vanity of vanities.

Although I was an only child, I was never really conscious of any disabilities or deficiencies. Happily, I had many aunts, uncles and cousins into whose house I would walk unhindered. I am speaking of the 1930's when we did not lock our front doors. I could simply enter and take my placed within a related family group. If the family was eating, I would join in at the appropriate course. No one waited for an invitation. Whatever problems afflicted the community, loneliness was not then one of them.

Like many children. I was never too sure of the borders of our family, nor did this concern me. There was a blurring of distinction between cousins and cousins-several-times-removed, between uncles and close friends of the family. But, if I was sometimes in doubt as to who stood in relationship to whom, I was always clear as to who was the source of authority and guided all its affairs.

At the head of my family was my maternal grandfather, Hirsch Hurwitz. He was a biblical figure; tall and distinguished with a dignified white beard. He was the rabbi of our community and undisputed king of the tribe. I was very proud of the respect shown to him. When we walked in the neighbourhood park on the Sabbath afternoon people would rise from their seats and greet him. I would hold his arm to guide him — his eyesight was failing — and bask in his reflected glory.

He preached in our synagogue only twice a year, to a "full house". His language was Yiddish — warm, expressive and sad — now rapidly disappearing. He was a master of oratory in the manner of the homiletical preachers and story tellers. Like the Welsh he would gradually change the pitch of his delivery and raise his voice into a kind of chant which bordered on singing. He could conjure up laughter or tears within moments of commencing his two hour discourses. He lived into his eighties and made a major impact on all who knew him.

With him, I studied Jewish scriptures and the Talmud, for some two or three hours each evening, when my day's studies at school had been finished. He and most of his children, including my mother, were born in Lithuania and came to this country at the turn of the century. He was my link to an understanding of the life of the Jew during the dark years of persecution, before the age of enlightenment and emancipation into which I was born.

SYNAGOGUE

How wonderful it is, how pleasant
For brothers to live together in harmony!
                              (The Book of Psalms)

The synagogue has several names in Hebrew; they
each well describe an aspect of its purpose. It is a
House of Prayer, it is a House of Study, and it is a
House of Assembly. In Hebrew, there is only one
word for both "house" and "home"; and the latter
term might be more appropriately substituted.

The synagogue has a number of distinctive features. For example, synagogues face towards Jerusalem. We turn in our prayers to Zion and the site of
the Temple (as Daniel did, and as Moslems turn to
Mecca). There is an "Ark" — an ornate cupboard —
on the eastern side, often built into the wall. It is the
main feature and focal point of the synagogue and
hence is often decorated and elevated; surrounded by
steps reminiscent of the approaches to the Temple.
In front of the Ark hangs an embroidered curtain.

Inside the Ark are contained handwritten scrolls
of the Five Books of Moses — the Torah. These are
extremely valuable in monetary terms (they take

about a year to write) and also in religious terms. They are surmounted by silver bells and a silver breastplate, and are covered by a suitably decorated mantel of rich material. A silver pointer hangs alongside.

In times of persecution, Jews would seek to rescue the scrolls of the Torah in preference to any personal wealth or possessions. Some scrolls are ancient, and some are famous for their history, having been owned by great rabbis, or having belonged to special congregations. Many have been carried from exiled or dying communities to find new homes in England, the USA or Israel.

There is a reading ("Lesson") from the Torah every Sabbath and Festival and on other special occasions. This is a central feature of the service. The ceremony of taking the Scroll out of the Ark and returning it subsequently is one which non-Jews visiting the synagogue for the first time and witnessing a service, always sense as being a high spot in the proceedings. Incidentally, all services are open to any visitor. There are no secret ceremonies.

Reading from the Scroll is a highly-skilled profession. The text is unpunctuated, there are no vowels; nor do the musical "notes" appear, which regulate the pattern of the traditional chant. There are special chants (they can hardly be termed "tunes") both for the reading from the Torah and for the reading from the Prophets (the "Second Lesson"), which follows. These derived naturally from the dramatic nature of the reading. They were probably improvised at first, in the days of Ezra when regular readings were instituted, but later became stylized and standardized. Certain books of the Bible, for example Esther and Lamentations, have their own special chants. The "flavour" of the occasion is gently suggested by and through the tune.

Selections from the Five Books of Moses are read each Sabbath, so that the Pentateuch (as it is called) is completed in an annual cycle. Between three and seven persons are "called up" to the Reading, depending on the occasion. On the Festivals a special, prescribed text relates to the particular occasion.

Prayers are led by a Reader who stands on a raised platform which is usually in the centre of the synagogue, but sometimes is close to the Ark. The prayers also relate to the special occasions being celebrated. Men and women generally sit separately; in many buildings. there is a gallery for the women. In my synagogue, as in many synagogues in the western world, there are stained glass windows.

Our prayers are in Hebrew, which Jewish children learn at an early age. Initially, I found learning to read the Hebrew script quite difficult. But later, with regular usage, I was able to establish a reasonable fluency in that language. When corresponding with my grandfather, for example, we would both write in Hebrew.

Hebrew is the key to Jewish religious thought. Our classical literature and our prayers are in Hebrew and hence, when I pray, this common language unites me with every Jew throughout the world who offers his prayers in the same language. Thus is enhanced the feeling of solidarity and togetherness which is such a powerful feature of Judaism.

Israel Zangwill describes the small prayer meetings held in the East End of London — in "rooms" as contrasted to the larger and often colder synagogues. He admitted the ignorance of most of the worshippers, but lovingly recounted the warmth of their piety and the depth of their sincerity. "When they prayed", he wrote, "they did not understand a single word, but they meant every syllable".

Today, many Jews read Hebrew, but cannot understand it. For them the prayer book is a series of sounds, without meaning, but they are aided by a translation into English which most Hebrew prayer books now contain.

Jews frequently repeat the same prayer. The three statutory prayers each day contain the same basic invocation called the "Amidah" (the standing prayer) said silently by each individual. The same "Grace After Meals" is recited after every meal and it is a long prayer lasting about five minutes. But this does not cause boredom or insincerity. The words are often mere vessels or containers. The contents and feeling poured into them are individual, spontaneous and evergreen. The words are abstract paintings which can reflect the viewer's own interpretation and can change with the mood of the beholder.

Jewish prayer is introspective. Its primary target is self. Hence the meaning of the Hebrew word for prayer is "Le-hitpallel" — "to judge oneself". We aim not so much to change God as to change ourselves, not so much to impress God as to express ourselves.

Prayer involves a contemplation of the infinite. I try to reach out to the infinite. I try to make contact with the One who is the Master of the Universe, Lord of all Creation, Our Father and Our King. I try to fathom the meaning of Creation, and to understand my place in it.

To do so, I examine myself and draw up a kind of spiritual profit and loss account. I believe that the most difficult task for us in life is to know ourselves. Our description of our own image is rather like the portrait of Dorian Gray — the view from without rather than the insight. I try to examine to what extent I have accomplished any of the aims which I set for myself. Sitting in the synagogue, I study rabbinic commentaries and consider whether I have succeeded in living up to the ideals which are expounded in our Scriptures, in the Torah.

But these two functions alone — meeting God and meeting myself — do not fulfil me as a Jew. In addition, within my House of Prayer, within my synagogue, I want to meet and encounter my fellow Jew; to have communion with him, to argue and discuss with him, to tell him of my successes and my failures, to talk to him of my family events and to learn of the latest chapters in the chronicles of his life.

Each Sabbath morning in my synagogue (as in synagogues throughout the world) worshippers are called forward to the Reading from the Scroll of the Torah — the Law. Separately, each mounts the platform and a portion of the lesson is read, accompanied by a blessing. If anyone has experienced any particular event within his family, a special prayer is said, either to extend condolences on a bereavement, or to offer congratulations on the birth of a child, or to express our hopes for the restoration to good health of a sick relation. The whole of the community participates in the personal event. We all call out "Mazal Tov" (Good Fortune) to somebody who is engaged, or married, or has had a child. We call out "Speedy Recovery" to someone who suffers illness.

Our community is concerned with each and every individual, and, reciprocally, the fate of the individual is bound up with the fate of our community.

What has always deeply impressed me is a custom on Friday evening when the first part of the service has been completed. A person who has lost a near relation (a parent, a wife, a child, a brother or a sister) during that week, enters the synagogue at that point, and is specially announced. The whole congregation rises, greets the mourner and expresses its condolences and good wishes.

I have experienced it twice; when my father died, and when my mother died. Previously, I had always been among the members of the congregation greeting the mourner. When I was on the receiving end, I was immensely moved by the surge of warm fellowship which seemed to wrap itself about me — like the Jewish prayer shawl — and comfort me in my grief.

For hundreds of years, during the Dark Ages and continuing into this century, many Jews would use the local synagogue as a hostel. In Poland and Eastern Europe the traveller had no inn to which he could afford to repair for the weekend. The synagogue then became his temporary home and the local community would ensure that there was food provided.

Today there is a happier replacement. After the Sabbath morning service, we frequently have a "kiddush", especially if there is some event to celebrate, either personal or communal. "Kiddush" literally means "sanctification" (of the wine). But it is far from being a sacrament alone. Drinks are offered, generally liberally. Whisky as well as wine. Nuts, crisps and cucumbers and cake are set out on the tables. All of this light refreshment I enjoy. Who would not? But above all, I enjoy the opportunity of seeing my friends who, during the week, are busily engaged on their own activities.

We must all constantly try to keep our friendships in repair. Regrettably, we infrequently do so. The synagogue provides Jews with an opportunity to try at least to repair some of our worst sins of omission.

Jews experience a strong bond of tribal kinship. A Jew can travel throughout the world — as I have done in Europe, Russia and the Far East, for example — and, going into a synagogue and meeting a fellow Jew, can stretch out his hand and say in sincere greeting, and deep-rooted friendship: "Shalom Aleichem" — Peace be unto you! I am a fellow Jew!"

SABBATH

"Observe the Sabbath and keep it holy. You have six days in which to do your work, but the seventh day is a day of rest dedicated to me. On that day no one is to work — neither you, your children, your slaves, your animals, nor the foreigners who live in your country. In six days I, the Lord, made the earth, the sky, the sea, and everything in them, but on the seventh day I rested. That is why I, the Lord, blessed the Sabbath and made it holy".

(The Ten Commandments)

Significantly, it is the mother of the home (the wife *is* the home, said the rabbis), who inaugurates the Sabbath by the simple act of lighting two candles. Like all Jewish practices, it is accomplished by the recital of a short blessing: "Blessed are you, O Lord Our God King of the Universe who sancitified us with his commandments and ordered us to kindle the Sabbath lights". The wife covers her eyes with her hands as she recites this blessing. She adds a silent, private prayer for her family. The physical light of the candles is enhanced by an almost palpable spiritual enlightenment which spreads over the home. The Sabbath day has commenced.

For me personally, the Sabbath is the zenith of my week and the point of my greatest attachment to Judaism. Like all Jewish festivals, it starts on the preceding evening. From then until nightfall on Saturday (about 25 hours later) I know I shall beholden to no man and to no machine. The telephone loses its power to summon me in response to its imperious ring. I simply ignore it — and feel liberated.

Most people fail to read that Fourth Commandment correctly. Most people think that it is just a command to rest on the Sabbath Day. It is not. The preamble is part of the commandment. It is an exhortation not only to rest, but also to work. "Six days shall you labour"! Working for six days, trying to give of our gifts of mind and the skill of our crafts to the community, is an essential prerequisite of our day of rest. If we have not worked, we cannot really rest.

The prohibition against work on the Sabbath is not determined by the *labour* involved in an activity, by the amount of energy expended. This is often not perceived by Jews who, in this modern age, argue that certain prohibited works can be readily performed by pushing a button. The ease of performance does not decide our attitude. Rather, the works listed as transgressing the Sabbath are *creative* acts, irrespective of whether they are tiresome to carry out or not.

Observing the Sabbath does not lie just in refraining from weekday activity. A mere cessation from work on the Sabbath is not sufficient. The whole purpose is not just being lazy and engaging in recreation of the physical being, but in re-creation of the soul. I have time to read and to study. I also have time for my family, my children. After the candles have been lit and the Sabbath Evening Service sung, I bless my daughters: "May God make you like Sarah, Rebecca, Rachel and Leah. May God bless you and protect you; may God give you light and be gracious unto you. May God favour you and grant you peace".

There is a need for a regular meeting of the generations based on love, and common interest, not on confrontation. The meal on Friday night, and again on the Sabbath day, is unhurried. No-one is going anywhere fast. We all have the time to be together, to listen to one another, to hear the other person out.

Sabbath and festival meals start with the sanctification of the wine and the breaking of bread: two loaves, to symbolise the double portion of manna which the Children of Israel received each Friday in the wilderness. In common with many families, either immediately after or before the "Kiddush" (sanctification), I sing a portion of Proverbs, Chapter 31 which praises the mother of the home. She deserves special mention; she should not be taken for granted.

We then sing more general Sabbath table songs, interspersing the courses with melody. The tunes are catchy and are often handed down in family or community groups. The themes relate to the day of rest and to the aspirations of the Jew. The Grace after the meal is also sung and is a fitting, and rousing, musical and spiritual climax.

The food is frequently "traditional"; that is, it relates to the origins of the Jewish communities in Eastern Europe or Spain or the Middle East. Each of these areas had their special dishes, with local recipes and spices. I can tell the origin of a Jewish family by the food they cook, especially for the festivals.

Because of the probibition against cooking food on the Sabbath, many of the dishes are pre-cooked and then put into the oven on a low flame just before the Sabbath. They can slowly simmer for 16 to 20 hours until they are required and the long, slow cooking improves them. They are then served piping hot.

The quality of the meal, the concern for good food, is very much a part of Jewish living. It is specially important on the Sabbath, when the choicest dishes are served. Jews in former, less affluent days, who could afford little or no luxury on weekdays tried to serve a special choice meal on the Sabbath, and they would skimp and save for six days in order to do so.

Because of the special fare, it is also a great privilege to entertain guests at one's table on this day. In the Synagogue, on the Sabbath, members of the congregation would once compete amongst themselves for the honour and pleasure of inviting travellers and strangers to their homes. For the joy of the Sabbath to be complete it must be shared with others, particularly the less fortunate.

This same thought prompts a custom which is,

sadly, less observed today than in former years. The parents of a bride invite to their wedding not only family and friends but also the poor and the needy within the community. Moreover, they must not be relegated to a corner of the hall but must be seated in a honoured position. Often the father of the bride himself waits upon them at table. Only thus can a truly Jewish wedding be celebrated.

The Sabbath is a taste of the World to Come. "One sixtieth part" said Rabbis — that is, a minute fraction. On that day of joy, despite all outside distractions, and whatever the weekday harassments, even the poorest Jew has been able to sit at his table, look over lovingly and admiringly towards his wife, regard her and address her as a queen, and feel himself to be a king.

One element of the greatness of the Sabbath lies in an area that non-Jews might criticize as being too "legalistic", namely the precise moment that the Sabbath commences. Each week, with the changing seasons, the time that the Sabbath starts changes. In order that we may know the exact time, to the minute, it is carefully calculated and published in Jewish calendars and the weekly Jewish press. Within England, the times of the start of Sabbath for all the major towns are published, although they differ by only a few minutes.

Such a concern for detail makes sense to me. I do not regard this as a matter where the "spirit" should count most; for we are usually so possessed by our work, by the pursuit of wealth, that it is essential for us to face the discipline of an absolute and clear command to desist. Were a "period of grace" granted, we would push one more article across the counter, drill one more hole, spray one further branch of a tree, take another telephone call, sign another letter. As Jewish Law has wisely legislated, no discretion is left to the individual; he simply stops. And the working week comes to an end. It is like the sounding of the factory siren to down tools. Appropriately, in Jerusalem and some other cities in Israel, the Shofar (Ram's Horn) is blown to signal the arrival of the Sabbath.

I find it difficult to convey to those who have not personally experienced the Sabbath eve, how the peace of the Sabbath descends upon me. Probably the greatest test for me was after the death of my mother. Her funeral was on a Friday. Returning home, I sat in mourning, in accordance with the Jewish customs governing this traumatic period of one's life. But I knew, and had always deeply reflected on, the regulation which laid down that one may not mourn on the Sabbath. I found I was able to fulfil this ruling, strongly aided by the knowledge that my mother herself would have wished it so. I was able to interrupt my mourning for the Sabbath and the grief was lifted from my heart as I sat and celebrated the Sabbath as always, with its songs and its rejoicing.

"More than Jews have kept the Sabbath, the Sabbath has kept the Jews", said Achad Ha'am, a Jewish philosopher and essayist of the beginning of this century. He was totally right. I know that whatever the pressures of the week, whatever problems are left unsolved, the Sabbath moves me completely into a style of living which is not related to the ephemeral but to the eternal.

The Sabbath is for the living; for us, our children, our servants and our animals. Yet is is even for the dead, asserted the rabbis! They, too, are entitled to a respite. Each seventh day, as long as we, here on earth, observe and enjoy the Sabbath, so long they too, wherever they may be, are granted remission.

I am not concerned with the literal truth of this assertion. I am concerned with the greatness of the concept and the total humanity of those who conceived it. This, for me, has elevated Judaism, has moved it far above the philosophical speculations of those disciplines which are not God-centred, and has inculcated an abounding and abiding compassion within us, which is the primary virtue of man in relation to his neighbour.

LIFE IS FOR LEARNING

"Thus taught the Baal Shem Tov: Study for the sake of scholarship is desecration. It is a transgression of the commandment against bowing down before other gods; the idol being mere learning. The study of the Torah is a matter of the heart's devotion."

(Hasidic Saying)

In all the Jewish homes I have known, there has always been a place for books. Whatever else had to go out, books had to come in. In my grandparent's modest home, one room was specially dignified and styled "The Study".

A home without books, without learning, is not a truly Jewish home, because study is fundamental and essential to Judaism. It is part of prayer, being the key to any meaningful examination of self. Many parts of our "Siddur" (Prayer Book) are simply long extracts from the Bible or Rabbinic teachings. They are introduced not to be "prayed" or "said", but to be studied and considered.

Study is also the spur and guide to action. "An ignorant person cannot be pious" argued the Rabbis.

On the face of it a little unfair, but, on deeper examination, a basically sound proposition. Judaism is an involved religion, covering all aspects of life — private, public and collective. The laws and customs governing behaviour are detailed and intricate, they must be known and understood in order that they may be practised. An ignorant Jew is an unfulfilled Jew.

Dedication to study — against the background of our deep faith and our undying optimism — has kept our people alive. When the walls of the Ghetto closed around us and our physical horizons were harshly circumscribed and severely limited, Jews enlarged the world of the spirit and the mind so that the locking of the ghetto gates each night became meaningless. Those inside immersed themselves in study so that they soared into the limitless realms of philosophical and metaphysical speculation. Possibly this has given the Jew such a notable bent for disciplines such as theoretical physics. At all events, far from deteriorating under conditions of oppression and restriction, Jews often reached out, way beyond their jailers. The deeper the cork was depressed in the water, the higher it shot out when finally released.

Dominating the image of the Jew during the middle-ages has been the Merchant of Venice stereotype. There were, indeed, Jewish money lenders. In many instances, as for example in England before the Expulsion of the Jews in 1290. Jews were generally forced into moneylending because most other occupations were barred to them. And individuals could amass a great deal of wealth. But those who achieved fame, such as Aaron of Lincoln and Aaron of York (12th and 13th Centuries) probably acted for a wide consortium. On every money lender were dependent twenty to thirty families. The occupation was fraught with hazard. Aaaron of Lincoln's property was confiscated on his death. Aaron of York died penniless; his wealth was taken in taxation even before he died.

The money lending experience educated Jews in banking. New procedures were devised, such as letters of credit which could be discounted by Jews in other countries. This was the forerunner of the merchant banking system, which brought some families into world prominence, notably the Rothschilds, the Sassoons and the Ezras. However, these were the rare, rare exception.

The ordinary Jew had little opportunity to accumulate wealth, he was often prohibited from owning or even renting land. He therefore looked either to petty trading or to certain crafts and professions where study and skill could promote his progress.

He was, for example, drawn to jewels and gold, where a high degree of skill could be very profitably exercised, utilising a small amount of costly raw material. His stock could not deteriorate. Rarely would it go out of fashion! If local conditions proved unfavourable — politically or economically — he could put his "shop" into his pocket and migrate.

Tailoring, shoe-making and furniture were also, but at a later stage, favoured occupations. They still are the main areas of Jewish involvement in the retail trade and especially in the multiple-stores. "Take it from your belly and put it on your back" was ancient rabbinic teaching, urging Jews to eat less but dress well.

Whatever professional or business outlets the Jew acquired, it still remained his aspiration to pursue his spiritual and cultural life, within his home and within his community. "Integration" was an unknown concept and the problem of assimilation hd not yet been posed. Rejected by the wider society around him, the Jew could only look inward, to his religion and its unbounded treasure house of wisdom, the simple key to which was study.

The basic "textbook" for study has always been the Bible — more exactly that part termed by Christians: "The Old Testament". (The New Testament is not part of the Jewish Bible.) Like our Prayer Book — another book indispensable to the practising Jew — it is an anthology, and should be approached and studied in this light. Poetry and law, history and ethics, philosophy and genealogy, prophecy and song; all these elements blend into one book and within Judaism there is a blurring of distinctions between disciplines that is a key to an understanding of the Jewish character.

The Bible tells of our history — the stirring events which created our people and shaped our destiny. It speaks of the word of God and relates the visions of his prophets. It also contains the primary code of law which governs Jewish life.

Many Gentiles believe that Jews are obsessed with the concept of the law, that we are too "legalistic". The Five Books of Moses the first part of our Bible, is called "Torah" in Hebrew. Often this is translated the "Law", but the true meaning is the "Teaching". As such, the term is often applied to the whole corpus of Jewish teaching.

When I carry out what I believe to be the will of God, I want to do so fully — in all its details — and correctly. I want to apply my mind, my heart and my soul — my reason, my love and my will — to all the commandments of God.

Hence I do not regard the legal instructions telling me how to perform the "Mitzvoth" (commandments) as restrictive and inhibiting. I do not regard them as obstacles preventing me from pursuing my true purpose, in my own way. I regard them as signposts for my journey, as helpful guides, as the distilled wisdom of former generations anxious that I should benefit from their experience. Far from being hinderances, they are spurs. The Rabbis taught that because God wanted us to acquire merit he *increased* the "Mitzvoth" we have to perform.

In light of this, every detail, each rubric, is an object of affection and concern. Our emotion then prompts our intellect to examine the propositions more closely and carefully so that all minutiae are extracted. A rabbinic parable compares our attitude to a man invited to appear before Royalty. He is keenly concerned to ensure that his dress, demeanour and conversation will conform to protocol. But he also looks forward with excitement and pleasurable anticipation to being presented. Similarly, a Jew should regard himself as daily standing in the presence of the King of the Universe. He should be thrilled to learn and know how he can best behave. The Law is life, and thus is itself alive. It is not a dry-as-dust code to be circumvented, but a fountain of eternal living waters.

The "Talmud" is the encyclopaedia which expounds and expands the Torah. It was originally the Oral Law, in contrast to the Written Law of Moses. The latter needed explanations and commentaries. Precisely what work is prohibited on the Sabbath? What does a "Sukkah" (Tabernacle) look like? What are its dimensions? How were the sacrifices offered? A thousand questions needed to be answered; not only relating to our religious laws, but also to our civil and criminal code, and our social customs.

For many centuries the answers were conveyed orally, the tradition was handed down through judges, prophets, scribes and rabbis. This enabled the necessary adjustments to be made; to meet local conditions, to retain relevance in changing times. Jewish law was therefore termed "Halacha", from a root word implying movement. There was nothing static about the observance and the law needed to answer the problems posed by progress.

Eventually, however, the sheer size of the code and the growth and geographical spread of the disapora, dictated the committing of the Oral Law to writing. There were two sections: the first, the code of law itself (Mishna), edited at the beginning of the second century; and the second, the discussions as to the basis of the law and the reason for the decisions (Gemara), compiled several centuries later.

There is a Palestinian Talmud and also a Babylonian Talmud, reflecting the differences between the two major regions of Jewish settlement at that time. The Babylonian Talmud is the one more generally studied and considered more authoritative. It is written in Hebrew and Eastern Aramaic. It has 63 volumes — and contains over 2½ million words — and is lengthier than the Palestinean Talmud. References in Rabbinic writings are to the Babylonian Talmud, unless otherwise stated.

Over the centuries, the Talmud has attracted further commentaries, and these are usually printed alongside, and are indispensable to a study of the main work. These commentaries alone are treble the size of the Talmud.

It is this work the Talmud, which has been the main subject of traditional, higher Jewish study for nearly one and a half thousand years. As I have already explained, every Jewish child was early taught to read Hebrew. The basic prayers were already familiar to him even before he acquired a reading

51

skill. He would, therefore, begin by studying the Pentateuch, move on to the major commentator (*Rashi* — a French scholar of the 11th century), start Mishna at any age from six or seven onwards and be well into the Talmud by the age of ten or eleven, possibly earlier.

Depending on the talents of the individual, studies would then be pursued at a "Yeshiva" (Talmudical College) a "seat" of learning. The Jew immersed himself in the study of the Talmud. It became for him his whole life.

Some would aspire to be teachers and even heads of academies. Their initial studies could readily last twenty years. Some youthful prodigies emerged, still in their teens. Many would continue at the Yeshiva even when married. The whole community supported these scholars. Institutions which attained fame could look for financial help throughout the disapora.

Modern Jewish literature has frequently described the life of a Talmud student. During times when Jews were depressed and even when nearly half of the Jewish population — especially in Eastern Europe — had to be totally supported out of charitable funds, students were still considered a top priority. However, the assistance they could be afforded was often minimal. To sustain themselves they would "eat days", (as the Yiddish phrase described it) that is, they would be regularly invited to the homes of different families on different days of the week. Not all meal times would necessarily be accounted for. There were also "blank days", which the student would then designate as a fast-day, so that at least some religious merit would attach. It was the ambition of every father to eventually marry his daughter to a renowned scholar. Economic status was disregarded. Fathers were happy to support a son-in-law for many years so that he could continue to pursue his studies.

Of course, there have been many Jews skilled in other branches of learning, notably in mathematics, astronomy and medicine. Great rabbis frequently did not exercise their rabbinical function for financial gain. They would practise a trade or profession. Some were cobblers, blacksmiths, shop-keepers and, later, many were doctors. A trade was always considered honourable. The years of study at a Yeshiva were not intended to lead to a professional career in the rabbinate. Study was for its own sake.

Study afforded the Jew the opportunity to transcend the life of here and now. There is no end to knowledge. When Adam took of the fruit of the tree of knowledge, he started on a road which is without end. Some rabbis envisaged the "World to Come", not as a place where we will indulge in unrestrained pleasure (as we presently construe pleasure on this earth) but as a place where we will indulge in the endless acquisition of knowledge.

Study for the Jew is the chief joy of the mind. To learn is part of worship, a part of Divine Worship. It is conducted in the home and in the synagogue, as well as in the school of learning. The scholar, the student of the Talmud, is the aristocrat of Jewish society.

But learning is not merely a process for oneself. It is a contribution to others. For it is through study that we learn what we, as members of society, must do for others; what our contribution to the world must be.

This is the function of Jewish study — the accumulated wisdom of the ages is transmitted to future generations. We can move then towards the establishment of the Kingdom of God — not in the Heavens, but here, now, on earth.

JEWS FOR ALL REASONS

Now the Lord has told us what is good.
What he requires of us is this: to do what
is just, to show constant love, and to live
in humble fellowship with our God

(The Prophet Micah)

The favourite question asked of the Jew, by others and by himself, is: are Jews a race or a religion?

I believe we can speak only very loosely of the Jews being a race. There are Jews of every colour from white (or pink), to yellow and shades of brown and black. Any visitor to the State of Israel, travelling on an Egged bus, is struck by the variety of types featured among the passengers, all of them Jews. Certainly, Jews are not one race in the ethnic sense.

The physical features frequently described in the West as "Jewish" — what one might almost term the "stage" Jew — do not have general application. Insofar as these features exist, they are common to many peoples of the Middle East, and could more properly be described as "Semitic". Gesticulation and mannerisms often categorise people more than facial appearance. I was born into a family which "spoke with its hands" and I do likewise. In the multi-cultural society of England today, I find this is increasingly acceptable and does not attract the adverse comment it once did.

Over the centuries, certain groupings emerged among Jews which related to geographical areas and hence there are now many physical differences which can be quite easily observed. "Sephardi" Jews for instance, are of Spanish, North African and Oriental descent. They have distinctive religious customs of their own, so do the "Ashkenazi" Jews — those deriving from Russia and Central Europe. The former are generally darker skinned. Although the bulk of Anglo-Jewry today is Ashenazi, Jews in England range from blue-eyed, blonde-haired Jews through "ginger" (quite a high proportion of Jews are red-haired) to the stereotype image of dark-haired Jews.

In most countries of the world, these two groups are merging, but synagogues still tend to follow the liturgical patterns and Hebrew dialect of the one or the other. Jews from one group feel quite at home in the synagogue of either group. (That is if they feel at all at home in a synagogue.) Intermarriage between Ashkenazim and Sephardim is now common and attracts no special comment.

Furthermore, Judaism is not exclusive, and any original racial features have long since been lost. Many people have converted to Judaism, starting from Ruth (in Biblical times) including the Idumeans (bringing Herod to the throne), and such diverse characters as Lord George Gordon (of the Gordon Riots fame) and Marilyn Monroe.

Contrary to common opinion, converts certainly can be accepted, but conversion must be based on an understanding of the faith, and sincere acceptance and practice of Judaism. The process generally takes a year, often longer, sometimes even five or six years. It involves a study of Judaism, the Hebrew language and Jewish history. The prospective convert must know the customs and practices of the faith. It is not sufficient to evince a general interest or a "balanced preference". Nor is the wish to marry a Jewish partner acceptable as a motive for conversion. Indeed, this would raise doubts as to the sincerity of the intention of the prospective convert.

Males must undergo circumcision. The final ceremony for both males and females is total immersion in a prescribed ritual bath (mikveh). A new Hebrew name is given to the convert (the Christian custom of baptism derives from this) who is regarded, and termed, a son (or daughter) of Abraham.

The convert obviously ceases to practise his or her former faith some time before final acceptance into Judaism. No form of renunciation or denunciation is required. All Jewish obligations and responsibilities devolve on the convert once admitted and converts must in no way be criticized or reminded of their former allegiance. Significantly, it will be from Ruth, a convert, that the Son of David, the Messiah, will eventually be born.

The movement between the faiths has not been in one direction only, as many Jews have given up their religion to become Christian or Moslem. Either they have been literally forced to do so or, much less frequently, they have opted to do so of their own free will. During certain periods of Jewish history, notably in medieval Christian Spain, but also under Islam, descendents of Jews who had been converted to the dominant faith (either voluntarily or because of presure) sometimes reverted secretly to their Jewish origins. They would carry out religious practices within the privacy of their home. The Spanish Inquisition was specifically concerned with such "Marranos". Many, when caught, suffered death at the stake, because their immortal soul was at peril!

In more recent times, some Jews have simply faded away, because of apathy or convenience, but have not joined any other religious group. Essentially, they are lost to the Jewish people. We can no longer even recognise them, let alone count them.

Since the Age of Emancipation, many new types and degrees of Jews have emerged, the 'hyphenated-Jew" as Rosenzweig termed it. Previously, one could apostasise — though this was viewed by the Jewish community as being one of the gravest sins — but all those who remained *within* the community had little choice but to conform to the established religious patterns. Heretics were few. Excommunication was rarely practised. When it was, it was generally for reasons of political policy rather than theology.

Those inside Judaism related so closely to their fellow-Jews — socially, economically, intellectually — that deviation was rare. With the advent of the period of the Enlightenment, it has been possible to be a secular Jew, that is, a Jew without Judaism, identifying as a Jew, expressing pride in one's origins, but not "religious".

The term "secular" or "non-practising" Jew can cover a wide range; embracing, for example, fluent Hebraists (culturally relating to the Jewish people), and "stomach" Jews (who simply like Jewish food). The common factor is that the religious observances are either disregarded or treated as of minor importance. Some of these Jews may well follow a pattern of disciplined living, aspire to intellectual attainment and adhere to high moral standards which stem in great measure from Judaism and the history of the Jews; a fact which they might not acknowledge. But, in any event, they would not automatically accept the "Mitzvoth" (Commandments of Judaism) in the same way as a professing *religious* Jew.

There are also many Jews whose degree of observance is selective; who observe only certain precepts and disregard, or do not accept the contemporary validity of, others. Jewish thinkers have continually explored, examined and speculated on the reason for the divine commandments, other than the laws of morality or those relating to criminal and civil procedures. Whilst many reasons have been advanced explaining certain commandments rationally, the orthodox approach has demanded observance because of the divine nature of the command and not because of the human assessment of its purpose. The meaning and relevance of individual laws are subordinate to the argument for the Law, and that was quite readily accepted even by the rational philosophers.

Since the early 19th century (and disregarding the Karaites of a thousand years ago who accepted only the written Biblical Law) different attitudes have been expressed. The Reform Movement, collectively, asserted preferences and were prepared to regard certain precepts (for example the dietary laws) as deriving from hygienic and sanitary reasons and hence now outdated.

Furthermore, they queried the basis of the "Halacha" (Jewish Oral Law) as it had been interpreted down the ages, and as it was presented as almost unalterable by the contemporary rabbinic world.

Orthodox (more correctly "ortho-praxis") Jews, whilst individually selective in their observance, as a group subscribe to the whole corpus of Jewish law, as successively presented in the classic Jewish codes. Today, there are many Jews who must be described as "nominally" orthodox. Their synagogue is orthodox, and they as its members, recognise the validity of "Halacha" but they do not themselves adhere to all the laws. [This issue of Halacha must not be equated with the question of Fundamentalism as it is understood by Christians.]

Scattered among the different synagogue groups, or even outside them, are those who have been termed "cardiac" Jews, so called because they generally introduce any discussion on their personal attitude with the phrase: 'I'm a Jew at heart". This emotional, rather than rational, approach covers a wide spectrum.

Both the secular and the cardiac Jew may well feel and express a degree of pride in being Jewish. They may still retain synagogue membership out of a sense of loyalty, nostalgia, parental respect or tradition. Frequently, they may associate themselves with a particular field of communal endeavour, for example by working on behalf of Israeli causes, or participating personally in Jewish welfare work. As Judaism has placed great stress on "works" they can sit very "religiously" on the committees of the community and find total social acceptance among Jews. They should not be lightly dismissed. In the eyes of Jewish law, sinners are still fully Jewish.

One final category has also emerged, that of persons who are Jewish by descent (that is, they have a Jewish mother and hence are *fully* Jewish) but they have no connection whatsoever of their own choosing — religiously, culturally, philanthropically or emotionally — with the Jewish people. They are Jewish only because a label has been attached to them (by the non-Jewish world) which they have not actively sought to remove or, having tried, have failed.

Society recognises all these types and groups as being Jewish. Indeed, so far can a Jew, as an individual, wander from Judaism that there are such charged terms as: "a Jewish-Christian" and there are those in the Soviet Union who describe themselves as: "atheist Jews". In a Jewish religious sense this is contradictory, but in the social sense, there clearly exists a Jewish people that is not tied to, or dependent upon, the religion of Judaism as such. Some would use the term "race" to describe this phenomenon.

But I, personally, am not so worried about how others identify a Jew. I am much more concerned with how a Jew identifies himself. Does he keep Jewish traditions? Does he associate himself with Jewish problems and seek their solution? Does he actively ensure that his children will know of their heritage and will wish to pass it on to *their* children? Does he add to the ethical and moral legacy which each generation of Jews should try to bequeath to mankind.

For me, a Jew is a blend; an amalgam of religion, of peoplehood, of history and faith. Sokolow once defined the Jews as being: "a confederation of families". That implied mixture of common descent, of inter-family connection, and of tribal loyalty seems right to me.

I am a Jew because I adhere to the faith of Judaism, because I share with fellow Jews a common way of life and the hope of a common destiny. Of all my aspirations, my Jewish aspirations rank highest.

THERE'S NOTHING QUITE LIKE DYING

"When Rabbi Bunam was lying on his deathbed, his wife wept bitterly. Thereupon he said "Why are you crying? All my life has been given to me merely that I might learn to die".

(Hasidic Tale).

Quite a number of Jews are three-times-a-year synagogue goers. They attend on the two days of the New Year and on the Day of Atonement. Even this attendance may be perfunctory and only for part of the service. But it is nevertheless a significant act of association and identification. The eve of the Fast of Yom Kippur (Day of Atonement) sees the largest attendance of all. Most synagogues are completely unable to cope with the large number of worshippers wishing to attend. Extra chairs are intoduced, aisle space is reduced, classrooms are converted into temporary synagogues and outside halls (including cinemas) are hired for "overflow services". No other event — social, political, philanthropic — draws a crowd even remotely comparable in size to that evening.

It is ironic that the joyful occasions in the Jewish year — Tabernacles, for example, which is described as the "time of our rejoicing" — does not summon forth a half or a quarter of that number which attends for the solemn Fast, which is demanding and restrictive. The opportunity to repent for commandments transgressed is more attractive than their actual performance. A Fast has more appeal than a Feast. We seem to respond more to heavenly sticks than to earthly carrots.

An interesting exception is Soviet Jewry. There, the largest crowds of the year — including many young people — are drawn to the synagogues, and they overflow into the surrounding streets on Simchat Torah, the concluding day of the festival of Tabernacles. This is the most joyful day in the calendar. It celebrates the annual completion of the cycle of Reading the Torah and the recommencement of that cycle afresh. (The completion of the study of major Jewish writings is celebrated; but always a new book is opened and its study immediately started). It is a day of unrestrained jubilation when dancing and merrymaking in the synagogue is not merely tolerated but encouraged. Soviet Jews need the fortification of a religion of joy, not merely the spur of the forgiveness of sin.

Strangely, the present solemnity with which Yom Kippur is vested did not always attach to that day. In Temple times it was a day of happiness and many elements of the liturgy still reflect this. After all, the opportunity afforded by the day for repenting of one's sins towards God, (sins to man require reparation and forgiveness) was magnificent, calling for celebration. "Rejoice in trembling" said the Psalmist and this strange mixture of emotions is the key to understanding the Jewish approach. It is a day of paradox when God, as ever, is our Father, but when he is also our King. Paternalism and sovereignty inspire in us different feelings, blending love with awe.

Whether an instinctive, inherited, insight calls the Jew to prayer on this day or whether he, as many others, responds more to challenge and demand than to acceptance and gracious receiving, the "Yom Kippur Jew" — and there are many — clearly indicates his lack of more sustained interest by his selective response.

The Rabbi is never sure whether he should welcome him on the rare occasions he does attend synagogue, or reprimand him for his failing to associate more frequently and meaningfully.

Unhappy as we may be with such members, there is a further category, the "three times a lifetime" Jew, who parallels those in other faiths. Many only see the inside of a House of Worship — be it church or synagogue — if they are propelled there in perambulator, wedding limousine or hearse. For the three ceremonies surrounding birth, marriage and death — the milestones of life — are still significant and there is a wish to associate formally with ones religious group.

The initiation into Judaism for a male is circumcision. Once it was quite usual for this to be performed in the synagogue. Today, it is generally carried out in the hospital or in the home. Hence the need for synagogue attendance occasioned by birth has been reduced. A girl is simply named in the synagogue when the father is called to the Reading of the Law. Neither the child nor the mother need be present.

Circumcision was the first custom introduced into the Jewish religion. It was carried out by Abraham upon himself and his two sons. Hence, the duty to circumcise a child has devolved upon the father, but, as he is generally not competent, the operation itself (which, in the Jewish manner lasts but a few seconds) is performed by a qualified practitioner. It is carried out on the eighth day after birth.

The "Covenant of the Sons of Abraham" is sealed into our flesh and whatever its origin and medical significance, the Jew carries it out primarily in fulfillment of a commandment of God. However, if for whatever reason it is not performed, the child concerned is still Jewish.

Boys aged thirteen, are privileged to be called to the Reading of the Law for the first time and they enter on their duties and responsibilities, religiously, as adult Jews (Bar-Mitzvah). Today it is a time for celebration and congratualtion and it is seen as an initiation rite, whereas formerly, and until as recently as the beginning of the century, it was a simple event, marked only by immediate members of the family. The large parties are new and are intended to stress the joyous aspects of Jewish responsiblities. For girls, some congregations have a parallel ceremony; but the more orthodox communities are less likely to mark the occasion within the synagogue.

These are the initiation ceremonies, and the vast majority of the community participates in, and experiences the ministrations of the synagogue in the early years of life. Most Jewish children (some two thirds) do receive some religious education, often in classes arranged by the synagogue (Sunday School) but, now increasingly (nearly 25%) in Jewish Day Schools. They learn to read Hebrew — so that they can follow and participate in the service — and are taught the basic beliefs and practices. But for many children this education is minimal: for some, even this minimum is non-existent.

The ceremony of marriage, especially in modern times, seems to draw fewer folk. Whether there are simply fewer marriages taking place, or whether there are fewer Jews in Gt. Britain, or whether more Jews are opting for a registry office marriage (at one time a rarity), is not clearly known. All of these are likely to be the case.

Jewish marriage is basically a contract between two persons, entered into freely before a congregation. Blessings are invoked, but it is not the rabbi who *performs* the ceremony so much as supervises it, to ensure that all the legal requirements are fulfilled.

Naturally, it is a religious occasion, but two Jewish persons living together (and both eligible to marry) would be deemed married in Jewish law — sufficiently so to require a divorce should they separate and one of them wish to marry another partner.

A Jewish wedding can be a very wonderful occasion. The ceremony takes place under a canopy, which is a very romantic setting for this major occasion in the life of the couple. I enjoy the traditional style of wedding, with a lot of singing and dancing; the Bride and Groom are lifted aloft on chairs and their friends dance round them. Even today, and in Britain, we can see the "bottle-dance", which started out as an East European folk dance, and is tremendously exciting. The musicians and the jester too have not quite disappeared from the scene. "Every bride is beautiful" said the rabbis, and we should dance in front of her and make her happy.

The purpose of marriage, certainly its main purpose, has been regarded by Judaism as being the procreation of children. A childless marriage was deemed tragic.

But marriages break down, although the parties will make strenuous efforts to keep together especially when there are children. If the two cannot be reconciled, then divorce is deemed quite correct, in the hope that the parties will contract a happier and more successful marriage in the future. No stigma attaches to divorce by mutual consent (which was once a bar to English civil divorce — and termed "collusion"). Judaism has always severely disfavoured divorce resultant from adultery (which English civil law once regarded as highly satisfactory grounds for divorce). However, any divorce "causes the Altar to weep", said the rabbis, and is a last resort.

For many Jews, Judaism comes to life with death. Whoever slips through the net at iniation ceremony or marriage rites — whether by intention or inadvertently — is inevitably caught up at death. Overwhelmingly, and whatever the degree of affiliation with the community during lifetime, most Jews seek burial in a Jewish cemetery. This return to, or conclusion within, the Jewish fold, frequently brings in its train an increased interest, or a reawakened interest in Judaism by the relatives of the deceased. The whole procedure surrounding the Jewish reaction is geared that way.

While the belief in an after-life has been firmly accepted by mainstream Jewry, certainly for more than two thousand years, Judaism has throughout stressed *this* world rather than the next. Furthermore, the sanction (or promise) which an after-life can imply was rarely employed in the armoury of exhortation of the preacher. Rather was there a constant appeal to the all-seeing omnipresence of God to ensure awareness by man that he must adhere to the commandments. The phrase "I am the Lord" was invoked where only God could know what was contemplated in the heart of man; where fellow-man could not judge the motive by the action.

Hence, death was intended to be taken calmly but, naturally enough, very seriously. "Repent one day before your death" was guidance offered by one rabbi. This was intended to ensure continual self-assessment and repentance, as no man could know when he was to die. An element of fatalism does appear from time to time in Jewish writings but, the teaching that prevailed was "Charity redeems from death". Good deeds (works) were the opportunity offered to man to change his fate, even the fate of death.

Attitudes regarding death itself, and how it should be greeted, varied greatly. Some presented death as the precursor of aweful judgement in the afterworld, a judgement which would take place before the Supreme Bar of Justice, before a Judge who, could not be deceived, where our virtues and vices would be weighed in a scale, and final, inexorable judgement would be pronounced. Others put forward the less dramatic view; that of death as facilitating a simple passage from a transitory and often deceitful world of vanity and suffering into the world of permanence, where we will be reunited with our beloved kinsfolk and, under the cover of the wings of the Almighty, our souls will be "bound up in the bond of eternal life".

Judaism, however, never accepted the right of an individual to depart of his own accord from this world, for whatever future bliss might await him. Nor may one facilitate the departure of another person for whatever reason. "Mercy killing" is totally unacceptable to orthodox Judaism. And we should not tell an individual of his plight, in extremity, if such knowledge will unduly frighten him or weigh heavily upon him. Rather should he be sustained and encouraged, so that his end may come more easily. We can tell him "white lies". Even if the doctor is asked a direct question by the patient, the doctor must judge whether the patient can withstand the hard reality of the truth. If not, and if such communication will lessen the will to survive, then the doctor should not disclose his prognosis. We must never give up hope; but drugs *should* be used to suppress pain. In all of this Judaism is very similar to attitudes and practices in most parts of the developed Western World.

Where there is an essential difference, it is not in theology or philosophy, but in the practical response of the living to the *fact* of death, and, more especially, to the particular death of a member of one's family, or a friend. Whereas most Westerners frequently exhibit distaste at the showing of emotion, an "it's better to leave them alone to their grief" reaction, Judaism takes an opposite view. "I am *with him* in his sorrow" (Psalm 91).

It is a Jewish custom to facilitate burial as soon as possible after death, generally the following day. (Funerals, however, do not take place on the Sabbath). The fact of death must be quickly accepted. To leave a corpse unattended is considered an affront to the dignity of the human frame and its Creator.

It is a supreme privilege to attend to the preparation of the body for burial. Indeed, most Jewish communities once had (and some still have) a society of volunteers who were especially selected to wash the dead person and carry out all the ritual requirements prior to the funeral. It was deemed an honour to be allowed to be counted amongst their number. Fathers so privileged would encourage their children to follow them into that society.

Jewish funerals must be as simple as possible, no elaborate coffin, and — in most orthodox communities — no flowers. The differing displays and tokens might seem to imply a social inequality which, whilst apparent and inevitable in life, would be distasteful and meaningless in death.

Jews will always try to attend a funeral. It is rare and sad when only a few mourners and friends are present at the final journey of any person. Funerals of great rabbis, despite the speed with which arrangements must be carried out, will draw crowds of tens of thousands, many of whom will travel huge distances to be present to pay their last respects.

In many western countries, the womenfolk are accustomed not to go to the cemetery to witness the actual burial. This might be too disturbing for them.

Even in extremity Judaism seeks balance. At every wedding we introduce a note of sadness by remembering the destruction of the Temple. At every funeral we introduce hope by declaring our belief that God will rebuild Jerusalem.

After the funeral the relatives commence a period of seven days of highly formalised mourning. They gather in one home, remove leather shoes (and wear cloth slippers) and sit on low stools. They also tear one of their garments. Males do not shave during that period. Mirrors and pictures are covered or removed. All of these were ancient signs of mourning. They are still in force today because it is felt that there is need for *visible* expressions of grief, that sorrow should not be bottled up, that the "stiff upper lip" is the wrong reaction to the severe trauma of losing a near and dear relation. We want people to show their emotions and recognise the vital therapeutic need to do so.

Judaism does not seek to prolong the grief but, by a series of gradations in the mourning period, it ensures the steady diminution of sorrow and the ordered return to normal life. Among those things which, "if they had not been created would have *had* to be created" said the rabbis, was the gradual forgetting by the heart of the terrible grief we first experience when, for example, our mother dies. We could not live the rest of our lives with our grief at the same pitch of intensity. The terrible sadness we experience in a bereavement — like every profound sadness in life — does gradually fade.

Jews today have mixed feelings regarding the visitation that is customary during the seven days. Many attest to its wisdom, visitors pouring into the home where the bereaved are "sitting", to express their condolences and talk with the mourners. This enables the close relations of the deceased, the widow for example, to tell over and over again of the last moments of the life of her husband and so to "get it out of her system". The first few times there are many tears to accompany the tale and the recounting of cherished memories. But, bit by bit, that tale becomes less and less emotional with its repeated telling.

The crowd present can build up into many dozens, especially during the evening prayers. Visitors *do* chat among themselves; they are not all gloomy eyed and mournful. They *are* part of an outside world which is continuing to live its life, however much the bereaved feels that life has lost all meaning and purpose. Some visitors who are present for the first time at a Shiva (seven days of mourning) fail to recognise that this is good therapy. It may well be that assimilation of the Jew into a western culture is affecting our attitudes.

On the seventh day the mourners rise (there is no mourning on the intermediate Sabbath) and all return to work and normal life. Some minor outward signs of mourning are retained for the first month after the death. These are then diminished still further and completely terminated after one year. Subsequently, every anniversary of the death is noted (a candle is lit and a prayer is said). Also on the major festivals a prayer marks the communal rememberance ("Yizkor") by all members of the synagogue of their relatives who have died.

During the first year, the son of the deceased, (or the father or husband) recites a special mourners prayer, (kaddish) in synagogue at each of the three daily statutory services. Significantly, the prayer is simply in praise of God; it does not refer to the dead. "Magnified and sanctified be His great name, in the world which He has created according to His will", and it continues in that vein. It is basically a declaration of acceptance of the will of God.

When we hear good news, we say a blessing. Similarly when we hear bad news we bless God and acknowledge him as a true God and a true judge. We cannot arbitrarily worship a God just so long as he is on our side. This certainly does not answer the question of the existence of evil in the world, but it does help us to respond to the situation, even if that response is one merely of resignation and acceptance.

The daily recital of the Kaddish, necessitating as it does attendance at synagogue, has an interesting, almost strange effect on the individual concerned. Frequently he has not been a regular synagogue attender, even on the Sabbath. Now, filial regard and respect place upon him the duty to become a daily attender; and not simply once a day but both in the morning and the evening. He joins others who are on a similar mission. A kinship is built up between those who recite Kaddish together for months on end. Some one described it to me as a very exclusive type of club. Having been a "member", I can understand this and accept it. There is a bond of friendship which frequently helps to bring back to Judaism many who have travelled far away.

The cycle turns. With the death of the head of the

family, or the matriarch, duties devolve on a new generation. Whilst many would be reluctant to come forward of their own free will, few will refuse the responsibility which is placed upon them. With the disappearance of one life, somehow the seed germinates in the next in line. Even if the response is not immediate, it is still likely to be evoked at a later stage; when grandchildren appear, for example.

Thus is the continuity of the Jewish people maintained. Despite massive rates of defections and inter-marriage, particularly in the free countries of the West, the miracle of Jewish revival is daily demonstrated as the son stands in the synagogue and recites "Blessed, praised and glorified, exalted extolled and honoured, magnified and lauded be the name of the Holy One blessed be He. . . He who makes peace in His high places, may He make peace for us and all Israel; and let us say Amen".

DESTRUCTION

"Not one persecutor alone has risen up against us
to destroy us, but in every generation there are
those who arise against us to make an end of us but
the Holy One, blessed be he, saves us from their
hands."

(The Passover Hagadah)

I think it was in 1938, when I had just turned twelve,
that I read a book by Stefan Lorant called "I was
Hitler's Prisoner". It made a profound impression
upon me.

Lorant described his arrest and subsequent
imprisonment in the concentration camp of Dachau,
Germany. He managed to secure his release and came
to Britain as a refugee. Here he became the editor of
"Picture Post". His book describing his experience
was my first introduction to the frightening story of
the Nazi Third Reich. It was clear that a brutal regime
had seized power in Germany which transgressed
every moral code, which murdered, robbed and
tortured at will, which sought to destroy the soul of

man. But the world at large did not know, did not want to know, about Hitler — until it had to. Possibly it was too hard to believe that a human could be so inhuman!

One evening my family went to synagogue to a "special service", to pray for the Jews of Germany and Austria who had come under Hitler's domination. I felt considerable uneasiness, because I did not know what a "service of intercession" was. I was accustomed to the ordered flow of the festivals and the services that marked them. I also knew of the regular daily services. A 'special service' seemed ominous to me and it was difficult for me to grasp the significance of the occasion.

But I doubt whether any of the adults, at the services held throughout England and America at that time, really envisaged that, within five years, in addition to the millions of casualties of war, six million out of a total world population of sixteen million Jews would be exterminated simply because they were Jews. We did not understand then: even as, later, the slaughtered themselves did not understand. When they were forced to walk into gas chambers disguised as showers, most of them could not grasp that fellow human beings were going to butcher them simply for the reason that they existed.

Both the act and the dimension are still beyond my comprehension.

Towards the end of the war, I remember reading a message by John L. Lewis, the American Labour leader. He wrote that it would be difficult for a person, in his working lifetime, to count six million grains of sand. How impossible, therefore, it was to try to measure and assess the death of six million human beings.

Years later, twelve years after the end of World War II, I visited the gruesome site of Dachau. It was left as it had been — with cells, huts and gas ovens, intact. I have also frequently made pilgrimage to the bleak site of Bergen-Belsen, the camp of living skeletons liberated by the British. Among the survivors was a cousin of my wife. There, and at the many other extermination units set up by Hitler in Germany and, more especially in Poland, Jews were gassed, battered to death, or thrown live into graves, at the caprice of their captors. And all this was part of a master plan of utter madness to obliterate every single Jew from the face of the earth. It was termed "The Final Solution".

Unlike some of his predecessors, Hitler did not investigate the beliefs or actions of his Jewish victims. He was not concerned with ideologies or with conduct. The accident of birth was itself sufficient to seal a verdict of execution. To be a Jew, was — during the war years — to live in the shadow of the vallye of torment and death.

There is, and must be a deep-rooted feeling of insecurity within the heart of every Jew. When even the slightest alarm sounds; when a casual disparaging remark is overheard; when troops goose step; when too many flags are put out; when a rabble-rouser pollutes the street corner with prejudice and incites group hatred; the heart of the Jew beats quicker, the muscles flex and the protective barriers are lowered.

The Nazi persecution was the culmination of many similar attempts to wipe us out starting, I suppose, from the story told in the Biblical Book of Esther which we, as Jews, still read annually in our synagogues. Haman approached King Ahasuerus, seeking royal approval of a plan to destroy the Jews. The basis of his accusation was that the Jews were "different" and did not observe the laws of the land. Queen Esther's later intervention with her husband secured for the Jews the right to defend themselves. They were saved from slaughter and Mordechai, the uncle of Esther, entered the government. The Festival we celebrate annually in commemoration of these events is called Purim (Lots), because of Haman's lottery to ascertain the most auspicious date for the massacre of the Jews.

A strangely similar theme has run through all the tragic episodes in Jewish history. We have constantly been accused of being "different". Even today, Jewish children visiting areas where Jews do not generally live, have sometimes been asked by local children "Where are your horns?"

Far from Jews rejecting the laws of the land, Jewish law itself prescribes that both the civil and criminal code of the country must be observed by Jewish citizens. But then, when Jews do enter the life of the country, its commerce, its professions and its government — any success achieved can in its turn create jealousy, and that jealousy can beget hatred. So it was that the "Golden Era" in Spain ended in expulsion of the Jews and the establishment of the Inquisition.

Outside the State of Israel, Jews are but a small minority in every country. In Great Britain, for example, we are 0.7%. The USA has the highest proportion of any country, and the largest Jewish Community, and even that is only 3%.

Hence, for those who do not know Jews personally, the old myths of the Wandering Jew and the image of the Jew as the killer of Christ and the rejector of salvation all combine with the innate "dislike of the unlike", that xenophobia which is part of the psychological make up of all of us, to make "differences" a valid reason for persecution, expulsion or even extermination.

Every Jew is enjoined, in the relating of the Passover story, to imagine himself as if he personally had gone out of Egypt. Some Jews in North Africa, on the eve of Passover, dress in travelling clothes and take their walking sticks in their hands, to portray visibly the actions of our forefathers and enter into the mood of the Exodus. So today, and ever onwards, I think every Jew must imagine himself as if he personally had escaped from Auschwitz.

Because of all this, I therefore identify with those

many people throughout the world who have suffered, and who suffer, from a discrimination which rejects them because of 'differences', because of their creed or the colour of their skin or of their hair, or the shape of their nose.

REMEMBRANCE

"God inflicts upon mankind only as much suffering as it can endure."

(The Book of the Zohar)

In 1954, I again joined Her Majesty's Forces and became a Jewish Chaplain to the British Army. The following year I was posted to the Army of the Rhine. I lived in Germany for five years. I had never previously visited Germany but, like many Jews, I was — and am — obsessed by memory of the Holocaust and its six million Jewish victims.

I went to Germany with my wife. She added a further dimension to the experience, for my wife originally lived in Germany. As a small girl she had managed to escape, at the end of August 1939, to find refuge in England. She arrived on the last "Childrens' Transport" to sail from the Hook of Holland before the outbreak of World War II. Those of her relatives who remained behind in Germany, including her father and sisters, were killed during the war. She never again saw them or heard directly from them.

It was very strange for her to come back, fifteen years later, with a small daughter of her own. It was ironic that the frontier guards who had pushed her father over the Polish border in 1938 in a forced expulsion should now welcome her, the wife of a British Officer, with the fullest courtesies.

When we walked in the streets and looked into the food shops we saw mountains of food. Every conceivable delicacy was displayed. We gazed at the cafes, where the traditional German appetite — and its fulfilment — was much in evidence. We could not help thinking of the concentration camps in which my wife's family had starved for lack of a crust of bread.

We lived at an Army base, and so we were somewhat isolated from the German population generally. Contact was established only slowly. But, bit by bit, relationships were struck; with shopkeepers, domestic personnel, civilian drivers. I think it took a full year before I could really relate to people, before I could see them as human beings and not as part of the nation of the Third Reich.

I learnt from my German secretary of her experience before and during the war. She remembered the 10th November 1938, engraved on Jewish memory. On that night hundreds of synagogues through Germany were brutally destroyed, and burnt. The outside world knew of the event. It was reported in newspapers and on film.

My secretary was a schoolgirl at the time. She told me of her recollection of the morning of the following day. Her teacher assembled her class and gleefully told them: "Children, today you are going to have a holiday because the enemies of the Reich have been defeated. We are taking you to a bonfire. You will be able to have a wonderful time there".

How was a child to react to such teaching? Naturally she and all the children were delighted to have a holiday. They enjoyed the bonfire, and imbibed anti-Semitism. Poison is insidious because it can be injected slowly, unnoticed, over a long period. It does not give the warning of a direct frontal attack which causes the defences immediately to rally.

I met some members of the wartime Dutch, and also German, resistance movements. They were incredibly brave people. I listened to their stories and saw the places where their exploits were enacted. Although these heroes were few, the miracle is that they existed at all. Under a totalitarian system, it is difficult to be brave. Critics in free countries can hardly imagine conditions under a dictatorship. As a Jew I shall always pay tribute to the Righteous Gentiles who risked their lives, and the lives of their families, to save Jews. And there were some who, incredibly, so identified, that they walked alongside Jews into the gas chambers.

It is not for me to forgive. It certainly is not for me to forget. That would be to betray the memories of the grandparents of my children — children they never lived to see. My second daughter was actually born whilst we were stationed in Germany. Since my positing there ended, I have not gone back.

I believe it is important for mankind to know what happened under Nazi Germany. And above all not to distort, as a number of people are currently attempting to do, trading in sensationalism. We must learn and never forget the lesson of the Holocaust, of Hitler's destruction of tens of millions of people — not only Jews, but Russians, Poles, Czechs, Dutch, Belgians, French and others — the gypsies, the mentally deficient and those of the German people itself who opposed him.

This imperative of rememberance applies to the whole history of mankind. The key is to know. To know and to recollect what has happened so that we can avoid in the future moving along the terrible paths that have been trodden in the past. Not so that we may indulge in excuses or self-pity, and not in recrimination, but so that we shall resolve to build that better future which Jews first enunciated and in which we have always believed. A future when: "Judgement will run down as waters, and righteousness as a mighty stream". When we will indeed "beat our swords into ploughshares and our spears into pruning hooks", when "nation will not lift up sword against nation, when we shall not learn war any more".

A PEOPLE THAT DWELLS ALONE

"If only Israel observed two Sabbaths according to the Law, they would immediately be redeemed".

(Talmud)

An Israeli leader in New York stood at the head of a crowd of youngsters demonstrating on behalf of Soviet Jewry. They were waving placards with the slogan: "Let My People Go". He turned to them and said: "OK, then, get up and go!"

One simple, sad fact about the State of Israel, for whose rebirth Jews have prayed for nigh on two thousand years, is that the majority of the Jews who have gone there (and the same holds true currently) did so because they had to; because they were pushed rather than pulled; because of persecution or trouble in their country of origin. Jews in the Western World, in Great Britain, Europe and America number well over seven million — more than half the Jews in the world. They could simply book an air passage and go — if they really wanted to.

Whilst this must certainly be accepted as a strong and clear indication that Jews in the free world are, by and large, satisfied and happy in the land of their birth or their settlement, it does not mean that Jews do not support the State of Israel or have doubts about its necessity or validity. The over-whelming majority of Jews relate strongly and positively to Israel. They have links with Israel; business, professional and philanthropic connections, as well as links of kinship. Friendships forged on visits increasingly strengthen mutual concern. It is estimated that more than one in ten Jews from Britain visits Israel each year.

Israel is the only country in the world which is a Jewish country and where the majority of the citizens are Jewish. The mere fact of its existence causes many Jews to sleep more peacefully in their beds. It represents an ultimate asylum, should it be needed. And few Jews would ever categorically guarantee that Jews — in any country — will always live where they are safely. They would not rule out as absurd the possibility that, one day, they or their children might indeed buy that air ticket, for whatever reason. The uncertainty of the Jew in the world — even in the closing decades of the 20th Century — is still a very real factor in determining Jewish attitudes towards Israel.

Diaspora Jews are highly critical about many aspects of Israel; they will speak scathingly of Israeli manners, of the country's economic policies, of the political stance of its government, of religious attitudes, of social divisions and of its highly politicised system in so many of the country's institutions. There is a strong independence of thought amongst

Jews, which is zealously cherished. Jews enjoy criticizing — and they are experts in self-criticism. You can find Jews less extremist and more extremist than official Israel policy on any and every issue.

But criticism will generally be confined to private comment and rarely will it be uttered in the wider public forum. Israel is still far too tender a plant for Jews to be prepared to do anything to harm it. Hence the sensitivity of Jews is touched when Israel is attacked in the United Nations; by a body where power blocs reign supreme and where lonely Israel does not control, or exert any real influence over one single vote other than its own. In the face of attack, Jews are quick to unite. The degree of concern for, and identification with, Israel varies directly in proportion to the urgency of the situation and Israel's need for help and support. The historical consciousness of the Jew works overtime in emergencies.

There are Jews whose attachment to Israel is minimal — possibly a once-in-a-lifetime visit, or a correspondence with a friend or relation there — and others for whom it is maximal, involving the donation of large sums of money (beyond that which they can really afford) and even "Aliyah" (emigration and settlement). But, whether minimal or maximal, Israel, for most Jews, is not simply another country; it is *the* other country and support for it is very strong.

I know that when I went to visit the State of Israel for the first time twenty-seven years ago (I was the first of my family for many generations to do so), I felt that I was returning home for myself and also for countless others before me whose great dream it was to see the Land but who were never so privileged. I have been back many times since, and each time I find there is something special about it. I always find it an emotional and spiritual experience, a return to roots, drinking from the ancient wells of my tradition and my history.

Does this love for Israel affect loyalties to the country of one's birth or domicile? In no way. The world suffers presently from too *few* loyalties, not too many, and Jews have always sought to fulfil to the utmost their obligations and duties as citizens.

It is good — and it still seems remarkable for Jewish tourists — to see a country where stevedores, truckdrivers and policemen, tinkers as well as (the traditional) tailors, are all Jewish. After centuries of abnormal economic life, we like to gaze upon Jewish farmers, shepherds and market gardeners. It brings very strong and powerful reassurance. It is a living corrective of the "reversed pyramid" which has so long symbolised the economic structure of the Jews of the Diaspora.

As for the younger generation of Jews, for whom the State of Israel has always been part of their lives, the novelty of Jewish dockers does not greatly surprise or influence them. They are seeking more meaningful connection. Many of them *are* aware that the very first Command, given to the very first Jew (Abraham), was that of Aliyah — to settle in the Land.

The religious aspect of the contemporary Jewish State — notwithstanding its many real problems — seems to have Biblical undertones. A measure of prophetic fulfilment is apparent in its achievements. The Hebrew language has been revived. A unique system of social justice embraces the total living system of that quarter of a million of its inhabitants who live in the Kibbutzim and co-operative settlements. Israel has become the home of one-fifth of the Jewish people. The country has resisted the combined and repeated attacks of all its neighbours to destroy it. Half a million of its Jewish population derive from the the backward countries of the Middle East, whose civilizations are several hundred years behind the West. They have been absorbed into the modern, twentieth century culture and technology of Israel.

Whilst externally, the Arab-Israel dispute remains as intractable as ever — with occasional shafts of war and also rays of hope — internally one in nine Israelis is an Arab, a citizen of the country, with full rights, living reasonably satisfactorily alongside his Jewish neighbour. Much, much more remains to be done, but seeds have been planted which will fully blossom in conditions of peace.

All Jews hope for the time when Israel, as an ethically-based society, a living exponent of prophetic ideas, will live "in quietude and at ease, when none will make her afraid." We pray daily for peace. But until that peace comes, any examination of Israel's place in the world-beyond the bald expression of the ideal — is premature. Israel has to survive and so she forms her alliances and shapes her relationships in the light of that necessity. She would like to plan for the long term, but first must be sure she can survive the short term.

In the forefront of the issues which concern the Jew in relation to Israel is the place of religion in modern Israeli society and the official attitude of the country to the problems arising from being a 'Jewish State' and not simply a 'State for Jews'.

A member of a synagogue in Britain or America, who may himself be non-practising, is affronted if his rabbi fails to observe the precepts of Judaism. Similarly, Diaspora Jewry tend to expect the Israelis to be observant and are strongly shocked if they find this is not the case. Bacon can be contemplated outside Israel, but surely not in Israel.

There is certainly an inclination towards tradition among Israelis. Some third of the population (far larger than the vote for the religious, political parties) send their children to religious, state schools. All food served in the army and in public institutions is kosher. Jewish consciousness amongst Israelis has increased, especially in the wake of both the '67 and '73 wars. There is a strong awareness of the history of the first and second Jewish Commonwealths. Archaeology is a nationwide pastime. Bible quizzes on the radio and television attract peak audiences. Yom Kippur is almost totally observed in the country. (Each year the police generally report that, on that day, no crimes are committed.)

Can the religious demands of Judaism be reconciled with the modern requirements of a State? Certainly it was easy to proclaim Saturday as the Sabbath for the whole country and the Jewish Holydays as the official State holidays. But what about transport? The unpleasant situation has emerged that it is not possible for the poor person in most parts of the country to take a bus to the seaside on the Sabbath, but the richer person can take a taxi or his own car. Isaiah did not envisage such a compromise, inevitable though it may be deemed today.

The rights of the differing faiths in Israel are well-established. Each religion has responsibility for marriage and divorce, and for matters relating to personal status. But the person who calls down a plague on all your marriage houses and simply wishes to marry in a registry office cannot. Such offices do not exist.

Whilst a theocratic state is hoped for by some, the proposition does not seem likely to command a majority support. How else can a modern state be based, except on the freedom of the individual to follow or not to follow a religious faith? But, then, how can Israel be a Jewish country if each and every Jew may decide for himself whether he will or will not observe his religion? There are far more questions than answers. It would be over-enthusiastic and very naive to imagine that all of these problems can be solved quickly.

Concern is expressed by the Diaspora that Israelis should be Jews as well as Israelis. Israelis must know that their State did not just rise suddenly in 1948. They must feel and recognise that all that went before, the whole of Jewish history, is part of their own history and that of Israel. It is of primary importance that the legacy of the holocaust should be understood by young Israelis as being *their* legacy. The Ingathering of the Exiles must always continue to be a principle of Israel, so that any Jew anywhere in the world requiring a home in Israel, will know it will be there for him.

Israelis, for their part, look to the Diaspora for sustained support — material, moral and political. The one ally on whom Israelis feel they can always rely is Diaspora Jewry. Jews in the Diaspora *do* regard much anti-Zionism as being anti-Semitism and sense that the former is often a cover and a guise for the latter.

Jews in the West are rapidly assimilating. Intermarriage with non-Jews is nowhere less than 20% and in some areas as high as 40%. Those who are no longer observant of the traditional commandments often remain Jews only because of their concern for Israel. Once the religious imperative or Christian persecution kept Jews within the fold. Today Israel secures Jewish survival; and the major, positive identifying factor for most Jews throughout the world is Israel.

JEWS AND JESUS

"God is not in the world; the world is in God"
(Talmud)

I first became aware of Jesus shortly after I started school. Moving along school corridors, I heard the recital of prayers coming through from school assemblies. Although I did not identify the addressee with the God I spoke to in my Hebrew prayers and blessings, the prayers themselves seemed reasonable enough. What puzzled me was the constant reference, especially at the end of many of the prayers, to "Jesus".

At Christmastime, I started to acquire vague notions of this Jesus. The decorations in school and especially the models of the manger afforded me something visual. I sat mutely through school concerts and listened to the carols. I liked the tunes, but they added little to my scant store of knowledge. Interestingly, I do not think I identified Jesus as being Jewish. (The snow and Santa Claus further misled me.)

My Christian classmates, too, probably did not think of Jesus as being Jewish and almost certainly did not recognise the whole of the background of the rise of their Christianity as being part of Jewish history. They assuredly did not identify me with the Hebrews of the Old Testament, but rather with the Jews of the New.

I never attended a Church service. I do not consciously recall seeing a crucifix. We never had a Christmas tree at home and we did not exchange Christmas cards. Jesus was not mentioned in our home. I had only the vaguest knowledge of the Gospels. No copy of the New Testament featured on our bookshelves. Later, the nearest I came to learning of Jesus was through reading Jewish Biblical commentators, I studied their refutations of alleged Christological references in the Scriptures. I did not read the New Testament until well into my twenties.

But this did not affect my Judaism. Whilst it can be maintained that the Christian needs to know of his origins in Judaism in order that he may understand Christianity, the converse does not hold true. My ignorance of Christianity extended to religions generally. I knew more of Greek mythology than of Islam or Buddhism.

Jews may well recognise the historical person of Jesus. Some might even accept as true the account of the miracles attributed to him — although today many Christian theologians are re-interpreting them — because Judaism has never claimed that prophecy is restricted to the Jews. (Balaam, for example, was termed by one rabbi in the Talmud as "even greater than Moses". Job, according to another commentator, was actually not a Jew, but an Egyptian). Jesus's miracles do not present a theological problem for Jews.

Nor is there a major problem regarding the teachings of Jesus. Most of them were paralleled in contemporary Jewish teachings. Not only was the language of Jesus the language of the rabbis, his prayers their prayers, and his style their style, but his message, with some few exceptions, was the message of Judaism. And where there were differences, this was fully in keeping with the Talmudic spirit, where argument follows argument and even basic laws are expounded differently by the Talmudic schools. Differing and dissident views were acceptable, provided that the argument was "for the sake of heaven". It is by no means clear to me that Jesus intended to form another religion; if anything, I feel he did not. He spoke to the house of Israel. The break — and such it, of course, became — and the parting of the ways, started with Paul.

Even the issue of Jesus's messianism was not such as to place the early Jewish Nazarenes outside the teachings of Judaism. It is not certain whether Jesus himself laid claim to being the Messiah, the language used is equivocal and can be variously interpreted. But, in Jewish history, many Messiahs have arisen. Their claim, as such, to be the Messiah did not move them out of Judaism. Nor, indeed, did we regard their followers as anything other than unhappily mistaken. The famous Rabbi Akiva believed that Bar Kochba (the leader of the 132-135 AD Revolt against the Romans) was the Messiah. Events proved him wrong. No-one has ever detracted, because of this, from the respect and admiration accorded to Rabbi Akivah. He was one of the outstanding Jewish teachers of all time; and Bar Kochba is regarded as one of our great generals.

Judaism rejected, and rejects, Christianity because of the *divinity* it attributes to the person of Jesus. In Jewish teaching, *all* men are the sons of God. In that sense, and in that sense only, can we regard mankind as divine. But then we should have to so describe the whole of humanity.

Furthermore, the virgin birth, the relationships it posits, and the nature of the Trinity are concepts which are not comprehensible to Jews and which seem to us to contradict our understanding of Monotheism. Arguments which point out that there are mysteries in all religions fail to appreciate that there is not sufficient basis of acceptance by the Jew of Christianity as a whole, or faith in its teachings, so as to acquiesce in the doctrine of the Trinity as part of a "package".

Judaism, then, does not find any special place within its philosophy or teachings for Jesus. Christians may be surprised to know that Jesus rarely even features in Jewish history books. The single paragraph in Josephus (a Jewish historian of the first century) is so slight that many scholars believe it is a later interpolation. Only in modern times has there been an attempt by Jews, (in works of fiction as well as fact) to assess the character, teachings and place of Jesus and to relate him to his Jewish background.

In the course of many discussions I have held with Christians, one argument has frequently emerged; the success of Christianity (and, implied, the failure of Judaism). I find this a singularly unacceptable argument. I would imagine that, at any given time, vice might well poll more votes than virtue. That would not validate sin, any more than it would invalidate merit.

Can I account then, for the phenomenal growth of Christianity over the ages — and it has been a phenomenal growth?

Christianity demands a greater commitment of faith than any other religion. This has a great appeal; but now lessening in an age which worships rationality. Furthermore, the Christian doctrine of God-made-man (the doctrine which lies at the centre of Jewish-Christian disagreement) is immensely attractive. It affords the greatest comfort to believe that God totally understands us — our sins, our temptations and our backslidings — because he *has been* us. Whilst the Immortal might condemn the mortal, surely an Immortal-Mortal must be highly tolerant?

Christians of abounding goodwill still attempt to effect a "reconciliation" between Christianity and

Judaism, and particularly to persuade Jews to accept Jesus. A prominent Jew of the 19th Century (who became a Christian) reputedly said that no Jew could ever really be persuaded of the truths of Christianity, because no Jew could ever really believe in the divinity of another Jew.

ACROSS THE DIVIDE

Confucius
Confuses.

Jesus
Generally pleases.

Many are enamoured
With Mohammed.

While Buddha
Makes some shudder,
Brahma
Is definitely calmer.

Chairman Mao for China
Couldn't have been finer,
As they don't want Tao
Now.

Engels and Marx
Cause far too many sparks.
Mind you,
Even to follow Moses
Is no bed of roses.

Jews have lived in a Christian society for many centuries; but in my home as a child, as I indicated in the previous chapter, although we knew Christians — some neighbours, trades-people and so on — I had little knowledge of Christianity. If any zealous missionaries thrust a pamphlet through the letter box of our door, it was burned. If an evangelist set up his soap box at a street corner, his words were ignored.

By contrast, most Christians, pre-World War II, had some knowledge of Judaism, but rarely had personal knowledge of Jews. Their Jewish knowledge was almost invariably inadequate and often erroneous. Generally it was derived from New Testament parables and quotations. Had Christians known Jews personally, it is unlikely that the massive persecution of Jews by the Church could have attained the dimensions it did.

Jews were thin on the ground, contrary to the general impression (in the Middle Ages numbers probably only just exceeded one million) and were concentrated in specific areas.

Whatever my personal ignorance of Christianity, I knew Christians individually at school. I knew they were *people,* and so I did not feel that gaps in my knowledge concerning Christian doctrine needed to be rectified. Christianity was the Church — and the Church was all the frightful stuff I heard adults tell of and which, somewhat later, I read about in Jewish history books. Christianity and persecution were synonymous in my mind, but I did regard each and every

Christian as bearing the burden of the guilt of his Church.

My grandfather was very polite, even friendly, with our gentile neighbours next door; a teacher and her elderly mother. They were greeted by us warmly and treated with respect. They would help us out occasionally if we needed some particular operation of work to be carried out in our home on the Sabbath. We exchanged gifts, and I would visit them in their home. They knew which foods they might or might not offer me.

But, I clearly knew — and the lesson was continually reinforced — that there was the major Jewish taboo: "Thou shalt not marry a non-Jew!" So I never dated a non-Jewish girl, and I rarely had social contacts in the homes of non-Jewish classmates. I am not even sure whether there would have been a willing response had I made overtures. But I was aware — and the matter was never discussed openly in my presence — that forbidden liaisons had taken place. (So it *could* be done!)

My grandfather would never hold theological discussions with Christian clergy. He had no desire to convert or converse. He honoured them, but at a distance. "Respect but suspect!" We were not so far removed from the times when compulsory attendance was demanded of Jews at missionary sermons in Church. These were first instituted by the Council of Basle (1431-1448) which confirmed all the previous body of Church Canons against the Jews from the time of Pope Gregory I and also introduced a requirement for Jews to listen to conversion sermons, being brought to Church 'by force', if necessary. This ruling was periodically invoked, especially in Central Europe, Jews frequently responded by stuffing cotton wool in their ears before entering the church.

The changes in relationships which have come about in the post-war years are little short of phenomenal. In part, they result from a completely new approach of Christians to Christianity. In part, they stem from the rapidly-growing secularism of our age, which has reduced Christian numbers and thus stressed what we have in common rather than what divides us. Furthermore, enlightenment has destroyed or diminished the credibility of many of the super-stitions which once attached to Jews. On the Jewish side, since the establishment of the State of Israel, Jews and Christians have been able to talk together on equal terms, probably for the first time.

Some Jews, especially those engaged in talking with Christians in the various groups that now exist throughout the world, including Israel, may well be so taken up in their discussions that they no longer marvel at the huge distances that have been travelled, at the narrowing of the gap. It is now commonplace for the rabbi to sit down with the bishop.

The disputations of the Middle Ages between Jews and Christians, many of them recorded for us, were events which deeply disturbed the Jews. They could not afford to lose; they dared not win. The best they could hope for was a stalemate. Today, the process is termed "dialogue" and very free and frank discussions are held, with neither side striving for advantage.

Nevertheless, this may optimistically ascribe a success to the outcome which is not yet truly attained. Basically, we have not yet fully covered the course where both sides explain their particular way, conveying what their religion means to them, introducing the other to their thought-patterns, describing the meaning of words and concepts. Dialogue is still some way ahead. It will remain in the future so long as there is a vestige of suspicion in the minds of Jews that the ultimate Christian purpose is conversion. There are many Jews, especially those who have not personally participated in the discussions, who strongly reject the need, the desirability and even the feasibility of meeting together in inter-religion exchanges.

Often, on the Christian side and from the purest of motives, there is a desire for something which is seen as "positive" and not impinging on "differences" — to hold interdenominational services. The purpose is designed to illustrate and demonstrate that we worship one God, to fortify those who seek to repair the damage of the past, and to give encouragement and hope to those who wish to see religion once again shaping the life of the individual and the nation. All these are laudable aims. What is questionable is whether they can best be achieved by these means.

The real area for interdenominational demonstration of common interest, concern and purpose lies in the immediate future not in Religious Services, but in religious service — for the welfare of man, the relief of poverty, aid to the developing countries, medical care for the sick, the assertion of religious values in a society where standards of human behaviour have deteriorated. Inter-faith dialogue is basically an educational process and a very necessary one, but the main challenge for interdenominational consultation lies in the need for joint action of religious bodies for human rights, translating words into deeds, words which today seem very empty of meaning to most members of society.

Into this arena the forces of religion have barely penetrated as a joint operation. There may well be an acceptance that religious powers need to combine, but there is not yet the understanding as to how this can be achieved.

Judaism has not yet fully awoken to its part in meeting this challenge. Some of those Jews who *are* aware still share the hesitation of previous generations and are not sure that Jews are called upon — or need — to join hands with others. We are so convinced of our powers of survival — we are, after all, world champions — that we have not yet assessed what our position would be if we had to live in a secular society, instead of one cherishing the Judaeo/Christian heritage.

THE HEART OR THE MATTER?

The Kobriner Rabbi asked his disciples: 'Do you know where God is?' He showed them a piece of bread. 'God is in this piece of bread. Without God's manifestation of his power in all nature, this bread would have no existence.

(Chassidic Tale)

Russia is a country which declares, contrary to Judaeo-Christian teaching, that man *does* live by bread alone; that materialistic fulfilment is the goal of mankind. Marxism has certainly sought to relieve oppression and poverty and to restore dignity to man. But the concept that, primarily, change must be effected in the heart of man was dismissed.

Marxism saw its way as lying almost entirely in economic — and thence social — change. Furthermore, Marxist-Leninism was prepared to achieve its aims by depriving less deserving sections of society of their civil liberties in the hoped-for-good of the more deserving proletariat. Stalinism, subsequently, was not a departure from Lenin's teaching but its projection; almost its inevitable sequel.

As the direction lay in material growth, so the measuring scale of success applied was production. Hence the failure of the USSR in this field was the bitterest blow. It called forth drastic measures, particularly in agriculture, where the peasants were never considered by the Communists to be as good revolutionaries as the factory workers.

Paradoxically, though, in the very area that Communism choose to demonstrate and measure its success are evident its failures. Production is one of the idols, but the private sector of agriculture, some 3% of the total, achieves a productivity almost ten fold that of the collectivised sector. The free market in the big towns can thus give to the few, to those able to afford it, the tangible fruits that Communism strives to provide for the many. The peasant, encouraged to live by the creed of material success, wants the rewards for himself and not simply to satisfy and propitiate another god, the "Five Year Economic Plan".

There is constant comparison with the USA. "In another ten years we will have overtaken America in the production of . . .", is a recurring theme in conversation with Soviet officials. I have no means of gauging the truth of such forecasts. What intrigues me is that the very capitalist criteria decried by Communism are those it seeks to emulate. It is not the economic theory of Marxism that I attack, nor is it the capitalist approach that I uphold. I simply voice deep regret at any form of social management that disregards human rights and subordinates the individual to the party.

It was not the superficial exterior that interested me on my visits to Russia — the buildings, factories, streets, monuments — so much as the people and the below-the-surface attitudes.

World War II has left a bitter legacy. The fear of a further war has undoubtedly been exploited by the authorities to foster and strengthen suspicion of the West. Russian armament is always termed "defensive". American armament is always termed "offensive".

Slogans are bandied about and a series of equations builds up. Capitalism is Imperialism, is Reaction, is Racism, is Facism, is Hostile. By contrast, Communism (but not Chinese Communism) is Progressive, is Enlightened is Truly Democratic.

Hence there is little real understanding either of the successes or the failures of western society. Nothing good may be learned from any other system as, eventually, all other systems will be self-destructive. The questions, then, are often naive and painful.

"What is freedom *really* like?" asked one woman. And that about summed it up; the blind seeking to understand colour.

I had never previously been a totalitarian state, other than for a fleeting visit. I strongly sensed and resented authoritarianism, implicit in the attitudes of every desk clerk, in hotel, theatre or station. Even if I sought some simple piece of information, it was made quite, quite clear that I must not regard this as a right but as a privilege — to be conferred or witheld at the discretion of the official.

Suspicion of the written word was revealed at the airport examination — and confiscation — of books and newspapers. I found this the most significant and revealing of all the actions of Sovietocracy. The suppression of opinions contrary to the state, even the restraints placed upon the acquisition of knowledge, is only one short stage before the physical imprisonment of those the state judges to be its opponents.

I was told that no ordinary person can consult old newspaper files. (An even simpler device than the rewriting of history as in Orwell's "1984"). One can buy books in the bookshop and, indeed, I saw many customers crowding these shops. But one cannot order books beforehand. This would enable an individual or group to make systematic study of a subject. Such studies must be at a university library, by approved and known students, pursuing a registered subject. No anti-Marx could sit in Moscow as Marx sat in the British Museum Library in London.

I was moved by the plight of those who wanted to leave the USSR but experience severe difficulties in obtaining exit permits. Why should a country, confident in its lifestyle, not allow those who dissent simply to leave? I was reminded of the Berlin Wall which was built at a time I was living in Germany.

Many then spoke of it as intended to prevent people from "voting with their feet". Where the ballot box is suppressed such walls are inevitable.

I was impressed by those young people I saw who met together in a clandestine group to study the Bible and to learn Hebrew. I was depressed by the fact that children under 18 cannot legally assemble together for any form of religious instruction. This does not prevent religious feeling from penetrating the heart of man, but it hinders *informed* religious belief.

In Russia, the "world-today" tries to obliterate and remove the need for the "world-to-come". But true religion lives on in the hearts of the people. The over-sixties in the churches have all grown up under a communist state. The very need for virulent anti-religious propaganda and the repression of religious freedom are clear indications of the staying power of faith.

Religion is opposed, not simply because it was one of the tools of Czarism, but because it might deflect men of vision and capacity from the true pursuits. Opium! Russia today has not yet actually banned God, but it devotes a good deal of effort to trying to phase him out. There is an active propogation of atheism. Young people are actively discouraged from attending at church or synagogue. The congregations I saw were composed overwhelmingly of people aged sixty and over.

The churches are tolerated, but many restrictions are imposed to limit their influence. Priests who are too active in the cause of their religion are removed from office. Some are imprisoned or exiled. Spiritual faith is considered the enemy of the advancement of Communism.

The displacement of "conventional religion" has simply induced in Russia an alternative faith. For Marxism *is* a faith, despite the self-given nomenclature of "Scientific Socialism", and it is presented with trappings very similar to the religions it is attempting to supplant. Pictures and busts of Marx and Lenin have replaced the Crucifix; party ideology has replaced the catechism, the commissar has taken over from the priest — or tries to. The queues of men, women and children in Red Square, patiently moving forward towards Lenin's Tomb, are as devout as any pilgrims I saw in the magnificent shrines and churches in Zhagorsk, the seat of the Patriarch of the Russian Orthodox Church. The theme of "life-after-death" is common to both. Even a special language has been formulated, so that discussions in Moscow with Soviet officials seemed to me reminiscent of theological disputations elsewhere.

Marxism cherishes the belief that no god exists; that this life is the only life, and when it ends there is nothing else. Well . . . anyone who believes that must make the best of it, whilst it lasts! And why bother about others? Each individual will set himself, his own fulfilment, his own pleasures, above every other single person in the world. Why give to others what you yourself can enjoy? Do unto others before you are done.

112

"If I am not for myself, who will be for me?", asked Hillel, and then he went on: "But if I am only for myself, what am I?" Man cannot live by bread alone, nor can man live by himself and for himself alone.

Judaism certainly does not despise the material. We should enjoy those pleasures the world legitimately offers us Judaism does, after all, look towards a promised land of milk and honey. As Jews, we pride ourselves that we are a practical people. Like Jacob's ladder, whilst our head reaches into the heavens and we have visions of eternity, our feet are firmly planted on the ground. We feel obliged to make this life a good life, and to enjoy this world. We have experienced ascetic sects in our midst, but these have seldom influenced mainstream Judaism. Neither suffering nor deprivation are deemed virtues.

We reject neither the bread, nor that which comes forth from the mouth of God. We embrace both the material and the spiritual. "If there is no flour there is no Torah. If there is no Torah there is no flour." Without bread, there is no teaching of the word of God. But without such teaching, the bread is stale. The doctrine of "bread alone" must inevitably lead to the doctrine of self alone and self above others. Hence, the flouting of human rights in the USSR and, indeed, in all those societies which, whatever their economic concept, place the acquisition of goods above the pursuit of good.

Such societies will flounder, whether on drugs or

alcoholism, or simply, and more insidiously, because of strife and dispute, and greed. Because its human rights record is better, the western world is by no means free from criticism. We often argue over the distribution of a cake before we have even baked the cake. And the cake then burns to a cinder!

Only if we accept the concept of the Fatherhood of God does there flow the certainty of the doctrine of the common brotherhood — and the rights — of man. I know of no basis for a society other than the divine absolute.

THE DIGNITY OF LABOUR

"Days are coming", says the Lord, "when corn will grow faster than it can be harvested, and grapes will grow faster than the wine can be made. The mountains will drop with sweet wine, and the hills will flow with it. I will bring my people back to their land. They will rebuild their ruined cities and live there; they will plant vineyards and drink the wine; they will plant gardens and eat what they grow. I will plant my people on the land I gave them, and they will not be pulled up again."

(The Prophet Amos)

Towards the end of World War II, I served in the British Army. For a time, I was with the Jewish Brigade in Italy. Then I was posted to India. Happily, by the time I arrived there, the war was over. I was there for about a year. From India, I moved on to serve with the British Commonwealth Occupation Forces in Japan. There I spent a further year. During all these travels, I witnessed only too vividly the cheapness of life and the descent of man.

In wartime Italy the price of a woman was, literally, a bar of soap. A round tin of fifty cigarettes (one per soldier was distributed free each week) constituted wealth. The war had moved steadily from south to north, grinding all before it. The ravages and scars of battle and conflict were seen not only on the countryside but also on the face of man.

I sharply changed my European ideas when I moved to India. The scale of depleted values I learned in Italy had to be completely revised. In Italy, I saw the cheapness of life and I thought I had plumbed the depths of unhappiness. In India, I saw the cheapness of death, and I knew that there was no measuring the degredation man could endure. There I encountered starvation on a massive scale. I was startled to realise the value of a slice of stale bread or of a bowl of soup. And this was not in a concentration camp situation, it was no "freak" aberration or temporary breakdown, but normal life; that had been the norm for generations and seemed set-fair to remain so for generations to come.

For me, coming from a family where, although we certainly could not boast wealth, we experienced no want of basic necessities, all of this was vicious and startling; a sad revelation of aspects of an existence I had not dreamed of. Vague recollections came back to me of a geography text book I had studied at high school: "The average expectation of life in India is 27 years". That had seemed strange to me at the time, too strange to be believable, too remote to be meaningful.

Coming home after my demobilisation, to a depressed, post-war England, I tried to clarify my thoughts, my ideas and my plans. I was 21, unmarried, without any particular skills — other than those I had learnt in the Army, and they were hardly likely to help me find a job. I was looking for a vocation and planning a future. I had intended to go up to university, but the acceptances I received from the colleges to which I applied were for two and three years ahead. There was a long queue in front of me. The war had interrupted and delayed many careers.

I resolved that I would, at least for a time, help to produce some of the food that I consumed, that previously I had eaten casually and with unquestioning acceptance — the divine right of consumers. I joined a Jewish trainee group in Buckinghamshire, which was preparing youngsters who intended to settle in Palestine. I became a farm labourer and earned £4.10.0d for a 48-hour week. In summer, during harvest and with overtime payments, I could bring this up to about £7.

Each morning at seven o'clock, I left the hostel where we lived and biked to work. The morning milking and its aftermath occupied the first few hours of my working day. Subsequently, I moved to whatever job needed doing on the farm; hedging and ditching in the winter, cultivating in spring, harvesting in summer, ploughing and sowing in autumn. It was hard work, lasting sometimes until ten at night. I enjoyed it, once my hands hardened and the muscles in my back had learnt to take the strain.

The cycle of the year and the calendar of nature determined the pattern of my life. I felt I was doing something worthwhile. After four years in the army— destroying and being destroyed — this was productive, bring forth, creating.

Working on the farm gave me a great deal of inner satisfaction, even though it did not bring me much in the way of material gain. As "the reward of fulfilling a commandment is the opportunity to fulfil a further commandment", so the work itself was its own reward. The understanding I gained of the process of cultivation, the privilege of witnessing the magic of crops growing from the soil, this was an added, unexpected benefit.

Having been born and bred in the town, I did not have regard for the distinction between peasant and squire. I was keenly socialist but I held no grudge nor grievance against my boss and his family. They were more my co-workers than employers; they certainly did not seem to be getting rich or fat on the toil of my hands. In fact, at times, certainly in the beginning, I thought they had a bad bargain in me. Altogether, I spent about two years on the job. And now, whenever I eat the bread of someone else's toil, I feel that I was, once at least, his partner.

I worked later in a factory. This lacked the compensation of outdoor life, with its bonus of fresh air and sunshine. But the same principles applied. In factories, the meaning and purpose of a job is often not so obvious, and the less a job appears useful, the greater the reluctance of the worker to perform it.

I have always subscribed to the doctrine of the dignity of labour; the belief that any job that needs to be done is honourable and should be done well. The crucial consideration is the necessity of the operation. Work to no purpose degrades a human and enslaves him. If I work for mankind — as farm labourer, as factory worker, as teacher or administrator — if I contribute to the common weal of society, then, but only then, do I earn my place as a full member of that society.

FELLOWSHIP

"There are four characters among men. He who says, What is mine is mine and what is yours is yours, his is a neutral character. (Some say, this is a character of Sodom). He who says, What is mine is yours and what is yours is mine, is a fool. He who says, What is mine is yours and what is yours is yours, is a saint. He who says, What is yours is mine and what is mine is mine, is a wicked man."

(Ethics of the Fathers)

The farm in Buckinghamshire where, together with fifty other youngsters ranging in age from about 18 to 25, I acquired the rudimentary skills of farming, had a special raison d'etre; there was one force which strongly motivated us. We all wanted to go to Palestine (as it then was) to play our parts in the miracle of the rebirth of the Jewish people. Hence, everything was run as on a kibbutz.

Whatever we earned went into a central, communal pool. No-one drew individual expenses — all out-goings were met from the pool. "From each according to his capacity, to each according to his needs". It was more than a slogan for us. That is how it really

120

worked, insofar as any system can accurately rate capacity and need.

The accommodation was rather rough; but nobody minded. The work was certainly hard, but complaints were few. The food was not exactly of the highest standard, but, as we were ravenous it tasted delicious. Meat was a rarity. Generally, only on the Sabbath and Festivals did it grace our tables. We had plenty of potatoes and bread, so no-one went hungry. There was a feeling of satisfaction all round.

This sense of wellbeing derived from several causes. We felt we were doing a good job. Farm work may be hard, but it is work out of doors; it is healthy and satisfying. Furthermore, our social life was very full. When we came home in the evenings, even though we were tired, we arranged talks and lectures, sometimes by our own members, at other times we invited guest speakers. We subscribed to many papers and periodiclas. Our reading ranged from "The Farmer and Stockbreeder", to the "Tribune", "New Statesman", "Economist" and "The Listener". We subscribed both to "The Times" and to the "Daily Worker". We strove for balance and for "culture".

Periodically, we danced, or produced a play or celebrated in really high style the marriage of two members. Very few were married when we came; many married there. Happily, I was one of them. Weddings took place in the open air. Relations and visitors mainly came by coach. They were good "old-fashioned" celebrations, with lots of dancing in the

East European Jewish style and modern Israeli dancing.

The highlight of every week was, of course, the Sabbath. We scrubbed ourselves extra well and put on our white shirts. We scorned ties, considering them very bourgeois. We prayed together to greet the Sabbath and then we sat down at one long table, instead of separate tables as on weekdays. The meal on Friday evening was an extended one. We interspersed the courses with songs; not only the traditional Sabbath Table Songs, but also songs which told of our hopes and aspirations, particularly regarding the rebuilding of the Land of Israel, or songs based on prayers or portions of the Bible, especially the Psalms. These were often sung to popular modern tunes.

On Saturday, the Sabbath Day, we studied together the Portion of the Week — the lesson we had read on the morning in our improvised synagogue. I say "improvised" simply because we only had one large hall; which served as our dining hall, our lounge, our synagogue, our concert hall and our social centre.

Our Sabbath pleasures centred round that hall. Religious principle prevented us from travelling by vehicle on the Sabbath. We could only go as far as our feet would take us. In the summer, we could stroll in the countryside. During winter, and especially in rainy weather, we were confined to the few buildings of our hostel. But no-one found it restrictive.

We would engage in endless discussion. We were prepared to take on the re-shaping of the post-war world. Pervading everything was a tremendous sense of enthusiasm. We believed in the future of the world and had confidence in our ability to shape that future.

Our group was run on totally democratic lines. There were committees for everything; for cultural purposes, to look after the religious services, to run our finances, to arrange the duty roster. There was even one unofficial committee which tried to match-make! All committees were elected and had to report back to the general assembly. There we debated everything, from socialist ideologies to the price of potatoes. This general assembly, held monthly or as special need demanded, was also responsible for deciding to accept for "permanent membership" candidates who had been on probation for some three to six months.

Those who were rejected or could not attune themselves to this communal way of life simply left, either to go directly to Israel or return to their occupation in England. Many of the latter attempted to settle in Israel later. All benefited from their stay, and all found it a tremendous experience and lesson in living together — of co-operation rather than competition. Naturally, there were rough corners and sharp edges — which human system has not? But it worked well.

I believe it was Heine who said: "Man can soar into the skies like a bird, swim through the oceans like a fish. But he cannot live on the land like a 'Mensch' — a human being". This experience taught me that in some small measure he can.

TIME TO ENJOY

Blessing to be said on seeing trees blossoming the
first time in the year —

"Blessed are you, O Lord our God, King of the
Universe, for you have made your world lacking in
nought, but you have produced within it goodly
creatures and goodly trees which give delight to the
children of men."

(The Prayer Book)

I recall very vividly a purchase I once made which was
motivated by passionate desire. I was about 4½ years
old. I saw a small, tin violin in a shop window. I cannot really claim that, at that age, I nursed a deep love
of music. Nevertheless, this little violin stirred fires in
my soul, and it was the most delightful object that I
had yet encountered in the whole of my life.

I think the price was 4½ pennies; hardly a major
purchase! I knew I had some money at home. A visiting relation had left me a round, silver sixpence. (It
was silver in those days.) Rushing home, I took it out

of my drawer, and then hurried back to the shop. I handed over my sixpence, and identified my purchase. I received the violin, and I also received change of a penny-ha'penny.

Frankly, this puzzled me. I went out of the shop delighted with my purchase, but wondering what I was supposed to do with the remaining one and a half pennies which had been thrust into my hand. I had no further desires. Of what use, therefore, was the change?

I resolved the problem quite easily. I threw the money away! Clasping the toy violin to my breast, I went joyfully home. (Incidentally, the violin could not produce more than a squeak, and I never subsequently learnt to play any musical instrument, but I do not think this was cause and effect!)

Throughout my life, I have found that the greatest force of evil, the greatest tempter to wrongdoing, is envy and covetousness. Our other vices, by comparison, have little effect on oneself and even less on society. Pride, for instance, may sometimes be destructive of self, it rarely damages others. Indeed, there can be legitimate pride in achievement, in fulfillment, in having been of service to others. Pride, like sex, is no vice if rightfully applied.

Rabbinical teaching regarded all the physical appetites as being not merely permissible but indeed desirable. Through sexual desire the world is populated. Where restrictions are enforced by Jewish law — in eating habits, for example — it is to guard against excess and to ensure that both the natural and divine purpose is served.

But envy can never be right. It harms oneself — one's personality and pattern of life — and, being directed against others, inevitably harms them too. It never knows a measure of satisfaction. Its appetite grows with eating.

I know that many would argue and would head their list with "hatred"; but surely hatred mostly derives from jealousy and envy? Coveting our neighbour's possessions we are prepared to kill, rob and bear false testimony. It is the final prohibition of the Ten Commandments because transgressing it can lead us back to commit all the others.

I suppose it is unreasonable to expect human beings entirely to eradicate emotions of this nature. In today's society, one of our spurs is competition. We need to produce in order to live. And most of us work and produce — not out of a sense of responsibility to our country to assist in its economic effort (although we ought to); we are prodded and cajoled into working by the immediate needs and wants of our family, and by the desire to obtain some choice fruit that at present is out of our reach. Sometimes, a fruit that belongs to someone else, or a fruit forbidden to us. "Stolen waters taste sweet".

For me, the answer lies in a rabbinic saying: "Who is a rich man? He who enjoys his portion". There is the secret. Happiness seldom relates to a scale of income, increasing in direct proportion to salary.

Poverty is certainly no virtue and Judaism has not extolled it. Poverty can exist at all income levels; so can happiness. We must seek to extract happiness from that with which we *are* blessed.

The more we focus on enjoying what we have, rather than regretting what we have not, the more we will appreciate what we have, and count our blessings, and the less will be jealous of others.

In this peptic-ulcer age, contentment is the greatest tranquilliser. For envy gnaws not only at our stomachs, but also at our hearts. Contentment and happiness derive from a positive enjoyment of that which we do possess. When we examine them carefully, our possessions are often far more valuable than we imagine. And, even more than we require. Said the rabbis "He who increases possessions, increases worry".

Maimonides, observed that the objects we physically need rate inversely to their price. The primary requirement of our body is air; we can exist only a few minutes without it; and it is absolutely free! Next, we need water, and that is fairly cheap. At the other end of the scale lie gold and diamonds; they are tremendously expensive. But a man can live the whole of his life without need of them.

At the commencement of every festival, whenever we enjoy a new fruit that comes into season, whenever we put on a new garment, we recite a blessing: "Blessed are You, O Lord our God, King of the Universe, for you have kept us alive and granted us existence and enabled us to reach this season." This is a blessing for life and for the good things of life — in fact, a blessing for enjoyment. By not taking God's gifts for granted we realise the enjoyment we can and should derive from them, even from the small things. And small can be good.

To temper jealousy, we must distinguish between need and desire, and be ever conscious and thankful for what we already have.

BEYOND HORIZONS

"I believe with a perfect faith in the coming of the Messiah, and though he may tarry, I shall await him daily."

(From the Thirteen Principles of Faith of Maimonides, contained in the Prayer Book.)

For some three or four months, when I was aged nine, my parents moved to a small typical mining village in County Durham, in the North of England and I attended the local school there. I was living, for the first time in my life, in a totally strange environment. I had hardly known what the countryside was, other than glimpsing it from the windows of a train speeding by. I must have been a strange creature to my classmates, for, apart from my being a "townie" they had never met a Jew before. No Jews had ever lived there.

One day the teacher asked my class an interesting personal question, which still sticks in my mind more than forty years later. "How far have you travelled?", she asked each of us. The replies were revealing, but they must be understood against the background of the time — the depressed thirties; and the background of the place — a poverty-ridden hamlet sited not in relation to any great metropolis or river, but simply to a seam of coal under the surface.

Most of the children replied that they had travelled only as far as the neighbouring village, some four or five miles along the road, a village almost identical to the one in which we lived. Some had been as far as the sea, fifteen miles away, where there was a run-down holiday resort to which miners would take their families — if they were lucky — on one day's outing a year. Few had travelled further.

I had been further. True, I had not yet visited the great city of London, but neither had the teacher. I had been to the main towns of Lancashire and Yorkshire, and Durham — places at least one hundred miles apart. That distance seemed enormous to my classmates, and I swelled visibly with pride at their reaction.

I suddenly became aware that, as a Jew, I was cosmopolitan, although I did not then know the word. My mother had been born in a different country, in Eastern Europe. My father's family came from Ireland. We were a good mixture, like most Jewish families. Our experiences, and our allegiances were widely-cast.

I think I sensed then, too, arising out of my classmates response, something of the attitude towards the "wandering Jew" for I experienced within me a kind of impermanence and unsettledness on the one hand, but also of terrific horizons on the other.

My outlook, as well as my background, stretched much, much further than the next village. At that early age, I was already conscious of the fascination of travel, not only in the lateral dimension, but in time. I was very much aware of the vast panorama of Jewish history.

Within Jews, I believe there has gradually been instilled a special concept of time. Significantly the Hebrew language strictly has no present tense, only a past and a future. The present is not simply fleeting, it does not really exist and certainly cannot be grasped or frozen.

In so far as there is a present, it is simply an extension of the past. Hence the events of the long history of the Jew do not feel "dated", but close, almost immediate and certainly relevant. A Jew feels himself, in a very real sense, to be a link in the continuous history of the Jew.

There is, therefore a certain disregard, almost disdain, for the present, for current events. The transitory and the changing cannot be as significant as the completed, the established and the recorded. Life itself, the world, is simply a bridge between the partial revelation of the past and the fullest consciousness which we shall attain in the total revelation of the world to come.

When a Jew reads a daily newspaper, therefore, I think that he is subconsciously judging what he reads against a background of four thousand years of personal history and experience. In this way it is possible to overcome any collective sufferings of the *moment*. It is much more difficult to overcome the troubles of the *past*. Thus the sin of the Golden Calf, the baseless hatred which brought about the Destruction of the Temple, these still grieve the heart of the Jew.

My teacher's question prompted within me speculation in a third dimension, that of ambition and purpose of life. What did I want to be? What was I seeking? How would I get there?

Since living in that small village, I have travelled a good deal — as far as distance and time go. I have travelled over half the globe and have moved through the Holocaust and into the age of the rebirth of Israel. But I am not sure that I have travelled so far in the dimension of purpose.

Strangely — and I think happily — I believe I stand today substantially where I stood then. Many of the values which I dimly perceived in my childhood — inculcated within me by my family and religion — are the ones I still hold to be true. Honesty to oneself and to others. Job satisfaction. Dignity. Respect and concern for others. [In fact, most of the virtues it is fashionable today to "knock".] My subsequent experiences have endorsed them. I do not think I have discovered new commandments and I have not been able to strike out any of the old.

I have also learned to distinguish between what is essential and what is but a passing fancy. I know that wisdom far outweighs wealth. I say daily blessings for good health, for the use of my faculties, for my freedom, for the good things I and others enjoy.

I know that in order to flourish, in order that we should not be stunted in our growth and impoverished in our legacy to others, in order that we might move into the future, we need companionship, love and — above all — hope.

And so, Jews who walked into the gas chambers of the Nazis actually sang the traditional Jewish song of hope and belief in ultimate redemption. It was not simply an expression of hope in God — that is the easier part. It was also an expression of hope in man.

I know of no greater courage, of no greater testimony to the creator God and of no greater lesson for the journey on which everyone of us is embarked.

JUSTICE

"Judah, the son of Tabbai said: In the judge's office, act not the counsel's part; when the parties to a suit are standing before you, let them both be regarded by you as guilty, but when they are departed from you, regard them both as innocent, the verdict having been accepted by them."

(Ethics of the Fathers)

The components of justice are the law and mercy. They must walk hand in hand; there are always individual circumstances to be taken into account. Counselled the rabbis: "Judge no man until you come into his place". We must try to understand the mentality of the lawbreaker, to penetrate his frame of mind. "Mercy and truth are met together", said the Psalmist, in what is, to me, one of the most remarkable verses in the whole of the Bible. Truth *alone* cannot decide. It must combine with compassion.

Over the years, I have become interested in the procedures of a variety of courts. In my childhood, I watched my grandfather preside over his rabbinical court, Beth Din (literally: House of Judgement) and

I had the special treat of sitting in to observe. During my army service I witnessed proceedings in military courts of inquiry and courts martial. Currently, being involved, as part of my own occupation, in trying to resolve many legal problems and conflicts, I have some measure of acquaintance with the English legal system. Three different approaches — religious, military and civil — to the task of ensuring justice; that concept which is so difficult to define but that all of us strive for.

For that reason I have always been fascinated by Judaism's approach to the practical application, rather than theoretical definition of righteousness and justice. Both of these words, incidentally, derive from the same Hebrew root word, as does also the word "charity" — a clear indication of the Jewish thought process.

If two disputants — one rich and one poor — had to appear before an ancient Jewish court, an interesting procedure was followed. In order that the rabbis who constituted the court might not be prejudiced, the rich man was given two options. The clerk-to-the-court would tell him that, either he could appear dressed in shabby garments (such as the poor man was wearing) or he could lend some of his richly adorned clothes to the poor man — so that both of them would appear equal before the Judges. Despite themselves, the rabbis might otherwise be influenced by the appearance of one of the litigants, and it would be as wrong to discriminate in favour of the poor as it would be to discriminate against him.

Judaism has long been deeply concerned with the concept of justice, and has always tried to introduce into the procedures of the court as many safeguards as possible to ensure righteousness in judgement. For example, exactly as in a court martial in the British Army — where the junior officer must announce his verdict first — so the junior rabbi must declare his view first, so that he will not be influenced — and perhaps overawed — by the opinion of a senior colleague. No judge sits alone. A court comprises a minimum of three members.

No interpreter might appear before the Sanhedrin, the Supreme Court in ancient Judea. The judges of that court were expected to provide from among their 70 members one who was himself fluent in the language of the defendant. An interpreter might change, even inadvertently, the meaning, or the shade of meaning, of the testimony. The judges must hear for themselves. Similarly, the court could not convene at night, as the judges must also see for themselves. They should be married and have children; for it was felt that only a parent would fully understand the concept and practice of compassion.

Jews are frequently accused of adhering rigidly to the letter of the law. In particular, "an eye for an eye and a tooth for a tooth" is cited as demonstrating that Jews demand a justice based on a crude measuring-scale concept, devoid of mercy. That is totally untrue. Historical records show that this was not taken literally. Indeed, the Talmud specifically rules that monetary compensation must be paid, and it would be illegal to inflict a parallel wound. The phrasing of the Pentateuchal instruction should be more correctly translated "an eye *instead* of an eye"; that is, the award of such compensation as would help to serve instead of the damaged organ. This applied to all limbs and to bodily injury, and it was necessary to compensate for the pain, the doctors bills, loss of income and psychological damage.

But when a life was taken, then money could not constitute restitution or compensation. A human life, any human life, and even for the smallest span of time, is infinite in value. So capital punishment was known in Jewish law, and could be exacted. But it was rarely exacted. (Once in seventy years?) The legal requirements gradually demanded by courts were so difficult of fulfillment that it was almost impossible to impose the death penalty. Principally it had to be established that, before the act of murder, two independent, reliable witnesses had jointly given explicit warning to the murderer of the consequences of his action. This and other requirements were specifically intended to reduce the possibility of capital punishment and, hence, it was almost totally excluded by our law some fifteen hundred years ago.

The State of Israel has followed that tradition. In thirty years, only one man (Eichmann) has been judicially executed. Terrorists captured, including those who have committed mass murder on innocent

138

Jewish and non-Jewish civilians — for example at Lod Airport — have not been executed.

Where homicide had been committed and no culprit could be found, where no one was arrested to stand in the dock, Mosaic law laid down that the elders of the nearest city must attest that they personally had not shed the innocent blood. Rabbinic teaching sought to explain this paradox; for surely no one could suspect the elders of such a crime? The practice, they said, was instituted so that the responsible leaders of society would understand that their community might have been inadequate and hence created the conditions whereby a crime could be committed. We all bear some measure of guilt for every crime.

One further major principle underlies the Jewish approach. In the book of Deuteronomy, we read: "Justice, justice shalt thou pursue". Why the repitition? asked the rabbis. Because even justice must be justly pursued. Ends do not justify means. Even the courts cannot take the law into their own hands.

Without justice, without courts to which individuals can bring their complaints and grievances and before which individuals can be arraigned and fairly judged if they contravene the laws of the land, society will perish. Of the seven basic laws for humanity (the "Seven Laws of the Sons of Noah") the only positive command of the rabbis was to establish courts of law. The absence of judges and judgement is the ultimate corruption of mankind. When justice departs, violence, and the rule of the mob enters. Values, human rights, are at an end. The ultimate rebuke to the Almighty, is that which Jews would shout out, when oppression was rampant and the voice of unreason prevailed in the land; "There is no judgement and no judge!" No more bitter cry could be uttered in accusation against a God whom we acclaim as the "Merciful One, blessed be He, Judge and Protector of Widows and Orphans."

But we cannot just direct out criticism upward. The maintenance of order is the concern of every individual. The pursuit of justice may seem unexciting and abstract. But, ultimately, therein we shall uplift mankind.

ATTAINMENT

What is Man? Psalm 8

All that the Holy One blessed be He created in the world, he created in man.

(Midrash)

I am sometimes depressed when I consider the deterioration in human relations, the increase in brutality and violence, the growing divide between ethnic groups, the proliferation of weapons of destruction. Every newscast, every paper contains the latest daily list. I once used to read newspapers from cover to cover, but no longer. I understand and have sympathy for the person who reads only the sports news. That, at least, contains a record of the achievements of man, not simply an account of his dismal failures.

I suppose it is ironic that we have now managed to accumulate a sufficient storehouse of weapons so that we can, literally, blow the whole of mankind out of existence but, by bitter contrast, we have not yet marshalled the resources of the seven years of plenty even to maintain and sustain the population of the globe — let alone to clothe and house all its occupants.

A Chassidic rabbi once gave a follower some good advice. He should write out two notes. On one, should be written: "Man is but dust", and on the second he should write: "For my sake the universe was created."

The man was to place the notes in his left and right pockets. Whenever he felt too proud, too smug, too self-satisfied, he should read the note which reminded him of his lowly origin. If, on the other hand, he became despondent and lacked hope, he should comfort himself with the thought of his ultimate destiny, that he was a unique being, the majestic creation of the Almighty God.

To use the language of the Talmud — when a human being stamps out coins, each of them is identical, but when the Holy One, Blessed Be He, creates life, each being has its own unique characteristics. Whoever sustains a living being, it is as if he has sustained an entire universe; but if we destroy a single human being, it is as if we have destroyed an entire universe.

We are, each of us, such beings, standing at the summit of creation, equal to the whole of humanity.

I often think of the symphony orchestra as one of our supreme achievements. It speaks an international language, possibly our only international language. It is an organism which requires the highest degree of mutual co-ordination and co-operation. It uses, for its raw materials, the simplest products of our society such as wood, metal and skin; but it refines them, to attain an extraordinary degree of sophistication and perfection.

Aircraft too have an international language. They overfly the political boundaries of states, and transcend the physical boundaries of geography. Once an aircraft is in the air, we are all concerned to see that it reaches its final destination. In other fields of endeavour, we compete one against another and exult in the failure of others. But we are all devastated when there is an aviation crash. All countries are prepared to co-operate in a search for survivors. It symbolises the working together of all peoples. In any kind of rescue operation, it is heartening to see how much effort we put in, how we spend without reckoning the cost, in order to save a single life.

But if I ever become a little too sure of myself, a little too complacent, then I remind myself that the same fate awaits us all, whether we are Einstein, or Schweitzer, Karl Marx or Rockefeller — that from the dust we came, and to the dust we shall return. Ultimately, we will all have to stand judgement.

But we will not be judged on the basis of whether we were as great as Moses. We will each be judged by the standards of our own unique potential and capacities. Did I fulfil *my* special potential? Instead of spending my life vainly mourning opportunities lost, did I seize the chances I was given? Instead of apologising for goals I could not attain, did I reach the goals I could attain? Every single day, I must justify my existence on this earth — in however small and humble a measure; providing it is *my* measure.

These, then, are the two stars by which I try to steer my course. If my spaceship moves towards the planet 'Pride', I try to give a boost of the corrective which is marked 'compassion and humility'. But if I lapse towards despondency, I look at the planet 'Potential' which shines brightly in the reflection of the uniqueness and greatness of every single creature of God.

BETWEEN MAN AND MAN

"And the Lord God said: It is not good that man should be alone."

(The Story of Creation)

I place people at the centre of life. It is all very well speaking highmindedly about abstracts — values, hopes, ambitions — but, at the start and at the finish, I believe that the touchstone of our existence, the justification of our being, is how we relate to other people; not in the mass, in the generality, but in the specific and particular.

I am suspicious of those who speak finely of our duties to mankind but reject the plea of a particular member. I have tried to make my contact with individuals the basis of my life, my feeling for others the gauge of my feelings for myself.

We only exist insofar as we are acknowledged and reacted to by other people. We often know ourselves better by our reflection in the eyes of others, by their attitudes to us, than by looking inwards within ourselves. We can so easily lie to ourselves! We do not, possibly cannot, mark our own examination paper fairly in the test of life.

Let me go further; I believe I live only insofar as I relate to other people. I do not think this is a negation of self, I think this is a fulfilment of self. The celibate hermit, the monk in his cell, are not part of the authentic Jewish tradition. Moses and Elijah encountered God in the solitariness of the wilderness but both were commanded to return to their people. Contemplation cannot in itself be completion.

"Not the exposition but the deed" taught the rabbis. These deeds fall into two categories: the commandments between man and his fellow man, and between man and his Creator. Significantly, the Fast of Yom Kippur atones only for the latter. In order to make atonement for the former we must rectify the wrong and seek forgiveness from the person we have wronged.

The Torah is described as a "Tree of Life". Its ways are ways of pleasantness and those who observe them are part of life and must direct themselves primarily towards the living.

All life is encounter and relationship and must involve reciprocity. Life is the responsibility of a "me" for a "you". We all experience a terrific longing for relationship. Loneliness is terrible. "Give me companionship or death." prayed one Rabbi.

I have daily contact with many people. I meet people with a variety of pains and problems. Firstly, I try to listen to what they have to say, to listen, not merely to hear. If I am listening properly, then part of their distress communicates itself to me, so that I feel an ache, so that my heart is moved. I must, in some measure, share their burden — and they must realise that I am sharing it. To listen properly is difficult and revealing.

The same applies to disputes. In order even to attempt to resolve disputes we must listen so carefully to each side that both parties really feel we understand them. Frequently, we are listening not so much that we may comprehend but that we may reject or rebut. We are seeking to expose the flaws in an argument presented to us instead of seeking to grasp its assertions. Also we all too readily judge a case not so much on its merits as on the merits of the one who presents it. "Please ask me nicely".

I was once engaged in a particular dispute, pleading the cause of one side. Although the structure of the dispute was somewhat academic, I felt very strongly on the issues. After we had stated our respective cases, the moderator turned to me and said: "You have heard what your opponent has said. Tell me in your own words what you think his case is. Present it to me as if you were on his side!"

I did so and found it a strange experience. As I spoke, I had to re-evaluate in my own mind the arguments which, when they were presented by the other side, I had mentally mocked at and rejected. Now I found that I was forced inwardly to concede certain points. Occasionally the insincerity of my voice seemed so obvious to me that I was sure it must communicate itself to my listeners.

When I truly regard the "You" as part of the "Me", and an essential part of the "me", when I really start to "love my neighbour as myself", then much of the bitterness and hatred within me subsides.

Who is my neighbour? Every human being. Significantly the Hebrew word for neighbour used in Leviticus is the same as the expression used earlier in Exodus to denote an Egyptian neighbour. Everyman is my neighbour. Indeed, one rabbi in his commentary emphasises this still further. His translation of the famous phrase is: "Love your neighbour *because* he is like you" — a fellow creature of God with the same or similar hopes, desires and aspirations and similar fears and frailities.

Implicit is the commandment is not merely the right but also the instruction to love oneself, to have regard for oneself. We are our brother's keeper; we are also the guardian and custodian of our own selves. We may not neglect our health or wilfully injure ourselves or even place ourselves unnecessarily at risk. To continually deprive ourselves of food for instance, cannot be meritorious. We are commanded to enjoy ourselves on the Sabbath and Festivals; to eat and to drink.

If I restrict myself, I shall be only too ready to assess the needs of my neighbour on a lower scale. Jewish teaching asserts the contrary. I must judge his needs, even his basic needs, generously. "If he falls on bad times, but in his former position he drank wine with his meals, then he must be given wine".

The love which we should bestow upon our neighbour does not even have to be earned. A famous modern Rabbi, movingly and from a depth of human understanding, urged that, just as there is "baseless hatred", hatred without cause, dislike within reason; so there should be "baseless love", love without cause, reason or foundation.

Of course, we are very far from fulfilling this basic precept, which we were taught in the Old Testament and which was again highlighted by Jesus in the New Testament. But the decisive issue in life is not whether we attain final success, not whether we reach the end of a particular road, but whether we make an effort to start out on a particular task, whether we attempt its fulfilment.

I am an unrepentant optimist. I am also a gradualist. I believe that if I do my bit, however small, it will add to the mite of my neighbour.

I cannot remove blemish from the heart of man by one incision of the surgeon's knife, but I can make my start by following the injunction of a famous rabbi in the Talmud: to "greet every one of God's creatures (my partners in life, who are part of my life) with a cheerful face".

BETWEEN MAN AND GOD

When Rabbi Zalman was nigh unto death, his friends came to his bedside and asked him to recite the "Confession". The Rabbi smiled and said "Friends, do you really believe a death bed confession contains much merit? No, friends. A man should confess when he is seated at his dining table and eating the good food thereon.

(A Hassidic Tale)

One night, in Japan, when I was stationed there after World War II, I was woken by a tremendous noise — eerie and unearthly. I realised that my bed, indeed the whole room, was shaking violently. I got up, but it was impossible to move more than a few yards without being thrown down, because of the movement of the ground. All was dark. I realised I was experiencing an earthquake; but it was impossible to do anything, other than wait — and pray. I was fortunate, but more than a thousand people were killed that night, over 30 years ago. I saw some of the devastation in the days that followed.

We can face death in many ways. Logic plays little part in reassuring us. I know that my accident insurance policy — skillfully calculated — indicates that the likelihood of my being killed in a motor car accident is three times higher than my being killed in an aircraft. But I am still ten times more nervous in a plane than I am in a car.

I think the difference lies in this. If I feel threatened by man, then I feel that the solution — the removal of the threat — lies within the power of man. I feel that there is a natural way out. So I look first to man, and only then to God. But as no man has yet been able to regulate an earthquake or a typhoon, I am pressed back on my final resort — appealing to the power of God. I am totally dependent on Him. Only He can help me.

In such situations, then, do I create Him out of my desperation? Is He a figment of my frightened imagination? Is He my extra-terrestial insurance policy; taken out after the aircraft has left the ground, or after the ground has given up its normal solidity and dependability?

Frankly, I do not think that is a fair question — and the answer would not be meaningful. No man — and no God — should be judged by actions in extremity.

For me, if God lives, He must live in my everyday life, in my attitude to Him in the rush and hustle of catching my morning train, of being crushed in the bus or on the tube on the way home, in my reciting a hurried grace before a quick meal, in my relationship to God during celebration rather than in fear. Can I dance before God, as David danced before God? Is He real for me and do I bear witness to Him in my prosperity, not simply when I am in desperate search for Him in my adversity?

Judaism has taught me to seek God and relate to Him in the small things, in the mundane. I do not know whether I quite capture the concept of the magnificence of God, and reach Him in all His majesty and glory when I stand before Him, in a congregation of thousands, on the solemn, absolute fast of the Day of 'Atonement. But I *am* concerned to feel Him present with me, and the few members of my immediate family, in my home, when I wash my hands before a meal, and say a blessing to Him, when I have a few private words with Him in the rushed minutes of the morning prayers.

It is easy to feel awe in the presence of God when we are part of a crowd in a house of worship. "In the multitude of people lies the majesty of the King". I reckon that the real test of me, and of my attitudes, lies in my actions when I am alone; and in small matters rather than large. I rarely face earthquakes, but yet I am tested every day, by little experiences and trials.

What thoughts move me when I see a beggar in the street? Do I see God standing at his right hand? And do I not merely give him a coin but also add a kind word — as Jewish tradition instructs me?

When I see a deformed person, do I shrink in revulsion? Do I move away, avert my eyes? Or do I recite the blessing prescribed by my faith: "Blessed are You, O Lord God, King of the Universe, who has created various kinds of creatures", to remind myself *that* all creatures are formed by God, that I must respect every one of them?

Do I respect the injunction to feed my animals before I partake of my own meal? Do I say a blessing over a rainbow and affirm my belief that total destruction will never threaten mankind again? Do I answer a simple "Amen" to the blessing of my neighbour's: "May His great Name be blessed for ever and ever." (A child merits heaven after he answers his first "Amen", taught the Rabbi.) Do I realise that waste is a sin against man and against God?

So I try hard with the little things of life. I am urged by Jewish teaching: "Be as careful with a small commandment as with a large one". I try to look out especially for those small acts which are easy to do and because they are easy I do not always do them.

"Know Him in all your ways". Try to seek Him, not in the thunderstorm, but in the small puff of wind. For, after all, that breath, and each breath, is the totality of life.

EPILOGUE

Once our problem was
Too many tin cans littering
Too many bottles guttering
Too many cars polluting
Too many people commuting
Too many mouths consuming.

Soon our problem will be
Not enough fuel for powering
Too few jobs for producing
Too much dissension
Too much time
And too little hope to fill it.

Plenty created greed,
Will shortage foster brotherhood?